Haunting Bollywood

Haunting Bollywood

GENDER, GENRE, AND THE SUPERNATURAL IN HINDI COMMERCIAL CINEMA

Meheli Sen

University of Texas Press *Austin*

Printed in the United States of America
First edition, 2017

⊗ The paper used in this book meets the minimum requirements of ANSI/NISO Z39.48-1992 (R1997) (Permanence of Paper).

LIBRARY OF CONGRESS CATALOGING-IN-PUBLICATION DATA
Names: Sen, Meheli, 1976– author.
Title: Haunting Bollywood : gender, genre, and the supernatural in Hindi commercial cinema / Meheli Sen.
Description: First edition. | Austin : University of Texas Press, 2017. | Includes bibliographical references and index.
Identifiers: LCCN 2016007500
ISBN 978-1-4773-1157-8 (cloth : alk. paper)
ISBN 978-1-4773-1158-5 (pbk. : alk. paper)
ISBN 978-1-4773-1159-2 (library e-book)
ISBN 978-1-4773-1160-8 (non-library e-book)
Subjects: LCSH: Motion pictures—India. | Motion pictures, Hindi. | Motion picture industry—India. | Gender identity in motion pictures. | Sex role in motion pictures. | Horror films—History and criticism. | Supernatural in motion pictures.
Classification: LCC PN1993.5.I8 S437 2017 | DDC 791.430954—dc23
LC record available at http://lccn.loc.gov/2016007500

doi:10.7560/311578

For my parents, Syamali and Debaprasad Sen

Contents

Acknowledgments

Books cannot be written alone, and first books incur many debts. Numerous people across the globe have made it possible for me to research and write this one.

My friends in Bombay and Pune have provided me with homes and families in those cities over many years; their warmth and generosity has enabled me to do the research that supports this book. I thank Sudeep Chatterjee, Moumita Chatterjee, Sandeep Chatterjee, Meghna Kothari, Subarna Ghosh, and Indranil Ghosh for all they have done to make my work possible. Sudeep's contacts in the film industry have opened many doors for me, and I am grateful for his help.

I am indebted to Arti Karkhanis and the staff of the National Film Archive of India (NFAI) at Pune for the invaluable assistance they have provided in locating print resources and images, many of which appear in this book.

Colleagues in the South Asian Studies faculty writing group at Rutgers University have been the core of my intellectual community for several years. I thank Anjali Nerlekar, Preetha Mani, Asher Ghertner, Nida Sajid, Mukti Lakhi Mangharam, Jessica Birkenholtz, and Triveni Kuchi for reading and re-reading huge chunks of this book from wobbly first drafts to more polished versions with care, attention, and enthusiasm. Their collective and impressively interdisciplinary feedback has been enormously valuable to me throughout the writing process. Anjali has also translated some Marathi film reviews into English for me, and I thank her especially for these. Beyond intellectual labor that they have expended on the book, these folks have provided more ineffable kinds of support as well—I am thankful for the numerous meals, beverages, and conversations they have shared with me. These exchanges have sustained me no less than their scholarly insights.

I am deeply grateful to Susan Martin-Marquez and Anupama Kapse, who have taken time out of their extremely busy schedules to read and comment on specific chapters. Their feedback strengthens this book. Neepa Majumdar has provided support and critical advice on matters both scholarly and quotidian on numerous occasions; I thank her for being a mentor, friend, and scholar extraordinaire—an all-in-one source of wisdom, kindness, and generosity.

I thank the three anonymous reviewers approached by the University of Texas Press for their comments. Amit S. Rai has provided some of the most incisive and productive feedback on an earlier version of the manuscript. Monika Mehta recommended the University of Texas Press to me several years ago, and I am grateful for her suggestion. My indefatigable editor, Jim Burr, deserves special thanks for shepherding this book to its completion; I appreciate the thoughtfulness with which he has handled years of anxious e-mails, the pressures of deadlines, and frantic last-minute inquiries.

Colleagues at Rutgers—Alan Williams, Alamin Mazrui, Ousseina Alidou, Charles Haberl, John Belton, Dianne Sadoff, Janet Walker, Sandy Flitterman-Lewis, Chie Ikeya, Christian Lammerts, and Rhiannon Noel Welch—have been supportive of this project from the beginning, and I appreciate their unstinting kindness and collegiality.

Over the years I have had numerous conversations with fellow film/media scholars at conferences and meetings, both formal and informal. Many of the ideas that have cropped up in those conversations have also pollinated this book. I thank Sangita Gopal, Corey Creekmur, Tejaswini Ganti, Rosie Thomas, Girish Shambhu, Priya Jaikumar, Ashish Avikunthak, Usha Iyer, Anuja Jain, Claire Wilkinson, Suvadip Sinha, Jay Beck, and Allison McCracken for their enthusiasm for this project and for willingly engaging with different aspects of it. Allison—the terrific trooper that she is—has also watched numerous horror films with me in blustery Chicago when no one else would. Nandana Bose is a source of support in my life both professionally and personally. We have navigated the thorny thickets of film studies together across multiple continents for almost two decades now, and I thank her for being a friend in every sense of the term.

Adviser, mentor, and friend, Matthew Bernstein has been a constant source of kindness since I began my graduate studies in the United States. I thank him for always being there for me, across long and short distances.

Friends in Kolkata have nurtured this book in multiple ways. My debt to Moinak Biswas is too vast to be adequately expressed in words. His teaching and scholarship have taught me some of the most important things about cinema and cinema studies. I continue to learn from him every day.

Haimanti Deb Roy watched many of the films with me late into the night as I conceived of this project many years ago in Atlanta. Rongili Biswas has sustained me in more ways than one through many years. As always, I thank Debargho Sarkar for the gift of music, and for sharing his considerable love of 1980s Hindi cinema with me.

My family, and especially Susie and Rodney Webb and Lara Glenum, have been remarkably supportive of this project from the beginning. I am grateful to them for excusing my frequent absences from family gatherings, outings, and vacations. I also thank Sanjukta and Sandip Mukerjee and Kamal and Koyel Sen for providing me with family ties here in New Jersey.

My parents have also put up with years of odd behavior and writerly tantrums. They have remained supportive even though much of the material I work with perplexes them considerably. For their unwavering love and understanding, and for allowing me to always chart my own path, I dedicate this book to them.

Finally, Philip Webb has been with this book since its conceptualization several years ago. He has watched dozens of films with me, navigating ghosts, snakes, and assorted monsters with remarkable patience and good humor. From reading and commenting on drafts of chapters to keeping our household afloat over many months as I absconded from all other responsibilities, he has been my most reliable ally in all of this. Simply, this book wouldn't have been written without him.

Introduction

In the summer of 1989, a childhood friend invited me to watch a film at her home in a small campus-town in West Bengal. This was during our summer vacation, when school was out and parents were away at work. My friend's family owned a VCR—a thrilling luxury in the pre-liberalization years—and she had managed to obtain a video copy of the Ramsay brothers' horror film *Veerana* (1988), a film that, in those days, could only be watched in secret. As a bunch of us gathered around the television set to watch our first A, or adult-certified, film, the air was thick with a heady sense of transgression. Someone had to keep a watchful eye on the door for returning parents, because getting caught watching this particular film would have had fairly serious consequences. Its reputation for being "sexy" was already common knowledge among sheltered, middle-class teens like us, and my intrepid friend risked a fair bit in initiating us into the joys of forbidden images. The other particulars of that viewing experience are hazy now, but I clearly recall being utterly dazzled by the combination of horror effects and sex scenes that littered the film, pleasures that could never be owned up to. My love of supernatural films was born in that synergy of breathless excitement and mounting dread at the thought of being "discovered," an affective state not uncommon to the reception of many of the films and genres I engage with in *Haunting Bollywood*.

This book delves into what the supernatural is and what it reveals in and about the Hindi film since the late 1940s. In the chapters that follow, I argue that the supernatural invites us to consider questions of film form, history, modernity, and gender in South Asia in especially pointed ways. Dispersed along multiple genres, and constantly in conversation with global cinematic forms, the supernatural is a labile and plastic impetus, and one that has routinely pushed the Hindi film into new formal and stylistic territories. And yet Hindi cinema's most enduring pleasures—from songs and stars to myth and melodrama—continue to inflect, infect, and undergird the supernatural: this is a story of mutual hauntings, and it traverses multiple sites of contact, contagion, and promiscuity. Crowded with abominable creatures, unproductive love stories, and unspeakable appetites, *Haunting Bollywood* demonstrates that the sheer heterogeneity of figures, styles, ideologies, and genres that the supernatural enfolds demands new modes of inquiry. While the bulk of my engagement situates the films/genres within their historical and political contexts, I also track the unintended pathways along which these films continue to travel, make meaning, and affect new audiences in the era of the Internet and new media. Historical and ideological scaffoldings provide some explanation for the continuing popularity of these genres, but many of these assumptions are reconfigured by the complexities of new media ecologies. For the most part, the films and genres I consider are B products—made on modest budgets and lurking in the margins of the mainstream industry; others, however, have enjoyed brief spurts of respectability. Some genres and their monstrous figures have even infiltrated single-mindedly bourgeois living rooms and elite multiplexes. In other words, the story of the supernatural is far from predictable and continuously emergent; *Haunting Bollywood* shows that its unruly energies do not capitulate to neat and singular methodological grids, and my analyses, likewise, resist the temptation of neatness and closure.

Hindi commercial cinema—often simply "Bollywood"—has received an enviable amount of scholarly attention in recent years. While this undoubtedly suggests a less Euro-American focus in film studies globally, it should not be taken to mean that *all* kinds of non-Western cinema have been enjoying their day in the sun. This book is about Hindi films that have not been discussed very often, or are only beginning to be engaged with in more "revisionist" histories of the form.[1] Although scholars of Hindi film routinely interrogate this cinematic formation's disregard for realism and its penchant for the irrational and the fantastic, analyses of the supernatural in Indian cinema have largely been limited to the incursions of divine beings such as gods/goddesses or saints in, for example, the mythological or devotional genres.[2] Orientalist, fantasy, and magical films that were staples of the silent era, and which provide some of the iconographic tropes for the genres I discuss here, have been explored with care and attention.[3] However, other forms of supernatural entities—ghosts, vampires, animal shape-shifters, monsters, malevolent spirits, and the like—have remained curiously absent in this literature, until recently.[4] The oversight remains especially noteworthy because South Asia's rich narrative and performative traditions—oral and written, religious and secular—have routinely invoked such figures to entertain, educate, and enthrall their audiences. *Haunting Bollywood* addresses this lacuna in Indian cinema studies by exploring some of Hindi cinema's least studied genres: ghost films, snake/animal films, horror, and so on.

The relative obscurity of the supernatural in scholarly inquiries of Hindi film (in spite of the vast number of films and cycles that belong in the category) can be partially explained by the marginal status of many of these films in relation to the commercial mainstream: as mentioned above, with few notable exceptions, the supernatural impetus has tended to lurk in the B and C categories of cinematic fare. Alphabetical tags not only correspond to industrial matters such as budgets or stars but, as I demonstrate in the chapters that follow, simultaneously signify putative audiences and gesture toward notions of taste and vectors of social identity. In the journalistic parlance that gathers around Hindi cinema, supernatural films have historically been made for "the masses"—working-class and often non-metropolitan audiences that, in Ashis Nandy's words, account for Hindi film's "slum's-eye" view of all things.[5] Whereas the contours of an academic field are often drawn by various determinants that have little to do with these broader considerations, it is difficult to deny that most of these films were simply not considered to be worthy objects of scholarly inquiry until now.

Haunting Bollywood traces some of the ways in which the supernatural film has mutated in Hindi cinema since the late 1940s. However, this is also a story of striking continuities; the supernatural congeals as a set of specific formal and narrative preoccupations in the Hindi commercial film, and though historical breaks exert certain pressures on these clusters, their overall resilience is remarkable. In other words, while the modalities of haunting sometimes shift and transform—creatures who haunt, for example, come in an array of forms and guises—how Hindi film *allows itself to be haunted* is a telling instance of its most enduring characteristics. Notwithstanding that specters have been flitting through Hindi film for a very long time, their presence in the humanities and social sciences received a new fillip in the 1990s.

HAUNTINGS IN THE HUMANITIES

The publication of Jacques Derrida's *Specters of Marx* (1993) infused new life into the specter as a figure, revitalizing the idea of haunting in the humanities and spawning "a minor academic industry."[6] Derrida's ghost is, above all, a deconstructive trope, aligned to broader poststructuralist imperatives: "[H]auntology supplants its near-homonym ontology, replacing the priority of being and presence with the figure of the ghost as that which is neither present nor absent, neither dead nor alive."[7] This ability of the specter to unsettle binary modes of thought "and the linearity of historical chronology"[8] accounts for much of its extraordinary fertility in literary and cultural studies.[9] For my purposes here, the ghost's ability to narrate/articulate (embody and make manifest) forgotten, repressed, and disavowed histories remains key: "[T]he ghost is that which interrupts the presentness of the present, and its haunting indicates that, beneath the surface of received history, there lurks another narrative, an untold story that calls into question the veracity of the authorized version of events."[10] In other words, the ghost's presence gestures toward concealed archives of events and memories that could not be unearthed, except by taking recourse to a figure that is revelatory: "[T]he ghost ceases to be seen as obscurantist and becomes, instead, a figure of clarification with a specifically ethical and political potential."[11] Whether literal or metaphoric, real or projected, the ghost exposes fissures and cracks in history, ontology, and text with an urgency that no other figure harnesses.

Ghosts in dominant narratives, histories, and chronologies do not necessarily reveal themselves easily; often they have to be carefully looked for or listened to. But their presence remains foundational to modern technologies like the telegraph, radio, television, and cinema, making these hauntological media par excellence. In Ken McMullen's 1983 film *Ghost Dance*, Derrida (playing himself) notes with customary prescience, "The cinema is an art of ghosts, a battle of phantoms. . . . It's the art of allowing ghosts to come back. . . . I believe that modern developments in technology and telecommunication, instead of diminishing the realm of ghosts . . . enhances the power of ghosts and their ability to haunt us." More recently, Jeffrey Sconce has shown how the entire history of telecommunications has been haunted by the sense that something uncanny, some sentient "presence" lurks in our familiar, everyday machines: "Sound and image without material substance, the electronically mediated worlds of telecommunications often evoke the supernatural by creating virtual beings that appear to have no physical form." Sconce goes on to elaborate how media technologies can themselves "take on the appearance of a haunted apparatus . . . telephones, radios, and computers have been similarly 'possessed' by such 'ghosts in the machine,' the technologies serving as either uncanny electronic agents or as gateways to electronic otherworlds."[12] A critical insight of Sconce's work—and one that remains important to my own inquiry here—is the historical mutability of the idea of haunting: in other words, how certain technologies are perceived to be haunted or to harbor "invisible entities" is historically contingent, and constitutive of various strains of contemporary discourse. However, as Derrida cautions, the relationship of haunting and history is far from simple and may unsettle the notion of telos and progress altogether, because "haunting is historical, to be sure, but it is not *dated*, it is never docilely given a date in the chain of presents, day after day, according to the instituted order of a calendar."[13] Unpredictable, unruly, and sometimes profoundly anachronistic, ghosts and hauntings force us to reckon with time, history, chronology, linearity, and the contemporary in fundamental ways.

As an iconic product of modern technology, the cinema comes to be embedded in this complex terrain in specific ways. Cinema's allegiance to the magical and the fantastic—harnessed by the wonder of the moving image in its earliest days, for instance—imbues it with a certain kind of richness in this context: cinema is simultaneously rational *and* magical, utterly modern yet capable of generating persistent enchantments.[14] Tom Gunning has demonstrated how "the convergence between phantoms and photography may prove more than fortuitous." Through a masterfully detailed consideration of "Spirit Photographs," scientific discoveries of optical tools that enabled different modes of perception and visuality, and philosophical tenets in the modern era, Gunning shows that modern media are foundationally imbued with hauntological possibilities: "[P]hotography was the first great breakthrough—a way of possessing material objects in a strangely decorporealized yet also supernaturally vivid form. But still more bizarre forms of spectral representation have appeared in the twentieth century—the moving pictures of cinematography and television, and recently, the eerie, three dimensional phantasmata of holography and virtual reality."[15]

This complex body of work on ghosts and specters informs *Haunting Bollywood* as a whole, but I also examine how Hindi cinema remains haunted in other and more specific ways. Playback singing, for example, overlays a prerecorded music track atop the image track and imbues the form with an added layer of spectrality; not only do ghostly forms flicker via the apparatus, but ghostly voices of absent others (and shards of times past) accompany them in the present of the projected moment. Hindi cinema's phantoms are, thus, both literal—ghosts, spirits, and other supernatural creatures when they appear as diegetic entities—and also symbolic, as they speak to and for other narratives, beyond the ones they inhabit. The dovetailing of real and metaphoric registers of ghostliness are typically highlighted through the formal particularities of Hindi film. The emphasis on hauntings may imply that supernatural beings are exclusively spectral and insubstantial in Hindi cinema, but this is not the case. Indeed, most of these films invoke the materiality of the body in a foundational manner. Supernatural entities in this setting remain stubbornly corporeal,[16] often eliciting correspondingly visceral responses in the audiences as well.

EMBODIMENT: HORROR, AFFECT, AND QUEERNESS

Since the 1990s, film theory has overcome its long-standing reluctance to address questions of bodies and embodiment; in fact, some of the most exciting theoretical breakthroughs since then have directly engaged bodies—both on and off screen. Linda Williams observes that one of the shared characteristics among excessive "body genres" is that they tend to display (especially female) bodies in the throes of extreme sensations: "[T]he body spectacle is featured most sensationally in pornography's portrayal of orgasm, in horror's portrayal of violence and terror, and in melodrama's portrayal of weeping. . . . Visually, each of these ecstatic excesses could be said to share a quality of uncontrollable convulsion or spasm—of the body 'beside itself' with sexual pleasure, fear and terror, or overpowering sadness."[17] Building on Carol Clover's work on horror, Williams goes on to argue that the binaries of male/female, active/passive, sadism/masochism are complex and fluid when it comes to questions of fantasy, identification with bodies on screen, and gendered notions of film spectatorship.[18] Williams's insights remain especially valuable for this book, because first, horror is one of the most important sites for the elaboration of the supernatural in Hindi film, and second, because most of the genres I look at are melodramatic at their core and deploy bodies accordingly, and finally, some teeter precipitously on the brink of pornographic titillation, especially when presenting the female body as spectacle.

Alongside Barbara Creed, Clover, and Williams, Jack Halberstam has opened up particularly productive ways of thinking about unruly, queer, posthuman, and monstrous bodies in horror and beyond. In considering Gothic horror, Halberstam has shown how certain notions of deviance and monstrosity are constitutively gendered, corporeal, and infinitely fecund when it comes to generating meanings. In *Skin Shows*, Halberstam writes,

> Gothic novels are technologies that produce the monster as a remarkably mobile, permeable, and infinitely interpretable body. The monster's body, indeed, is a machine that, in its Gothic mode, produces meaning and can represent any horrible trait that the reader feeds into the narrative. The monster functions as a monster, in

> other words, when it is able to condense as many fear-producing traits into one body. . . . Monsters are meaning machines.[19]

Although the figures I interrogate here are by no means uniformly monstrous, Halberstam's insights continue to be useful when looking at the multiplicity of meanings that supernatural entities effortlessly embody in given cinematic constellations. The attention to historical context—the fact that what gets designated as deviant, monstrous, or terrifying shifts across time, "that fear and monstrosity are historically specific forms, rather than psychological universals"—is a key aspect of Halberstam's work that informs *Haunting Bollywood* as a whole.[20]

While this excavation of the body vis-à-vis specific representational terrains began within feminist film scholarship still grounded in psychoanalytic theory, it has since moved farther afield, following the resurgence of interest in Gilles Deleuze's work. Steven Shaviro remains one of the most important voices in shifting the critical conversation to what has been called the "affective turn" in cultural theory. Marshaling his cinephiliac desire against the distanced and disembodied ruminations of psychoanalytic film theory, Shaviro writes, "In film viewing, there is pleasure and more than pleasure: a rising scale of seduction, delirium, fascination, and utter absorption in the image. The pleasures, the unpleasant constraints, the consuming obsessions of writing theory . . . cannot be separated from the bodily agitations, the movements of fascination, the reactions of attraction and repulsion, of which they are the extension and elaboration."[21] Arguing for a radical reconsideration of bodily sensations invoked by the cinema, Shaviro suggests that images affect the body viscerally and without mediation; that we initially encounter films as pure sensation, "before having the leisure to read or interpret them as symbols."[22] Unsurprisingly, many of Shaviro's favored texts for affective interpretation and reading come from the horror genre—from George A. Romero's "blank, terrifying and ludicrous"[23] postmodern zombies to David Cronenberg's horrifyingly mutant bodies, which make his films "violently, literally visceral."[24] Indeed, of all the "body genres" identified by Williams, horror has possibly benefited the most from the critical turn to affect, because—as Larrie Dudenhoeffer pithily notes—in a certain sense, "*all horror is body horror.*"[25]

While this large corpus of interdisciplinary scholarship on embodiment, corporeality, affect, monstrosity, and queerness[26] informs *Haunting Bollywood* in productive and constitutive ways, it is also crucial to note that Western cultural theory can only have limited purchase when discussing such formations as the Hindi popular film. A considerable degree of retooling and repurposing is required in order to do justice to the contextual valences of the films in question. For example, supernatural bodies do not quite function like human bodies in this context; in Hindi cinema, the body of the ghost, shape-shifting animal, or monstrous creature is often shot through with mythic and sacral intensities. Questions of ontology, corporeality, and subjectivity, therefore, have to be calibrated in accordance with the figurative energies that the supernatural entities harness in their bodies. Some of these bodies are quasi-divine, demanding our awe as well as fear; some others invite our desire and repugnance in equal measure. The mobilization of sensation or emotion in South Asian performative traditions is further complicated by, for example, the notion of *rasa* or "mood," a term that is derived from Sanskrit dramaturgy and one that is often deployed to address the manner in which Indian cinema inscribes emotions in depersonalized terms.[27] The notion of "queerness," likewise, permeates this book but means something very specific in this context: it ranges from the thanatic passivity of the Gothic hero who literally wants to "waste away" for the ghostly beloved in Chapter 1, to the unspeakable appetites implied by the human-snake romance in Chapter 3, to the more familiar sexual excesses and deviances of the Ramsay monsters that I explore in Chapter 2. Thus, although Western theory inflects my readings in important ways, I have remained attentive to the specific textual and historical terrains that tether these genres, even as they travel through the diffused and ghostly pathways of electronic and digital media in recent times.

The spectral and the corporeal, the affective and the psychological are held in productive tension in many of the genres I discuss in *Haunting Bollywood*. And the theoretical insights from affect (and gender) theory come to be enormously productive precisely at moments when ideological or historical analysis alone leads to critical impasses. Throughout this book, I move between various methods, using tools that the heterogeneity of my material demands. The manner in which bodies in films and the films themselves circulate through media economies and ecologies have much to do with the generic and formal peculiarities of the Hindi film.

GENRE, FORM, AND THE SUPERNATURAL

Hindi commercial cinema's most universally recognized aspect is its formal assemblage, the heterogeneity of its narrative structure, or its *masala* form. Any study of the form has to reckon with its "attractional"[28] format—song and dance, action, melodrama, romance, all strung together—and most scholarly inquiries tend to frame it as sui generis, which mutates only under extreme pressures that attend to the political economy, such as transformations in the state form.[29] While some historical phases have engendered a more integrative form—for example, the Social film in the 1940s through the 1960s, which often included themes of social importance[30]—others have witnessed its progressive unraveling into a tentatively held-together system of spectacles, such as the overwrought *masala* film of the 1970s, whose impulse toward the frontal solicitation of the spectator remains remarkably consistent. Either way, until very recently, the Hindi commercial film's unruly energies—both in terms of industrial organization and textual proclivities, which overlap with each other—could hardly be corralled into neat generic categories of the kind that scholars of Hollywood cinema can easily mobilize. For example, in his seminal work on Hollywood genres, Rick Altman describes film genre as a "complex concept with multiple meanings," which include the following:

- genre as *blueprint*, as a formula that precedes, programs, and patterns industry production;
- genre as *structure*, as the formal framework on which individual films are founded;
- genre as *label*, as the name of a category central to the decisions and communications of distributors and exhibitors;
- genre as *contract*, as the viewing position required by each genre film of its audience.[31]

Altman's fascinating study—which also complicates the unities sketched above—gives us a template for examining Bollywood's more recent, millennial restructuring; however, it remains inadequate, or simply inappropriate, for understanding the commercial cinema's industrial structuring, historical forms, and trajectories. Having said that, in *Haunting Bollywood*, I am calling for a recalibration of the portmanteau terms—"Social," "*masala*," and so on—in order to see how fledgling *generic impulses* operate within these more capacious categories.[32] In other words, I will use generic labels as a heuristic approach, despite their eventual absorption into the larger umbrella categories; here, I argue that attending to these "generic" preoccupations reveals something that remains occluded via the more general optics. What I shall call the "genres of the supernatural" include Gothic films (at the time, often advertised or consumed as thrillers), snake films (labeled and marketed as folklore or some variation thereof, and which I designate as a historically circumscribed cycle), horror films (unmistakably so, but qualified as equally *masala*), and recently, more generically consolidated novelties such as zombie films or creature-features. In *Haunting Bollywood*, I argue that the supernatural congeals as a specific set of *lateral* impulses in given historical junctures, and the concept of genre—traditionally defined—can enable us to uncover social as well as textual meanings that remain otherwise obfuscated.

The optic of genre—even if most of these films did not traverse through the production-distribution-exhibition triad of nodes and contracts that Western genre films typically do—is also productive in terms of the hybrid allegiances of the supernatural in Hindi commercial cinema. The generic clusters and cycles I look at in this book remain haunted on multiple registers: first, I argue that contrary to the commonplace notion that this cinema remains embedded within local narrative idioms, the supernatural genres, in fact, integrate international genre-film conventions into the local textual idiom, creating foundationally hybrid and unabashedly promiscuous formal modes: "It is not . . . a 'primitive' but rather a 'heterogenous' form that selectively (and whimsically) imports Hollywood norms even while remaining embedded in its historical and cultural milieu."[33] Second, and for my purposes quite pivotal, is the question of generic continuities in the commercial form: my readings demonstrate that certain conventions come to be recursive in distinct generic formations and the commercial cinema redeploys these in new guises in specific historical moments. For example, the figure of the singing ghost—the spectral siren who lures the hero away from a predetermined telos—appears in arguably distinct genres like the Gothic, the "snake film," the "reincarnation film," and the overblown horror film from the 1980s. In other words, here I trace generic "tropes" through both synchronic and diachronic axes. In this sense, the filmic iteration of the supernatural comes to be doubly haunted—bearing traces of the "uncanny foreign" as well as inscribing signs and traces of its own textual forbears.

A few concrete examples would sharpen this point further, and the reincarnation film—which I do not discuss in any detail, but which shares significant traits with the Gothic and several other genres that I do investigate—provides an excellent template for tracking the motility and plasticity of supernatural tropes.[34] Two key motifs that constitute generic propensities of the reincarnation film include the thematic of sexual violence and a patterned use of the song sequence. The foundational act of rape (real or potential), which often sets these narratives in motion, features in films ranging from *Madhumati* (1958) to *Kudrat* (1981) to *Dangerous Ishq* (2012). While the blockbuster *Om Shanti Om* (2007) does not incorporate rape, the chastity of the dead Shanti (Deepika Padukone) is indeed compromised by the villain Mukesh (Arjun Rampal) and must be avenged at closure. *OSO* famously pays homage to both *Karz* (1980) and *Madhumati*, and to the many pasts and genres of Hindi cinema, but even less reflexive reincarnation films repurpose the generic tropes in specific ways. The song sequence—in this case, the love song that the rebirth saga hinges on—is similarly deployed across films. If *Madhumati* features Lata Mangeshkar's haunting rendition of "Aaja Re" ("Come to Me"), then *Kudrat* mobilizes "Humein Tumse Pyaar Kitna" ("How Much I Love You") (sung by Kishore Kumar and Parveen Sultana) and *Mehbooba* (1976) incorporates "Mere Naina Saawan Bhado" ("My Eyes Rain Tears") in very similar ways, to jolt the reincarnated protagonists into an uncanny recognition of their previous lives/selves. Additionally, in many of these films, these particular songs are repeated, indicating the cyclical nature of death and rebirth in accordance with specifically Hindu belief systems. And, as I argue in the chapters that follow, the genres of the supernatural are especially prone to these recursive gestures; the history I map in *Haunting Bollywood* turns on the fulcrum of (re)iteration/accommodation, as generic clusters innovate and repeat certain formal and narrative preoccupations over time.

The advent of the supernatural in Hindi cinema dovetails closely with formal particularities; across genres, the supernatural impulse in Hindi film finds elaboration through what we can loosely call the "performance sequence." The most obvious modality of performance in the Hindi film is, of course, the song-and-dance sequence, "a deep structure of this tradition and crucial to the way it is described by both insiders and outsiders."[35] The song-and-dance sequence, as many scholars of Indian cinema have pointed out, not only attests to Hindi cinema's heterogenous mode of manufacture[36]—often shot and edited autonomously from the rest of the film—but it also remains a key commercial aspect of this cinema, used in advertising and marketing of films prior to their release on multiple platforms, on CDs, television trailers and programs, and now via the Internet. The song sequence—easily decoupled from the rest of the film—also speedily travels across the globe in diasporic and other locations worldwide;[37] indeed, the films as a whole often piggyback on the success of their music albums, and songs have been known to propel mediocre cinematic fare into box-office successes. Narratively, the song sequence performs multiple functions in the Hindi film, ranging from consolidating the romantic couple[38] to "serving as the kernel that contains the film's message and conveys the 'director's true intentions.'"[39]

In *Haunting Bollywood*, I argue that the song-and-dance sequence—a critical affective tool for Hindi film—also allows for the supernatural to be potentiated and elaborated; in fact, the supernatural subjects the formal grammar of Hindi cinema to extremes of the attractional format, as evidenced, for example, in the Ramsay horror film of the 1980s. But more broadly, the notion of performance is of key importance in this context;

so, for example, other types of spectacular set pieces stand in for song-and-dance sequences in the more recent Bollywood films that eschew the traditional portmanteau format. When the nature of the performance sequence is transformed—as in the new "songless" film, for instance—the supernatural comes to contort the formal domain in other ways, transforming generic modalities decisively. For example, in the recent *Go Goa Gone* (2013), extensive, spectacularly staged zombie attacks punctuate the narrative in lieu of more typical attractions. Throughout this book, the manner in which the supernatural imbricates formal aspects of the commercial film remains a central problematic.

The relationship between the supernatural and the performance sequence brings us to yet another key optic through which I read these genres—gender and sexuality. In *Haunting Bollywood*, I argue that gender is a particularly fecund terrain on which the supernatural rehearses its most basic compulsions. I suggest that the interface between gender and genre provides an especially productive lens for viewing the commercial form's negotiation of the supernatural in at least two ways: first, because generic particularities often congeal along certain kinds of gendered and sexualized representational modes, and second, because these films often address a specifically gendered spectator. The question of viewership—both the imaginary spectator addressed by the films and the fluctuating patronage of putative audiences—remains a critical component of my analyses; although this is not an audience study in the ethnographic sense, the discursive materials surrounding these genres—reviews, articles, interviews, and so on—give us a sense of who their intended audiences were.

Genres of the supernatural have always attempted to speak to specific audience segments: from the Ramsays to Ram Gopal Varma, filmmakers and production outfits alike pitch the supernatural to specific types of viewers. In this sense, barring a few exceptions like the more inclusive films from the 1960s, the address of the supernatural film remains narrower than most genres. This, too, is a matter of historical contingency, and I show how the supernatural films' audiences have shifted across time. The digital explosion and media convergence over the last decade or so have also garnered new audiences for these genres; in several chapters that follow, I demonstrate how new sites of reception have reanimated the genres that had become moribund in the intervening decades since their theatrical release and circulation. Ghosts, snakes, monsters, and other supernatural entities have been paradoxically infused with new life, as digital domains continue to host their untimely afterlives in perpetuity.

So far, I have only gestured toward one other theoretical scaffolding that undergirds *Haunting Bollywood* as a whole: the question of modernity and its many unpredictable habitats and trajectories in South Asia. Before tracking some of the complexities that constellate around the figuration of the modern in Bollywood film, it is worthwhile to recall that modernity has *itself* been described as an uncanny realm of experiences and representations; Jo Collins and John Jervis, for instance, have posited that "the uncanny may be a fundamental, constitutive aspect of our experience of the modern . . . the uncanny testifies to a distinctive sensibility, a fusion of feeling and reflection, hence to a distinctive aesthetics of modernity, along with the wider psychological and cultural consequences of this."[40] Sigmund Freud's famous 1919 essay on the uncanny is only a piece of the historical puzzle that demonstrates that a certain "uncertainty, at the heart of our ontology, our sense of time, place, and history, both personal and cultural"[41] has haunted the imaginaries of modernity since at least the nineteenth century. In his work on European modernist writers ranging from Arthur Rimbaud to Stéphane Mallarmé, Samuel Beckett, Paul Verlaine, T. S. Eliot, James Joyce, and others, Jean-Michel Rabaté similarly maps the "dim contours of a haunted modernity . . . a modernity that is by definition never contemporaneous with itself, since it constantly projects, anticipates, and returns to mythical origins, but that also teaches us more about the 'present,' which it historicizes."[42]

In India, of course, the hauntological imperatives of modernity are further complicated by the history of colonialism and Empire. One of the most important interventions in the humanities and social sciences—in disciplines ranging from history and literature to anthropology and sociology—in the last several decades has been the challenging of the universalist claims that the Enlightenment and Western modernity have been the engines for the propulsion of *all* histories. The basic thrust of this influential body of work—variously called "alternative modernities," and "multiple" or "other modernities"—has been to trace a "more complex genealogy of the modern,"[43] wherein the West and the rest are not bound in a relationship of delay (what Dipesh Chakrabarty evocatively calls being consigned to the "imaginary waiting room of history").[44] The idea is, rather, to engage with modernity as an emergent global phenomenon, wherein the non-West functions as the "constitutive outside" to the universalist European narrative. In this critical terrain, heterogeneous forms of social organization, identity formation, and modes of belonging and representation become essential components of that larger story. As Timothy Mitchell writes, "[E]very performance of the modern is the production of . . . difference, and each such difference represents the possibility of some shift, displacement, or contamination. If modernity is defined by its claim to universality, this always remains an impossible universal. . . . Modernity then becomes the unsuitable yet unavoidable name for these discrepant histories."[45]

For my purposes here, two themes that run through this vast body of scholarship remain especially critical: first, that the project of modernity continues to unfold and emerge, its various "posts" notwithstanding, and second, that arguably "non-modern" elements come to be *constitutive* of a certain kind of "modernity." Both of these insights remain important for understanding India, where the imbrication of colonialism and capitalism has bequeathed a fitful modernity, one that remains foundationally troubled by the feudal/non-modern.[46] Cinema—especially Hindi commercial cinema—comes to be entangled in this thicket of questions in specific ways. The heterogeneous mode of manufacture, which until very recently accounted for Hindi cinema's formal assemblage, remains something of a contamination of capitalism's neat, vertically integrated assembly lines; the industrial and technological and stylistic imperatives of the commercial film make it appear as "a-not-yet cinema, a bastard institution in which the mere ghost of a technology is employed for purposes inimical to its historic essence."[47]

From a formal mélange that constitutively flouts bourgeois modernity's most cherished mode of expression (realism, broadly understood), to narrative and ideological alignments that constantly seem to espouse some version of "tradition," "[t]his binary . . . figures centrally, both thematically and as an organizing device, in popular film narratives."[48] In the supernatural film, any traction that realism may have exerted in other formations—tentative at best in Hindi popular cinema—disappears entirely, generating fantastic thematic and formal terrains that push the binary to its limit. In *Haunting Bollywood*, I argue that the excessive, profligate energies of the supernatural genres throw down the gauntlet against modernity in a special way; in other words, this book demonstrates that the supernatural allows us an especially fecund, and so far underexplored, point of entry into the continuously emergent story of Hindi cinema's romance with modernity and its others. Most often, I use the term "feudal" to refer to the ethos and dispensation that occupies the other side of the binary axis. "Feudal," here, is a heuristic device to investigate an array of elements, starting from non-modern economic and social arrangements that these films include as content (the various *thakur*s [lords] in their *havelis* [mansions]) to the more latent ideological propensities where the feudal appears in transformed garbs and guises. As I demonstrate in Chapters 4 and 5, the supernatural's retreat from the rural *haveli* to the urban high-rise has not necessarily signaled a disabling of feudalism in this larger sense. Although modernity is certainly at large in post-liberalization avatars of the supernatural, it continues to be haunted by energies that remain inimical to its more familiar ontologies. If the narrative of South Asian modernity remains constitutively unsettled, forces of globalization have further complicated the scenario. Finally, I argue that far from becoming disenchanted under the aegis of late capitalism, Bombay cinema has incubated new habitats for the supernatural, in the era of its planetary dispersal. Put differently, the genres of the supernatural—perhaps more efficaciously than many others—demonstrate that the feudal/modern, past/present, myth/history binaries that remain so beloved to Hindi cinema, in fact, crystallize as mutually haunted categories. Time—the very notion of temporality—therefore, remains an important analytical vector for me. Recalcitrant shards of the past rupture and unsettle the present in the genres I discuss here. These genres offer a fractured, nonlinear version of history, wherein disjointed times and spaces jostle together to create meaning; under the auspices of the supernatural, Walter Benjamin's famous "messianic" and "empty" temporalities can almost seamlessly blend into each other, or, at the very least, exist in tandem. Ghosts, as Bliss Cua Lim reminds us, provoke, precisely because they "call our calendars into question."[49] Her work remains foundationally important to *Haunting Bollywood* also because she recognizes the supernatural as the most apposite site for the elaboration of a certain kind of temporal critique: "The supernatural is often rationalized as a figure for history or disparaged as an anachronistic vestige of primitive, superstitious thought. But from an alternate perspective it discloses the limits of historical time, the frisson of secular historiography's encounter with temporalities emphatically at odds with and not fully miscible to itself."[50] The Hindi film's constitutive capaciousness and plasticity makes it less resistant to alternate and non-secular temporalities; nonetheless, what Lim calls "immiscible times—multiple times that never quite dissolve into the code of modern time consciousness, discrete temporalities incapable of attaining homogeneity with or full incorporation into a uniform chronological present"[51]—offers a valuable framework for investigating the formation's predilection for invoking more enchanted chronologies. But time is important also because the supernatural film labors with equal ferocity to make manifest its contemporary moorings—from music to fashion and formal contortions, the supernatural genres are very much products of their immediate historical contexts as well.

THE STRUCTURE OF THIS BOOK

Haunting Bollywood maps the trajectory of supernatural genres from 1949 (the year *Mahal* was released) to the present. Although *Mahal* may have drawn on earlier formations—like Oriental and fantasy films from earlier eras—it nonetheless remains a watershed film that created a specific template for both the Gothic and the reincarnation genres in Hindi film. Mapping the supernatural chronologically also enables me to signpost certain key shifts that attended to the industry and social and political imaginaries over this sixty-five-year period. While the moniker "Bollywood" in the title is a convenient shorthand that allows me to gesture toward the entire corpus of Hindi cinema of this period, I use it more sparingly in the chapters themselves. For the sake of clarity, I—like many other commentators—use "Bollywood" to designate the slew of transformations that followed in the wake of economic liberalization in the early 1990s. For the rest of the book, "Hindi commercial film," "Bombay film," or some variant thereof refers to the products of the industry located in Bombay. In a somewhat contradictory move, I use "Bombay" and not "Mumbai" to designate the home of the film industry, because this book begins at a time when the capital city of Maharashtra still wore its anglicized—and considerably more cosmopolitan—name.

In terms of research material, films, obviously, constitute the bulk of my primary texts. However, whenever possible, I have juxtaposed these alongside reviews, interviews, and other elements from the popular press, whose coverage of the film industry is both prodigious and often acutely incisive. Often, these discursive materials allow us to glimpse how specific films, stars, or genres were received in their historical moment, and they remain crucial to my understanding of the larger context within which these formations were embedded. *Haunting Bollywood* is an interdisciplinary inquiry into the supernatural in Hindi cinema, and beyond the tools offered by film studies, I have drawn liberally from literary criticism, postcolonial studies, queer theory, history, cultural studies, and anthropology to frame my discussions of films and genres.

Chapter 1 looks at the emergence of the Gothic as a specific set of formal and thematic preoccupations in the late 1940s. Made at a time when the studio system was on the verge of collapse and the film industry was transitioning into a different sort of political economy, *Mahal*, as intimated above, is a foundational text in many ways. I argue that this particular film—and others such as the later *Bees Saal Baad* (1962) and *Woh Kaun Thi?* (1964)—lays bare some of the basic struggles that the popular form underwent in performing its role in the overarching national cultural sphere.

The Social—the dominant generic form that comes to be consolidated at this time—was often seen by industry insiders and outsiders as the prime textual site in which a "modern popular" could be made manifest. Alongside themes of social importance—Raj Kapoor's films of urban poverty and corruption, Guru Dutt's melodramas, the noirs from Navketan Films, and so on, were all Socials in industrial parlance—the Social sometimes incubated tendencies that ran counter to its larger ideological functions. The Gothic is one such remarkable genre that jostled against the basic reformist/pedagogic imperatives of the Social. In allowing the rational hero of the Five Year Plan (FYP) to veer away from his predestined telos and become dangerously besotted by female ghosts, the Gothic strained the very form that it was inhabiting; the postcolonial male citizen and the discourses of a disenchanted rational modernity were rendered perilously unstable within the Gothic as a generic formation, an instability that, I argue, had to be finally contained. The recuperative gesture that the Social finally mobilizes—suppressing Gothic femininities and the associated risks of decadence—is equally revealing of larger ideological imperatives of the time. In this chapter, I demonstrate that the Social had to perform an arduous but unavoidable task vis-à-vis the Gothic: in rescuing a rapidly unraveling modernity, the Social re-gendered the formation as the investigative thriller, a form far more appropriate for narrating the nation.

Although the supernatural was inevitably gendered feminine and could rarely be allowed to congeal in any real sense in the 1950s and 1960s, both the film industry and larger political terrain in India underwent massive shifts in the 1970s. Chapters 2 and 3, on Ramsay horror and snake films respectively, focus on the turbulent decades of the 1970s and 1980s, and the generic mutations of the supernatural that they engendered. These were monstrous times indeed, and the cinematic creatures they spawned remain testament to some of the horrors of this era. The 1970s witnessed the gradual dismantling of the Nehruvian imperatives that had characterized the years following national independence in 1947. The turbulent climax of this process of disassembly would come to be the declaration of the national Emergency: a twenty-one-month period beginning in 1975 when an increasingly authoritarian Indira Gandhi, then prime minister, suspended all civil liberties and centralized power in Delhi. In Chapter 2, I look at the emergence of the horror genre proper as a symptom of this larger process of disintegration of particular nationalist narratives that had run their course. As the integrated Social cracked under industrial and other pressures and mutated into the centrifugally organized, attractional *masala*, the stage was set for the inauguration of excessive horror. During this time, via the clever juggling of basic generic elements in the hands of the Ramsay brothers, horror both consolidated as a recognizable generic formation and enjoyed an unprecedented popularity with certain audience segments. The screen became awash with lurid fake blood, and plots began to include esoteric rituals and became inhabited by a series of bizarrely monstrous creatures—amorous witches, predatory werewolves, and lustful male and female vampires. The divorce between horror and a certain idea of "respectability" thus becomes firmly entrenched at this time; the fact that the middle classes shunned movie theaters in favor of watching films on video in the relative comfort of their living rooms is a matter of considerable importance when we interrogate the general contours of the horror genre of this era.

In Chapter 2, I argue that the supernatural takes on specific guises in this cinema that have as much to do with local political upheaval as with the international genre film conventions that the Ramsays unembarrassedly appropriated. Deep schisms in social relations and dramatic transformations in cultural imaginaries and public spheres inform the figuration of the supernatural in B and "exploitation" horror. Most important for my purposes, the horror genre continues the Gothic tradition of *staging* a confrontation with the feudal: these films *enact* a reckoning of sorts with what has come before and will not be easily left behind, or rest easily in the dungeons and grottoes of the feudal *haveli*. However, I also demonstrate that the story of Ramsay horror is far from simple: breaking these films down into their constitutive segments allows me to pay closer attention to those elements of the genre that remain recalcitrant to this familiar narrative of lowbrow exploitation; the Ramsays' successful penetration of urban living rooms via television shows further complicates bourgeois notions of taste and respectability. The Ramsay horror film, I argue, is not only very much a product of its unruly times but also a formation that lends itself well to cult veneration in the era of new media and convergence cultures.

Similar to the Ramsay film in some ways, but imbued with somewhat distinct energies, the snake film is one of Bollywood's most curious attractions. In Chapter 3, I look at the snake film as a specifically charged iteration of the supernatural in Hindi cinema. The life of the snake film as a prestigious cycle was relatively short-lived in Bollywood, but in its heyday, such remarkable films as *Nagin* (1976), *Nagina* (1986), and *Nache Nagin Gali Gali* (1989) provided its basic formal and narrative contours. While drawing on the robust body of myths and folklore that are based on magical, shape-shifting, semi-divine serpents in the subcontinent, these films also generated and assembled a vast array of filmic myths: tethered to the generic energies of the older mythological and fantasy films that have been made since cinema's earliest years, the snake film is an astonishing instance of the enduring power of enchanted traditions in Hindi cinema. In this chapter, I argue that despite the "ahistorical" nature of the materials incorporated and reassembled by the snake film, the formation remains aligned to the 1970s and 1980s in important ways, not least because its formal preoccupations are closely aligned to the *masala* idiom that dominated in this era. I also demonstrate how the genre is transformed by the muscularity of Hindu nationalism over the late 1980s, as a more inflexible religiosity supplanted the little traditions and folksiness of the earlier films. Much of the snake film's supernatural energy is constitutively enabled by cinematic technology—miraculous transformations that manifested on screen were typically accomplished by mobilizing the most basic of special-effects tools. However, through an analysis of the commercially unsuccessful Bollywood-Hollywood co-production *Hisss* (2010), I argue that the snake film resists a digital makeover in a fundamental way—its basic idioms cannot be meaningfully uncoupled from its generic and historical moorings. But just like the lowbrow Ramsay horror film, the snake film continues to enjoy a digital afterlife in a different sense: via numerous blogs, websites, online forums, and social media platforms, the magical female snake continues to seduce and enchant new populations of willing devotees.

The advent of economic liberalization in the early 1990s transformed the film industry as well as its products in fundamental ways. As the Bombay film morphed into what we understand as Bollywood proper,[52] the supernatural, too, underwent fairly decisive shifts. With the industry shifting its focus more toward middle-class audiences that returned to watch films in the reconstituted spaces of the urban multiplex, horror jettisoned its nonbourgeois trappings and excesses and became "mainstream" in the most literal sense. As scholars such as Sangita Gopal and Tejaswini Ganti have noted,[53] the multiplex phenomenon has not only changed the political economy of the industry but has also enabled generic differentiation in critical ways; the recent horror "boom" dovetails with these larger transformations. Successful horror films of this period would include *Raaz* (2002), *Bhoot* (2003), *Vaastu Shastra* (2004), *Phoonk* (2008), *1920* (2008), and *Haunted 3D* (2011), among many others. As I suggest in earlier chapters, these larger changes are often registered by the supernatural in formal terms; in knotty negotiations with genre conventions, some filmmakers such as Ram Gopal Varma have done away with song sequences, a gesture that brings these films in line with international horror, whereas others such as Vikram Bhatt continue to use songs in fairly traditional ways.

In Chapter 4, I argue that the potentially transgressive content of earlier decades has come to be diluted or lost in horror's rehabilitation to "A" status; a return to middle-class sensibilities has shorn the formation of the unruly energies that it harnessed in earlier iterations. I further argue that what characterizes this recent spate of horror films are fears and anxieties that involve the impact of globalization on the family—women entering the workplace, increased abortion rates, premarital sex, male unemployment, divorce, adultery, and the disintegration of the extended family. While a number of scholars have suggested that this new iteration of the genre endorses the current phase of consumer capitalism in no uncertain terms,[54] my own readings of the films focus on their deep ambivalence toward modernity at large. In fact, I suggest that the conjugal couple and the nuclear family—two of the most iconic symbols of the modern—emerge in this later avatar of the genre as the most beleaguered institutions of all.

Chapter 5 of this book looks at the generic novelties the new millennium has spawned within the terrain of the supernatural. Undoubtedly, the mammoth global popularity of franchises such as *Harry Potter*, *The Lord of the Rings*, and the *Twilight* series has imbued the fantastic with new energy in the last fifteen years. In the current industrial dispensation that has been called New Bollywood, the streamlining, corporatization, and vertical integration that began post-liberalization in the 1990s has acquired a definite and more organized shape. Hollywood entities such as Viacom, Fox, and Disney now partner with local production houses to make and distribute films in India, and products and fans are simultaneously wired into multiple digital media platforms and social networks. In other words, how movies are made, distributed, and consumed has transformed dramatically in the era of the digital and new media. I coin the phrase "planetary paranormal" in this chapter to gesture to the multiple shifts that characterize the genres of the supernatural in this contemporary moment. New Bollywood's global aspirations have sharpened in the last decade or so and now include a definite tendency to align in generic terms with internationally legible cinematic products. I argue that this desire for products that remain largely "undifferentiated" from other cinemas has contorted the Hindi film form almost beyond recognition. This disassembly of the Hindi film—the enduring portmanteau formula that has remained stable at least since the 1940s, as Social, *masala*, or some other variation—manifests itself in two somewhat related fashions: first, the industry is churning out generic novelties like creature features or found-footage films *as such*; in other words, the formation of the generic system in Rick Altman's sense is now finally applicable to the Bollywood industry. Products are advertised with generic clear labels, and audience expectations and consumption patterns fall in place accordingly. Second, a vast number of recent products take it upon themselves to self-consciously perform the dismantling of the popular form. So, for example, although many recent horror films such as *Ragini MMS* (2011) do not include songs in the traditional sense, *Go Goa Gone* (2013), Bollywood's first "zom com," includes a sequence that parodies the archaic "song-and-dance" romantic moment in telling ways. I finally argue that the irony, humor, reflexivity, and cinephilia that inform the planetary paranormal remain curiously disemboweled of the political in any recognizable way: New Bollywood's supernatural simply occupies an endless planetary feedback loop of winsomely packaged media commodities that remain, with few exceptions, curiously unmoored from their immediate context. When the political does return to the supernatural—as it does, I suggest, in *Ragini MMS*—it imbricates itself foundationally with questions of form.

The overarching narrative I chart in *Haunting Bollywood* is one of discursive and historical disjunctions, as well as generic and formal continuities. Fractious and recalcitrant, these films have propelled the Hindi film into new formal terrains, even as they continued to make room for its most enduring pleasures. The genres of the supernatural register and amplify Hindi cinema's undertow of enchantment in specific ways; certain types of irrationalities are thrown into sharp relief in forms that do not fully endorse the rational to begin with. Beyond the interrogation of specific generic constellations, this book demonstrates that the supernatural is considerably labile in Indian popular film, which enables it to incubate questions of social significance—such as history, modernity, and the contemporary—in particularly suggestive ways.

CHAPTER ONE

Haunted Havelis *and Hapless Heroes*

GENDER, GENRE, AND THE HINDI GOTHIC FILM

The spectre is an absent presence, a liminal being that inhabits and gives shape to many of the figurations of trauma that characterise the Gothic. The spectre is also a strangely historical entity that is haunted by the culture which produced it.

—ANDREW SMITH, "HAUNTINGS"

IT IS A STORMY NIGHT OUTSIDE THE CITY OF ALLAHABAD, exactly two miles away from the Naini railway station and on the banks of the river Yamuna. A stentorian voice-over signposts the location and introduces the story of the palatial mansion called Sangam Bhavan. The stately home, built as a love nest, was abandoned and has lain empty and desolate for many years. On stormy nights such as this one, the voice tells us, a boat appears out of nowhere and sinks in the river, and soon after, someone is heard weeping from within the mansion. Local people are afraid of the place and consider it unlucky, but an old gardener continues to live on the premises in a broken-down hut. And it is his telling of the strange story of a doomed love that keeps the mansion alive in popular memory.[1]

As we hear this on the soundtrack, Hari Shankar (Ashok Kumar), the new owner of this property, arrives at Sangam Bhavan. The old gardener picks up the thread of the tale and recounts the incomplete love story of the unlucky first owner of the mansion and his mistress, Kamini, both of whom died under tragic circumstances. Left alone by the gardener/storyteller, Hari Shankar is startled to discover a painting that bears an uncanny resemblance to him. Bemused, he wonders if he was the original owner, now reborn as himself in this later life. Almost immediately, the clock strikes two. Hari Shankar first hears and then sees a spectral woman singing a song of intense romantic longing, of a lover's return. This, then, is the ghost of Kamini (Madhubala)—the long-dead protagonist of the earlier, incomplete saga of love. What follows is Shankar's precipitous, indeed calamitous, descent into obsession, madness, and finally, death.

What this skeletal plot summary of Kamal Amrohi's 1949 film *Mahal* (*Mansion*) alerts us to is that the Gothic found a hospitable, if unusual, home in postcolonial Hindi commercial cinema. Or perhaps the Gothic's habitation of Hindi film is not so peculiar after all, because, as several scholars, including David Punter and Glennis Byron, have noted, the postcolonial is foundationally infused with Gothic potentialities, whereby "the attempt to make, for example, the nation in a new form is inevitably accompanied by the traces of the past, by half buried histories of exile, transportation, emigration, all the panoply of the removal and transplantation of peoples which has been throughout history the essence of the colonial endeavor."[2] William Hughes and Andrew Smith take this proposition a step further when they suggest that "there is a sense . . . in which the Gothic is, and has always been, *post*-colonial."[3] Emerging in the crucible of Empire in its most robustly expansionist phase in the eighteenth and nineteenth centuries, certain key affinities align the Gothic fiction with the colonial and postcolonial dispensations, including a preoccupation with radical otherness, "challenges to the boundaries of power and ownership, haunting of a repressed past, and embodiment of the frightening."[4] In the cycle of films I discuss here, these possibilities are allowed to germinate and develop to a degree that is extraordinary in the Hindi cinema of this time. However, as Philip Holden cautions, instead of a reading of "tropes" unmoored from history, "a commitment to historicism" and careful attention to the specific cultural context are critical, if we are to excavate the elisions, repressions, and silences that Gothic modalities seek to make visible within the postcolony. For my purposes, Holden's understanding of the *complexities* that underpin the processes of decolonization remain particularly useful:

> National movements struggled to make use of both Enlightenment thought and to rediscover indigeneity, to erase colonialism but also to claim access to forms of modern universality. Newly independent nations aimed to leave the legacies of colonialism behind, only to find that they returned, often with even greater violence, in the politics and the polities of the postcolonial nation-state. Indeed a simple focus on the postcolonial/colonial opposition erases these histories.[5]

As I will argue in this chapter, the domestication of the Gothic in the Hindi commercial film is a precise instantiation of these imbrications between Enlightenment discourses of rationality and persistent traces of older, feudal vestiges, between generic demands and ideological imperatives. Like postcolonial fictions from Africa or the Caribbean, the Hindi Gothic film "has the potential to excavate and explore anxieties attendant on nationalism, and in the transition from colonial subjecthood to national citizenship, and indeed to explore ongoing exclusions and internal colonialism after independence."[6] The Hindi Gothic film is a theater where the drama of gender and citizenship is most evocatively enacted.

In terms of scholarship on the Hindi Gothic, most studies have focused on specific films such as the Bimal Roy classic, *Madhumati* (1958),[7] or *Mahal*, which I consider at some length below. In an essay on the fiftieth anniversary of the latter, Rachel Dwyer, for example, notes that

> [e]lements of the Gothic are similar [to Hindi film melodrama] in that the Gothic novel focuses on emotion and the anti-rational and the non-scientific which often oppose or haunt the rational and the modern. The Gothic novel's concerns include the fantastic, the immoral, darkness, desire, the supernatural, delusions, the evil and so on. They are a part of an eighteenth century reaction to the Enlightenment in which reason and scientific thinking were presented as part of a form of modernity. One may detect links between the Gothic and the problems of an Indian modernity, rooted in the Enlightenment, which has often been presented as India's only possible modernity rather than considering the possible alternative of localized modernities.[8]

The idea that Hindi commercial cinema shares a vexed relationship with the modern has come to be somewhat axiomatic in Indian cinema studies. The problem is especially acute for the Gothic genre because its basic material remains decidedly and recognizably Western, British fiction, or Western film adaptations of this literature. Bombay cinema's romance with the Gothic is thus an appropriation and restructuring of an inherited colonial form.[9] However, contemporary reviews of the Hindi Gothic film suggest that the Gothic arrives in Indian cinema via a slightly more circuitous route.

Although the audiences (or reviewers) were occasionally aware of the literary source material for the films in question, more often than not the yardstick for comparison was the Hollywood films that were widely exhibited in India at that time. Consider, for example, the somewhat disgruntled review of *Kohraa* (*Fog*, 1964), which remains a decidedly *local* adaptation of Daphne du Maurier's Gothic novel *Rebecca*: "But the story—a very poor imitation of 'Rebecca' and other films—is undistinguished; the handling trite. . . . In 'Rebecca,' the audience was never given a glimpse of the dead woman. Yet so vividly was she present in the talk of the other characters, people left the theatres certain they had seen her."[10] Clearly, here the frame of reference remains Alfred Hitchcock's 1940 film and not the original novel, and given the aesthetics of the film in question, one suspects that this was true for filmmaker Biren Naug as well.[11]

Similarly, the treatment of the ghostly female figure in *Woh Kaun Thi?* (*Who Was She?*) is criticized by the unimpressed *Filmfare* reviewer because it fails to match the standards set by Hollywood:

> One of the most effective foreign films dealing with a ghost was "Portrait of Jennie." The film succeeded because it did not try to give a "natural" explanation. The loose end was allowed to dangle tantalisingly in the viewer's memory. "Woh Kaun Thi?" ends instead as a crime story. It is ironic that the film is most convincing when it deals with the improbable, most unreal when it brings in reality.[12]

This is actually a remarkably insightful reading of the film's formal capitulations, but more on that later. Although the readership of English film magazines was arguably limited to a particular kind of film viewer—who also watched Hollywood and was familiar with its formal and narrative practices—these disparaging takes on the Hindi Gothic film provide startling evidence of the challenges that the genre was up against in its own time. It is also worthwhile to note that the Hindi film industry underwent massive transformations in the period I explore in this chapter—the late 1940s to mid-1960s. From the dissolution of the studios and a restructuring of the political economy after World War II to the ascendancy of such auteurs and stars as Bimal Roy and Raj Kapoor, this phase is also considered to be the "golden era" of Indian cinema. However, the Gothic film remains something of an anomaly within this domain, as I aim to demonstrate below.

To summarize, although the recognizable motifs of Western Gothic texts—decaying manor houses, a history of violence/violation, madness, incarceration, preponderance of mirrors, doppelgängers, and unspeakable secrets—remain in place, Hindi film also grafts onto this cluster its own thematic concerns, such as narratives of rebirth and reincarnation, aligned with Hindu thought and philosophy.[13] *Kohraa*, in fact, provides an excellent template for the kind of retooling and repurposing the Gothic underwent in its Hindi film avatar. Unlike *Rebecca*, in which the second Mrs. de Winter remains nameless, in *Kohraa* the young protagonist is Rajeshwari (Waheeda Rehman), who marries a dashing aristocrat, Amit Kumar Singh (Biswajeet), and moves into his palatial home, Mayflower. Beyond these superficial changes, *Kohraa*'s most radical adaptative gesture is to change the dynamic between Rajeshwari and Daai Maa (Lalita Pawar, who plays the housekeeper, the Mrs. Danvers character) almost beyond recognition.

Whereas in the novel—and in Hitchcock's film—the sinister housekeeper's obsessive, erotic attachment to the dead Rebecca (named Poonam in the film) provides the narrative fulcrum for the dissolution of the second de Winter marriage, in *Kohraa* a monumental courtroom revelation elevates Daai Maa to the position of hero: it was she who killed her beloved Poonam (played by the actress Thelma), to put an end to her amoral, promiscuous, dissolute ways. Even before this climactic moment, Daai Ma and Rajeshwari's interactions and disagreements lack the twisted gravitas of the source material; as melodramatic protagonists of the Hindi film, they remain tethered to the overdetermined affective positions of mother-in-law and daughter-in-law, respectively. In the final moments when Rajeshwari symbolically touches Daai Maa's feet in respectful surrender to her benign authority and her self-sacrificing spirit, *Kohraa* congeals as a cautionary tale about properly consolidated bourgeois femininities and the inviolable sanctity of the Hindu marriage. Tellingly, unlike the doomed Manderley of du Maurier's novel, Mayflower survives the catastrophic legal/moral crisis, leaving Amit's feudal patrimony intact. The conjugal couple can thus be reinvented and reconfigured within the familiar portals of the modernized *haveli*. The reason I do not include this film in my discussion of the Gothic cycle—despite stylistic and structural similarities with the rest—is twofold. First, Poonam appears in *Kohraa* as a *real* ghost who actually haunts Mayflower and attempts to murder Rajeshwari. The other Gothic films in the cluster do not validate the supernatural in the same way. And second, the haunting of Rajeshwari instead of Amit also makes this film something of an exception in the way in which this generic terrain is gendered. As an exception to the rules, however, *Kohraa* remains a particularly important example of how the imported Gothic was reformulated and domesticated in Hindi cinema.

In terms of visual aesthetics, these films—beyond *Mahal*, my sample here includes *Woh Kaun Thi?* (Raj Khosla, 1964) and *Bees Saal Baad* (*Twenty Years Later*, Biren Naug, 1962)[14]—typically feature rich black-and-white cinematography with high-contrast images, striking chiaroscuro compositions that are often shot night-for-night, and fluid camera movements.[15] Mise-en-scènes are detailed and carefully crafted, the centerpiece of which are the feudal mansions, or *havelis*, with their ornate chandeliers, baroque spiral staircases, heavy furniture, paintings, weapons, mirrors—essentially feudal clutter and detritus, which the films lovingly and nostalgically showcase as remnants of a more gracious, if irrecoverable, past. The decadence of the

FIGURE 1.1. *Hari Shankar approaches the* haveli *Sangam Bhavan in* Mahal.

feudal mansion is instrumental in reinforcing its uncanniness, its sickness, its unnatural being in the present: "These objects conjure up memories, a past; their vestments, always slightly faded and dated remind us of those who came before; they embody dreams, delusions of presence now past. They possess aura, or transmit live memories of aura under the aegis of its decline."[16] The postcolonial Gothic genre fetishizes feudal splendor while simultaneously repudiating its excesses. While the deployment of a formidable array of cinematic technologies enables nostalgic affect to gather around the figuration of a bygone era, the larger discourses within which these films are embedded demand a rejection of that history. This discursive domain is able to gesture toward the supernatural only as a fleeting and illusory possibility.

Stylistically, intricate sound design is yet another important feature of the genre: under the talented stewardship of music directors such as Khemchand Prakash, Madan Mohan, and Hemanta Mukherjee, these films include beautiful music, both as hit songs and lush background scores.[17] Many of the most memorable songs are sung by Lata Mangeshkar, considered to be not only one of the most gifted but also the most ethereal of playback voices in Hindi cinema. Indeed Lata's singing voice comes to be a key trope through which the Gothic as a generic rubric is consolidated, and I return to this later in the chapter. Amrohi's *Mahal*, described by Vijay Mishra as "the first significant Indian gothic,"[18] would come to be the generic prototype; elements introduced in it would crystallize as generic conventions over the next decades.

Although critical ruminations on the Gothic note that genre's kinship with the horror film, most scholars are reluctant to overstate this relationship, either because the films do not inspire fear in the spectator or because the "ghosts" in question are ultimately explained away as phantasmagorias deployed to very specific ends.[19] I would, however, like to emphasize that the Gothic's relationship to horror in Hindi commercial film is very robust indeed. Following Brian Baker's argument, I read the "the modes of Gothic and horror . . . in a kind of generic continuum, albeit acknowledging that the two are not identical."[20] In fact, a lot of the conventional motifs deployed in later horror films—including the excessive Ramsay horror films of the 1970s and 1980s, which are radically different in tone and texture—can be traced back to the Gothic films under discussion.[21]

Furthermore, I am less interested in the "realness" of the ghost or the supernatural than in the *function* of ghostliness and spectrality in the Hindi Gothic. The ghost, in this analysis, and what Punter calls "the logic of haunting" inadvertently betray the apprehensions—indeed the horrors—of postcolonial modernity. Derrida's sumptuous *Specters of Marx* has revived academic interest in ghosts, spirits, and revenants, and it is telling that for Derrida, one of the most constitutive aspects of the specter is its liminality, its inbetween-ness between flesh and spirit: "[T]he specter is a paradoxical incorporation, the becoming-body, a certain phenomenal and carnal form of the spirit. It becomes, rather, some 'thing' that remains difficult to name: neither soul nor body, and both one and the other."[22] It is this indeterminate quality of the ghost—simultaneously immaterial and sensual, erotic and thanatic—that endows it with power in the Hindi Gothic film. The fundamental modality of haunting generated in these films is predicated on this paradox.

In this chapter, I argue that the Gothic ghost film jostles uneasily against many of the imperatives of the reformist "Social," the umbrella genre in the 1950s and 1960s designating all films set in the contemporary moment. This disquiet can be unpacked at different registers but is foundationally a problem of the Gothic genre coming into its own at a specific moment in the history of Bombay cinema. Starting with *Mahal*, the films are situated within, or alongside, the overdetermined terrain of the Nehruvian Social, which, more than any other Bombay genre, sought to define and concretize postcolonial modernity at this time; the reformist impetus, above all else, characterized the genre.[23] In what follows I argue that the "problem of an Indian modernity" comes to be particularly aligned to the figure of the masculine citizen-subject, the beleaguered hero of the Bombay Gothic film.

Especially interesting for my purposes here is the trajectory of the hero, both physical and philosophical. Countless films of the era enact the hero's journey from the village to the city; this itinerary, of course, resonates with the *bildungsroman* of the emergent nation-state—the nation was, discursively speaking, making a similar journey to modernity, development, industrial capital, and so on, the locus of which is the modern postcolonial metropolis.[24] This moment of arrival—we are reminded of Shambhu and his son's arrival in Calcutta in Bimal Roy's *Do Bigha Zamin* (*Two Acres of Land*, 1953), or of Raj Kapoor's wide-eyed first look at Bombay city in *Shree 420* (*Mr. 420*, 1955)—is a cherished event in Nehruvian cinema, around which congeals an entire universe of postcolonial discourses. The Gothic ghost film reverses this reified journey back to the village—or at least to an uncharted, unspecific non-urban space of profound uncertainty and peril. The hero travels to a place suspended in time, where the past remains present and palpable; the journey to the haunted feudal *haveli* of these films enacts a return to the remnant, the retrograde, and the regressive, a scandalous path for any modern hero worth his salt.[25] This initial break with the triumphant narrative of national destiny comes to be foundational—it sets in motion a ripple effect that eventually rocks the very construct of the Nehruvian hero and the discourses he so steadfastly embodies.

It is also important to underscore that contemporary contexts as well as larger terrains of identity—of family, class, and the like—so crucial to the Social films of the period, are almost entirely absent in the Gothic. When the hero travels to the feudal *haveli*, he almost always leaves behind public spaces, urban and rural, for a realm of interiors both architectural and psychological. His moorings within larger realms of belonging simply fall away. This is especially startling in a film such as *Woh Kaun Thi?*, which is ostensibly set in the city of Bombay, but we never see the bustling streets and urban neighborhoods so prominently featured in the films of the period. Beginning with *Mahal*, in the sections below I interrogate the tropes through which the dissolution of a certain postcolonial imaginary comes to be a core generic modality of the Gothic.

FIGURING THE HAUNTED HERO

As mentioned above, positing the modern citizen-subject of the new nation-state was a self-imposed task that the Social took very seriously at this time. Whatever the complications and entanglements of lived, quotidian, social worlds in postcolonial India, the Hindi commercial film imagined the Western-educated, modern, rational, male citizen with disarming simplicity. *Mahal*, too, is no exception, at least in the beginning. When we first encounter Hari Shankar as he steps into his recently acquired Sangam Bhavan, the signifiers of a "national modernity" are writ large on his person and demeanor. Garbed in a Western-style suit, Hari Shankar *introduces himself by name* to the old gardener/servant of the *haveli*, setting himself apart from the despotic feudal masters of the past. After listening to the tragic story of doomed love, he requests that the servant travel to a place called Georgetown, in order to inform his friend, Shrinath (Kanu Roy), of his arrival. Even this request is made only after Hari Shankar acknowledges the hardship the trip would mean for the old gardener. The bewildered employee, unused to such courtesy, quickly agrees to leave on the errand so graciously requested. This early exchange between Hari Shankar and the old gardener serves no clear narrative purpose in the exposition, except to buttress the modern sensibility of male protagonist—his commitment to a less stratified, more egalitarian worldview. Hari Shankar's validity as hero derives from his habitation of the discourses of modernity, and his status as an ideal postcolonial citizen is foundationally tethered to the larger philosophical imperatives of the developmental nation-state.

The dismantling of this universe—which commences with the reverse trajectory from the city—becomes inevitable with Hari Shankar's solitary encounter with the painting that resembles him exactly, in this first instance of Gothic doubling.[26] Startlingly, his immediate conclusion upon seeing the portrait is that he must be the old master of the *haveli*, reborn in another time. This observation is instantly followed by the chiming of the clock—an important motif in *Mahal*—and the strains of the song "Aayega Aanewala" ("My Beloved Will Come"), almost as though the hero has unwittingly opened the door to the irrational by his very words. Fascinated by the siren song, Hari Shankar follows the disembodied voice until he chances upon Kamini, the enchanting wraith/woman who restlessly wanders through the mansion, singing of her lover's imminent return. The thematic of return and repetition, of doubling back, of the failure of progress, is a critical gesture in *Mahal*, which I suggest comes to be modular for the Gothic genre as a whole in Hindi commercial cinema. Hari Shankar is immediately drawn to her, an attraction that swiftly becomes obsessive. After the first "sighting" of Kamini, he touches a burning cigarette to his skin, seeking to reassure himself of his wakefulness; for all practical purposes, he has already entered into a state of inescapable delirium.

The sprawling, baroque interior of the *mahal* is uncanny not only because Kamini's ghost haunts its ramparts but also because it remains *simultaneously* strange and familiar to Hari Shankar, "[f]or the home or house connotes not only the familiar but also what is secret, concealed, hidden from sight. When what is 'of or like the home' is synonymous with its opposite, we are quite close to the signifying field of the gothic narrative. The house,

FIGURE 1.2. *Hari Shankar encounters a painting of his doppelgänger in* Mahal.

in these films, is certainly uncanny."[27] This is how Mary Ann Doane, following Freud's famous 1919 essay, describes this slippage in her seminal work on the Hollywood Gothic. Similarly, it is no coincidence that Amrohi's film is titled after the mansion—the ghostly habitat forms the core of *Mahal*'s complex mediation of space, time, and desire. The mansion is the spatial locus of a suspended temporality—simply put, time is arrested within its stately confines. Hari Shankar, too, becomes suspended in time, trapped like an insect within amber, inhabiting a space-time continuum that is radically separated from the teleology he has left behind.

The hero's encounter with—and surrender to—the ghostly Kamini is also an acknowledgment of what is repressed within him; his capitulation to her charm is tantamount to a disavowal of modernity. As described above, the incursion of the irrational-supernatural-feminine remains fairly sudden, and the male subject's descent into irrationality, affliction, and madness is precipitous thereafter. It is important to note that Kamini is also insubstantial, a spectral wraith who always eludes the hero's corporeal, sensual desire;[28] it is altogether a different kind of attachment/submission she demands. Their love remains, constitutively, a non-reproductive love that will not beget the nation's future citizens. This non-productivity is resonant with the space and texture of desire that Hari Shankar feels for Kamini and the *mahal*. In a critical sense, in Hari Shankar's befuddled consciousness, Kamini and the *mahal* are one and the same—ghostly, sepulchral embodiments of stasis, inertia, stillness, and oblivion. The woman and the edifice also congeal for the audience as the topos of his fevered mind. Early on, at Shrinath's concerned insistence, he tries to leave Allahabad and the accursed *mahal*. But Kamini's haunting plaint, repeated through the aural motif of "Aayega Aanewala," ensnares him on the train, that iconic marker of modern technology and progress, just as he is about to exit, perhaps, the enchanted ambit of her voice. Hari Shankar eagerly returns to the *mahal*, besotted with the dialectic of Kamini's present voice and, in some ways, absent body.

GHOST VOICES, LATA MANGESHKAR, AND THE ACOUSMATIC PRESENCE

The unyielding strength of Kamini's spell is conveyed through the power of the "Aayega Aanewala" melody and the tenor and cadence of Lata's singing voice.[29] Kamini's song remains the most compelling signifier of the ghost's mesmerizing lure. In *Mahal* it develops into a musical leitmotif, repeated—in part or whole—over and over as Hari Shankar sinks farther into insanity and delirium. In terms of visualization, the bulk of the song is accompanied on-screen with images of Hari Shankar searching for a source of the singing, following the elusive Kamini around, as she glides through the mansion, tantalizingly just out of sight or glimpsed fleetingly in the corner of his eye. In other words, the disembodied song emanates from an imprecise off-screen space, an aural accompaniment to an obsessive game of hide-and-seek. *Mahal* also plays with internal and external diegetic sound: Hari Shankar continues to hear Kamini's song later, when he is traveling in the hills, clearly out of the sonic range of the mansion. Is he merely hallucinating Kamini's ghostly melody in these instances? Because no one else seems to hear the song, we are left to wonder if we are privy to the hero's troubled state of mind. The film creates a marvelous texture of indeterminacy; affectively bound to Hari Shankar, we are left floundering and unsure of what is real and what is a mere projection of his phantasmagorial attachment.

Philosopher of film sound Michel Chion has spent considerable energy expounding on what he calls acousmatic sound—a sound whose source or cause remains unseen. For scholars of Indian cinema, Chion's insights are important for understanding the implications of playback singing. Especially provocative for the purposes of the current discussion is Chion's elaboration on the acousmatic voice/presence and its allegiance to the ghostly and the spectral:

> He must [the acousmatic presence], even if only slightly, have *one foot in the image*, in the space of the film; he must haunt the borderlands that are neither the interior of the filmic stage nor the proscenium—a place that has no name, but which the cinema forever brings into play.

> Being in the screen and not, wandering the surface of the screen without entering it, the acousmetre brings disequilibrium and tension. He invites the spectator to *go see*, and he can be an *invitation to the loss of the self, to desire and fascination.*[30]

Kamini's song can therefore be read as an exemplary instance of Chion's acousmatic presence,[31] that which haunts the image and invites the listener to a surrender of the self.[32] In Hari Shankar's case, this invitation is also a seamless imbrication of eros and thanatos—in desiring Kamini, he longs to be unified with death.

Lata Mangeshkar's voice and style of singing is perhaps the most important tool in *Mahal*'s generation of the terrain of spectral enchantment. Interestingly, the "Aayega Aanewala" song is one of Lata's earliest hits, the song that lays the foundation of her aural stardom. Discussing this early hit, Neepa Majumdar writes:

> Here, both narratively and technologically, we hear a ghost voice, and at both levels the emphasis is on the lure of a disembodied voice. This song is now more closely identified with the star persona of Lata Mangeshkar than with the character played by Madhubala, although Madhubala's death at an early age certainly adds resonance to it. But the song's aural associations are stronger than the visual or narrative context of the film in which it appeared. In the fan discourse on Lata Mangeshkar, it also provides a kind of myth of origins for her identity as a playback star. The record of the song was originally released with the name of the narrative character, Kamini, credited as the singer, but it became so popular that "thousands of requests for the song used to pour in at the radio station along with a request to mention the name of the singer while playing the record. The radio officials approached HMV [His Master's Voice] to find out who the singer of this runaway hit was. As a result of this, Lata's name began to be announced over the radio."[33]

Lata's voice has thus been associated with the spectral from her earliest years, a fact not dwelled on very often by either critics or fans. For the purpose of my analysis, the slippage between Lata and Kamini is intriguing because if Lata is always already present in the ghost's seduction, then, at least in the case of *Mahal*, Kamini the character also "haunted" Lata's stardom in this early phase. There is an echo-chamber effect here, an intimacy and an affinity between Lata's stardom and the ghostly and the phantasmatic, that I would like to hold on to for the remainder of this discussion.[34]

FIGURE 1.3. *The ghostly Kamini on a swing in* Mahal. *Used by permission of the National Film Archive of India.*

Lata, of course, has become a legend in her lifetime for her prodigious musical talent as well as for the enormous number of songs she has sung over her almost seventy-year career. Indeed, Lata's industrial dominance as Bombay cinema's most prominent female playback singer had been almost absolute until very recently. The scholarship on Indian film music also regards her as the emblematic female voice of the modernizing nation, the voice of postcolonial, public femininity. For example, according to Sanjay Srivastava, Lata's voice is "the aesthetic epitome of Indian feminine identity"; he further argues that her "shrill adolescent-girl falsetto" not only helped purge Indian film music of its scandalous, disreputable connections with the Muslim *tawaif* traditions but also "provided another resolution of the 'woman question' in the post-colonial context: how to have women in public, but also within the firm grip of a watchful, adult, masculinity, such that the public woman became forever infantilised."[35]

Within the context of the postcolonial impetus toward sanitization, what is the adult masculinity that is so powerfully consolidated by Lata's "infantile" singing? In Srivastava's argument, the postcolonial Five Year Plan hero "represents, in a broad sense, a particular formulation of Indian masculinity where manliness comes to attach not to bodily representations or aggressive behavior but, rather, to being 'scientific' and 'rational.'"[36] This figure of modern postcolonial masculinity, aligned to the adult concerns of development, progress, and a vision of "national good," can be observed in countless films of the era, including the ones I am discussing here. He further argues that through various narrative ideological maneuvers, including spatial ones, the Hindi commercial film deployed Lata's voice in order to buttress the masculinity of the FYP hero:

> Lata's voice—her artistry—was also a part of the process where men from strong patriarchal backgrounds—the film industry people—sought to exercise control over the representation of women through both an expressive timbre and a vocabulary which resonated with more "controllable" environment: the village and the province. The city can, potentially, be a threat to male hegemony, and the presence of the screen-woman in its public places compounded this threat. So, if the heroine figure was infantilised through Lata's voice, she was also produced as familiar and speaking—or, rather, singing—in the language of "home" and the controllable domestic space rather than a recently produced public sphere, the nation.[37]

Certainly, Lata's singing voice becomes at this juncture a site for contestations over gender, nation, and a revamped traditionalism, and Lata's "chaste," desexualized public persona participated in these discourses to a very large extent.[38] However, to posit that Lata's "child-like" voice *always* performs the singular function of consolidating this nationalist-patriarchal figuration of the FYP hero is too simplistic a formulation. Lata has sung too many songs, and too many different kinds of songs, for us to be able to straitjacket her aural stardom into neat categories. In the Gothic film, for instance, the precise obverse of this process is elaborated—Lata's voice engenders an affective terrain that quite systematically ruptures the figuration of the male citizen-subject.

Let us consider another example of the Gothic film, Raj Khosla's *Woh Kaun Thi?* starring Manoj Kumar and Sadhana. In this film, the FYP hero, Anand, is a medical doctor, the profession emblematic of scientific rationality. On his way back from work one rainy night, he almost literally runs into a mysterious woman in white who refuses to introduce herself and rebuffs all of his questions. Intrigued, Anand offers to give her a ride, despite the oddness of her demeanor. His windshield wipers stop working as soon as she sits in his car, but with a vision that seems preternaturally sharp, the woman guides Anand as he drives through winding roads in the rain. At her request, a perplexed Anand drops her just outside an old cemetery, and we hear the first strains of Lata's song "Naina Barse Rimjhim Rimjhim" ("My Eyes Rain Tears") as the spectral form disappears into the mist. Soon after, Anand's girlfriend, Seema (Helen), is murdered and he begins to see the mysterious woman everywhere. Their second encounter is occasioned by a phone call that summons Anand to the site of a supposed medical emergency. Anand arrives at a dark, decrepit mansion—with cobwebs, creaking stairways, and unsettling shadows, where the conventions of the

FIGURE 1.4. *Sandhya enters a cemetery in* Woh Kaun Thi?

Gothic come to be clearly aligned with horror—and he realizes that the patient, already dead, is none other than the young woman he had driven to the cemetery. Disheartened and confused, Anand leaves the mansion, only to be told by a policeman that the mansion is a haunted house and on stormy nights, many an unwary doctor is summoned to the site of death. Anand rushes back to the house to find it chillingly empty of all inhabitants, dead or alive. Shaken by this second encounter with the "supernatural," Anand's sanity, rationality, and scientific temperament begin to unravel quite rapidly.

Woh Kaun Thi? stages the next steps of the FYP hero's dissolution through an unusual narrative twist—conjugality. Worried over her son's mental state, Anand's mother arranges his marriage to Sandhya, who—ironically and rather horrifically for Anand—turns out to be the ghostly woman's uncanny double![39] Although Sandhya (also played by Sadhana) resolutely denies that she was present at multiple locations and on separate occasions as Anand alleges, he is unable to come close to her. Her very presence takes him back to the mansion of ghostly encounters and reduces him to a nervous, confused wreck—a hysteric. Here, as in *Mahal*, Lata's song generates Sandhya as the acousmatic presence, Chion's "special being" whose "voice becomes invested with magical powers."[40] For Chion, the acousmatic voice often shares an imprecise relationship with bodies on the screen; its power lies precisely in its un-anchored freedom. Tellingly, the "Naina Barse" song refuses to remain confined to Anand's home, where Sandhya lives; it follows him everywhere, haunting within his own home and without.[41] Thus, the relationship between on-screen and off-screen space, the imprecise spatial organization and location of the *haveli*, and the ability of the ghost/voice to traverse heterogeneous spaces are all spaces opened up by the technologies and apparatuses of Hindi cinema, and they coalesce in the Gothic film in a compelling manner.

Sandhya appears and disappears, seemingly at will; she sings the same song and sketches the very same haunted house that Anand had been invited to earlier in the film. But she is simultaneously a resident in his own home, significantly destabilizing that foundational locus of bourgeois safety and selfhood.[42] Sandhya is both dutifully domestic and dangerously ghostly; she lives as his wife, yet remains fundamentally unknowable. She calmly addresses his frantic questions but refuses to provide satisfactory answers. Sandhya comes to be the embodiment of Freud's *unheimlich* in this context, and the film artfully explores the simultaneous desire and repulsion Anand feels for this woman who invades his home and his senses, but to him remains, constitutively, also a sign of certain death. Driven to anguish, Anand finally sends Sandhya away from his home, only to learn of her death—a second death essentially, as he has already seen her dead in the mansion—in a train accident. But, of course, this death does not bring closure, either. A ghostly Sandhya continues to sing "Naina Barse" to a now almost completely unhinged Anand in faraway Simla, where his friends take him to recover.

The trope of an unsuccessful marriage remains common between *Mahal* and *Woh Kaun Thi?*. In both films, the postcolonial FYP hero gradually comes to be obsessed and possessed, rendered helpless, passive, and impotent. In *Mahal*, Hari Shankar's impotence and emasculation come to be literal as he fails to consummate the marriage that his father arranges for him, in an abortive attempt to restore him to the time-space configuration of the modern, productive citizen. Just as Hari Shankar is about to lift his bride Ranjana's (Vijayalaxmi) veil—a symbolic gesture for the establishment of conjugal relations in Hindi cinema's shorthand—Kamini's song calls him away from the nuptial bed, blighting permanently the possibility of a procreative marriage. The only love he is capable of is pathological—an obsessive modality that afflicts his soul and within which his body is merely an encumbrance. Rachel Dwyer notes that "Hari Shankar has to reject his wife in order to try to become himself. The rejection of a beautiful and devoted wife and the companionship she offers in favour of a morbid and ethereal beauty is never challenged. Hari Shankar embraces what he knows he must reject."[43] In a near echo of the wedding night sequence from *Mahal*, in *Woh Kaun Thi?* the marriage between Anand and Sandhya remains an unconsummated failure, until the mystery of the apparition is resolved.[44]

We must note that alongside a descent into madness and hysteria, the

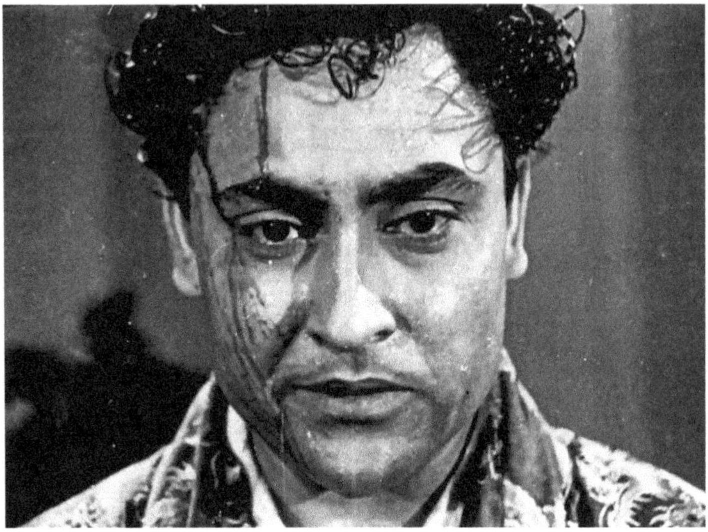

FIGURE 1.5. *A haunted Hari Shankar in* Mahal. *Used by permission of the National Film Archive of India.*

male protagonist in these films also becomes physically unstable and incapacitated—Hari Shankar keeps losing his balance, and he falls down and injures himself on at least three different occasions in *Mahal*. Anand in *Woh Kaun Thi?* takes a tumble down a hillside in Simla and is hospitalized; the very ground the male citizen walks on is rendered treacherous in the genre. The dismantling of masculinity can be unpacked on the aural register, too. Flouting Hindi commercial cinema's grammar of establishing heterosexual romance, these heroes almost never sing duets with their beloveds. As mentioned above, Lata's signature "ghost songs" are emphatically solo tracks; the hero can only mutely follow the singing wraith or be stalked by her voice. The affective terrain of partnership and mutuality demanded by love duets is never animated in these songs; the power to enthrall, seduce, and render silent remains with the woman/ghost.[45]

Biren Naug's *Bees Saal Baad* betrays some of the struggles that lie at the heart of the Hindi Gothic genre. A loose adaptation of Sir Arthur Conan Doyle's *The Hound of the Baskervilles*, the film's allegiance to a Gothic imagination coupled with an insistence on rational deduction makes it a special case. Since Sherlock Holmes and Dr. Watson do not feature as characters in the film, the task of logical deduction falls on the hero (the Henry Baskerville character in the original), Kumar Vijay Singh (Biswajeet). From the outset, Kumar is reluctant to accept the story of the vengeful *pretni* (female ghost) who murders all the feudal lords of Chandangarh, the film's fictitious location. It is to investigate and *solve* the murder of his uncle, the last *jagirdar* (landlord), that brings Kumar from London.

Armed with Western-style suits, rifles, and fedora hats, the male protagonist displays very few of the anxieties that Hari Shankar and Dr. Anand embody in the other texts under consideration here. Tellingly, Kumar seems perplexed when he hears the ghost's song—Lata's eerie rendition of "Kahin Deep Jale Kahin Dil" ("Lamps Burn and So Do Hearts")—but not mesmerized or terrified. He pursues the specter determinedly through a swamp, but this is a different, more confident kind of pursuit, unhampered by love or longing. The female ghost in *Bees Saal Baad* is subject to a masculine, rational, investigative gaze—one that seeks to demystify her very existence quickly and efficiently. The male protagonist remains in control of his destiny, and he falls in love with Radha (Waheeda Rehman), a village belle, instead of the spectral woman who sings and weeps in the swamp. Unsurprisingly, Kumar is able to sing love songs to Radha, unencumbered by ghostly passions.[46]

Concomitantly, the film invites a different sort of spectatorial engagement—we are participants in Kumar's investigation, asked to assess a host of slightly sinister characters who are proffered as possible architects of a nefarious plot against the hero. It remains true to the spirit of Conan Doyle, in that its indulgence of the irrational remains arguably brief; the mystery of the spectral manifestation is always already embedded in a whodunit format of the investigative thriller. The powerful uncanny harnessed by Kamini in *Mahal* or Sandhya in *Woh Kaun Thi?* is largely missing in this film. Ironically, in terms of aesthetics, *Bees Saal Baad* is superbly Gothic.[47] From Naug's masterful chiaroscuro lighting of the *haveli* and the restless, balletic movements of the camera, to the swamp of reeds and crumbling tunnels and temples, reminiscent of Shindo Kaneto's *Onibaba* (*Demon Hag*, 1964), to the unanchored spectrality of Lata's song—everything in *Bees Saal Baad* is poised to become the ghostly and the haunted.[48] However, underpinned by a sturdy scaffolding of deductive logic, *Bees Saal Baad* remains deeply and confidently masculine; the mesmeric lure of the "ghost story" is fleeting here, at best.

LOVE IN THE TIME OF GHOSTS

So far, I have focused almost exclusively on the spatial aspects of haunting in the Gothic film. However, time is also rendered profoundly ambivalent in this generic formation; the specter "de-synchronizes, it recalls us to anachrony."[49] In her recent work on East Asian horror cinema,

FIGURE 1.6. Bees Saal Baad *hero Kumar Vijay Singh descends the* haveli *stairs. Used by permission of the National Film Archive of India.*

Bliss Cua Lim argues that the ghost film interrupts what she calls "modern time consciousness," the time of clocks and calendars—the temporal axis that Walter Benjamin has famously called "homogenous empty time."[50] She writes, "Ghosts call our calendars into question. The temporality of haunting—the return of the dead, the recurrence of events—refuses the linear progression of modern time consciousness, flouting the limits of mortality and historical time."[51] In the Hindi Gothic film, this temporality—essentially the linear, progressive time of the modern nation-state—is suspended and rendered obsolete, not only within the confines of the *haveli* but also without. The male protagonist's struggle hereafter is a struggle to re-enter, re-inhabit the temporality of the modern.

It is no accident that in *Mahal*, Kamini's beckoning song always follows the clock's chiming two. Dwyer writes:

> The clock also represents the repetition of time, striking two every night (and afternoon) as well as its passing. The hero is lost in the present and seeks his place in the past . . . and wants to recreate the past in the future where this reunion will take place. He is willing to

> sacrifice his present by dying for the sake of this past and the future. The song "Aayega Aanewala" is repeated many times in the film; 'he will come,' the future tense repeated again and again within the song.[52]

What Dwyer's analysis alerts us to is the palimpsestic quality of time in the Gothic. I would suggest that multiple temporalities are not simply engendered or layered in the genre; distinct temporal modes collide and get radically fractured. The confrontation with the ghostly feminine in the feudal *haveli* and the hero's absolute surrender to her spell is a capitulation to a specific kind of past and an abrogation of all that the FYP hero is narratively and discursively aligned to. Time is rendered disjunctive, "out of joint," in another way, as Dwyer notes: through repetition. The "Naina Barse" song is repeated on at least five different occasions in *Woh Kaun Thi?*, punctuating the narrative and signposting the stages of Anand's progressively fraying composure. Even in the relatively straightforward narrative organization of *Bees Saal Baad*, the "Kahin Deep Jale" song generates an excessive pattern of repetition and return to the site of the successive murders.

Scholars of Hindi commercial cinema have often dwelled on the formation's departures from classical storytelling. But even if we bear Hindi cinema's penchant for meandering, non-linear plots and multiple interruptions, the repetition of the ghost's song is an extraordinarily powerful, and peculiar, convention in the Gothic. The repetition of the phantom's song resonates with a series of missed encounters with the hapless hero; what is engendered in the process is a narrative of replication and circularity where every movement is also, constitutively, a return to the same scene. Lim reminds us of Derrida's comment about the ghost: "One cannot control its [the specter's] comings and goings because it begins by coming back."[53] I use the word "scene" here also to draw on its rich psychoanalytic valences. The hero comes to be akin to Freud's famous hysteric: repeating the traumatic scenario compulsively and pointlessly until almost the very end of these films. The spectator, too, is bound up with the hero's psychological universe; we are, as mentioned above, typically, the only others who can hear/see the ghost.[54]

In terms of the basic generic and ideological preoccupations of Nehruvian cinema, the Gothic ghost film remains an extraordinary formation in the 1950s and 1960s. Although many genres of the period betrayed varying degrees of anxiety about the rapid modernization and industrialization that national independence brought in its wake, there is also an unmistakable optimism about the future of the postcolonial nation-state; this buoyancy is part and parcel of the Social's reformist-pedagogic impetus. As several scholarly studies have shown, however ruthless the modern, industrialized present, the hero's destiny is braided with the progressivist, purposive narrative of the nation. In the Gothic, however, one detects a certain kind of unwillingness—perhaps even an inability—to participate wholeheartedly in this forward-looking ethos. From the hero's initial turning back toward the feudal *haveli*, his path decisively diverges from that of the triumphant trajectory of national modernity and the relentless march toward a utopian future. Here, the FYP hero remains willingly entangled with the past, enmeshed in a special kind of seduction—his love for the female ghost is aligned with an enchantment with an arrested movement—with stillness, stasis, and inertia. Enfeebled, hystericized, queer, and nearly insane, the hero's inability to overcome the retrograde feudal and move forward is echoed by narratives of circularity, repetition, and pointless, meandering sojourns to nowhere.[55] This scandalous rejection of the modern and the rational-masculine is achieved in the Gothic via, among other components, the haunting cadence and tenor of Lata's singing voice. The refusal/dismantling of modern masculinity in the Gothic ghost story is a generic trope, a convention that is perfectly in keeping with the dominance of the feminine in these films. The ghostly feminine is irrational and anachronistic, but its power remains unquestionable in the films under discussion.

RE-GENDERING THE GOTHIC FILM: EN-GENDERING THE THRILLER

What, then, is to be done? The postcolonial male citizen-subject cannot be abandoned with his masculinity in tatters, cannot be deserted in the throes of irrationality and madness. The FYP hero must be restored to modernity, as it were. Historical and ideological imperatives necessitate that the narrative cannot remain in disarray, mired in returns and repetitions, either.

Hereafter, the films deploy a tricky sleight of hand to accomplish virtually an impossible task—recuperate the impaired/imperiled masculinity of the hero and reinstate him to the helm of narrative agency. This recuperative gesture, then, will also reinscribe him within the modern time-consciousness of the nation-state. The universe of meanings that have gathered around the "ghost story" must be, figuratively speaking, put to rest. Needless to say, this task proves quite arduous, and the only way these texts can guarantee the hapless hero's rehabilitation is by re-masculating the generic propensities of the Gothic film. In other words it is the *genre* that must undergo a radical re-gendering before the hero can be rescued from the dangerously emasculating spell of the female apparition. The reformist Social, which has lain dormant for so much of the proceedings, must be ceded to at this point.

The Gothic abruptly undergoes a chameleon-like transformation in the last half hour or so and morphs into the investigative thriller with our embattled hero becoming the putative detective figure, whose intelligence—especially his powers of rational, scientific deduction—physical prowess, and courage enable him to unravel the chimerical mystery of the female ghost.

This sudden turn is like the Radcliffian "explained supernatural" in Gothic literature, when the supposed supernatural finds rational explication.[56] The narrative, too, at this stage, regains some of its lost linearity. Often this "explanation" has to do with murky intrigue set in motion by the many shadowy characters that also haunt the margins of these films—nefarious villains appear almost by magic to lay claim to the events that have endangered the hero and contributed to the dissolution of his sanity. The phallic and moral economy of the investigative thriller is, therefore, constitutively aligned to the expulsion, or at least marginalization, of the female ghost—the rejection of the irrational-supernatural-feminine, which had heretofore insistently haunted and enslaved the male subject. This reorganization of narrative material would also come to be a generic convention of the Hindi Gothic during the 1950s and beyond.

The female "ghost" often turns out to be merely a mortal woman playing dress up, either to fulfill some deep psychological need or at the exhortation of villains who wield some sort of power over her. Thus, Kamini in *Mahal* is only Asha, the old gardener's daughter, who, having heard of the tale of the star-crossed lovers of Sangam Bhavan, created a duplicate fantasy world in which she played the role of the dead beloved in the splendid isolation of the deserted *mahal.* Struck by Hari Shankar's resemblance to the portrait of the mansion's past owner, she eventually falls in love with him. Asha continues to perform and sing as Kamini in the hope that when Hari Shankar finally sees them as one and the same, he too will reciprocate her feelings. As Wendy Hsu argues, the irony of this doubling is unmistakable, as "Kamini and Asha *should not* appear to be one and the same person, according to Shankar's perspective, but simultaneously, Kamini and Asha *should* in fact be the same individual, following the filmic reality."[57] In other words, in the film's reality, there never is a Kamini in the present tense; in Hari Shankar's anguished imagination, however, accepting Asha's existence is tantamount to the death sentence that, in fact, he finally receives.

Unsurprisingly, he continues to refer to Asha as Kamini, even after her confession about her origins and identity. This momentous revelation is made during the courtroom scene, in which Hari Shankar is wrongfully tried for the murder of his wife, Ranjana. It is crucial to note that the larger universe, the massive ideological apparatus that typically underpins commercial Hindi cinema—of the state, society, family, and so forth—which had largely receded with the hero's encounter with the apparition, somewhat abruptly returns to these narratives.[58] After almost two hours of unfolding as a supernatural ghost story, *Mahal* abruptly transforms into a courtroom drama wherein Hari Shankar's attorney and friend, Shrinath, valiantly defends his client's innocence in the matter of Ranjana's death, which is finally revealed to be a suicide.

In *Woh Kaun Thi?* the doubling of wife/ghost is literal because the climax reveals the existence of two women—biological twins, separated as infants. Ramesh (Prem Chopra), Anand's cousin and a minor character in the film, ruthlessly used Sandhya and her unnamed "bad double" in order to gain access to a legacy that Anand has inherited. The inheritance, mentioned briefly at the beginning of the film, stipulates that Ramesh will be next in line to receive it if it can be proved that Anand is unsound of mind. Thus, the two unfortunate sisters were merely pawns, tools in a game in which they became victims. Sandhya and her twin sister were both under Ramesh's control and were forced, therefore, to become instruments for Anand's destruction. Both Kamini in *Mahal* and Sandhya in *Woh Kaun Thi?* turn out to be flesh-and-blood women after all; this process of rendering them human is what Michel Chion calls "deacousmatization." The acousmetre becomes "dispossessed of its mysterious powers"[59] when the source of the ghostly singing comes to be connected to the face/body of a living woman. The mysterious lure of the ghost, the power of the enigmatic, is invalidated in the end. Embodiment makes these women mortal, modern, quotidian, and in some sense, banal. Sandhya can then become a suitable partner for Anand, the modern hero; shorn of the powers of spectrality, she transforms into the dutifully domestic, risking her own life for Anand's safety during the climax. This transformative juncture in the narrative is additionally marked by the hero's sudden revival as a physical being—for example, the climax of *Woh Kaun Thi?* is ushered in via Anand's fight sequence with the villainous Ramesh. Anand resoundingly thrashes Ramesh and his hired goons and saves Sandhya, thereby emerging with his courage, ingenuity, and physical prowess restored.[60]

The Gothic's capitulation to the supra-generic Social becomes especially evident in the "explanations" that accompany the dénouements. The rationalization for the "supernatural occurrences" remains excessively, almost defensively, detailed. In both *Mahal* and *Woh Kaun Thi?*, verbal explanations—from Asha in the former and the police officer in the latter—are accompanied by images of exactly how the ghostly encounters transpired or were manipulated.[61] These flashbacks are also *reenactments*: at the same time that the actors listen to the tales of trickery, *we*, the spectators, are made to revisit these earlier encounters through omniscient narration, and we thus reassess what we have seen before, in a different light. It is as though the films remain only tenuously convinced of the realist, rationalist explications that have replaced the irrational; dialogue, therefore, must be reinforced by strangely unanchored images to ensure that the spectator, too, has made the critical transition mapped by the narratives.

Although this recuperative gesture is typically both canny and efficacious in bringing about the pat closure, I would argue that it is only sporadically successful. *Mahal* is a particularly interesting case, where the ruse fails quite drastically. Having been exonerated in the case of Ranjana's murder, Hari Shankar avoids the death sentence, but even this instance of liberation is fraught with untimeliness. He arrives too late to prevent Asha's marriage to Shrinath, a calamitous turn of events, because he had, in fact, requested that the two marry after being sentenced to hang. Hari Shankar's attempted passage to the spatio-temporal modality of the modern nation remains as journey to nowhere—a trip that can only lead him back to death, in another moment of repetition. So longingly has he desired death that he finally dies, gazing fixedly at the spectral beloved—now embodied, corporeal, and married to his best friend. In this film, the entire process of generic transformation fails and the narrative is restored to circularity, as Hari Shankar vows to return to win Kamini back in their next birth. The time of revenants, of spectrality, and of enchantment is thus re-animated at closure. *Mahal* remains an especially interesting iteration of the Gothic in Hindi cinema because it was made during a period of transition, when the industrial and formal imperatives of Bombay cinema had not yet congealed into their seriously Nehruvian modes. Perhaps this is why Amrohi's film is able to retain its open-ended closure and so insistently celebrate an ethos of failure and un-becoming.

The postcolonial Gothic film allows us a different point of entry into India's post-independence rhetorical universe, giving us a fecund terrain on which we can unpack the nation's fraught struggles to negotiate a lingering feudal ethos and an emergent triumphant modernity. The Gothic film concretizes these struggles via a generic schizophrenia—an incomplete reconciliation between a feminine/feminizing ghost film and a hastily phallicized investigative thriller. The feudal, the feminine, and the supernatural must be abrogated by popular Hindi cinema of this time. However, while decadent and decaying, the feudal is also sensuous, voluptuous, and beautiful, something that rests uneasily alongside frugality, thrift, and the seriousness of the postcolonial dispensation. The Gothic is aligned to everything that must remain disavowed. But in this process of disavowal, the genre betrays a sense of loss, of yearning. It remains one of the only genres of the period that is able to mourn the passing of an entire universe with a degree of candor.

The Gothic took a specific shape in the years immediately following independence, but it continued to inhabit specific generic formations in Hindi cinema thereafter. The previously mentioned "reincarnation film" has emerged as one of the most hospitable ecosystems for the incubation and elaboration of Gothic tropes, and later films—complete with haunted *havelis*, singing specters, and wronged, murdered, and reincarnated lovers—include *Neel Kamal* (*Blue Lotus*, 1968), *Mehbooba* (*Beloved*, 1976), *Karz* (1980), *Kudrat* (*Nature*, 1981), and others. Even more recently, similar hauntologies have appeared in *Om Shanti Om* (2007), *Dangerous Ishq* (*Dangerous Love*, 2012), and *Ek Paheli Leela* (*A Secret Leela*, 2015). Although the Gothic and the supernatural have endured in Hindi cinema in more ways than one, they transfigured into one of its most interesting iterations in the Ramsay horror film, a genre I explore in the following chapter.

CHAPTER TWO

The Ramsay Rampage

HORROR AS EMERGENCY CINEMA

> *The Ramsay Brothers—the men, the movies, the money, the mockery, the memory—have found altogether new channels via which to haunt the contemporary.*
>
> —KARTIK NAIR, "TASTE, TABOO, TRASH: THE STORY OF THE RAMSAY BROTHERS"

BHAYANAK MAUT (WHICH ROUGHLY TRANSLATES AS "Terrifying Death") is a contemporary death/thrash metal band in Bombay that claims to have taken its name from a Ramsay brothers horror film. This claim is intriguing on at least two different registers: first, there is actually no Ramsay film with that title, and second, this discrepancy does not seem to matter in the least to the producers and consumers of the music in question. The fact is it *could* very well be a Ramsay film, and it is this vaguely associative resonance that seems to be of key importance in terms of branding.

Ashim Ahluwalia's globally acclaimed independent film *Miss Lovely* (2012) pays homage to the media environment within which a certain kind of horror cinema flourished in India. In a particularly memorable scene, a character enters where a scantily clad female actor is being mauled by a hairy monster on a B/C-grade set that is clearly reminiscent of a Ramsay film. Although not naming the Ramsays explicitly, *Miss Lovely*'s mise-en-scène and cinematography painstakingly replicate the texture and feel of kitschy, low-budget horror films from the 1980s—it remains, above all, a deliriously saturated and compulsively reflexive mediation on and homage to the trash cinema of the era.

It seems clear that the Ramsay "brand"—which has historically been synonymous with a particular style of B-grade, Hindi-language horror film in the 1970s and 1980s—today stands for much more: a cultish, edgy, provocatively dark ethos of hip, global-urban cool. The paracinematic impulse that Jeffrey Sconce identified in the American context in 1995 now encompasses diverse global "trendy trash" products, such as the Ramsay horror film.[1] The Ramsay film's contemporary global visibility is additionally buttressed by the availability of a number of these films on DVD: Mondo Macabro, a company that specializes in producing sleekly packaged trash and exploitation cinemas, has released six of the Ramsay films in the North American market in the last few years. These films now rub shoulders with classics of exploitation such as Juan López Moctezuma's *Alucarda* (1975), prompting a number of internationally reputed film magazines and publications—including the blog that accompanies the high-profile *Film Comment* and several other websites devoted to global cult cinema—to feature articles and write-ups on the once-lowly Ramsay film.[2] In tandem with these developments, the genre has also become a subject for serious scholarly research in recent years.

Clearly, the Ramsay film's fortunes have risen dramatically since its heyday in the 1980s, when it was consigned to the garbage heap by mainstream cinema, critics, and bourgeois arbiters of taste as the sleaziest of Bombay's cinematic offerings.[3] Beyond this curious—although not entirely unexpected—afterlife that the genre now enjoys, examining the formation within its industrial and social context allows us to unearth richly suggestive connections between the politics of genre and politics *as such*: the Ramsay horror film emblematically captures the zeitgeist of Emergency and post-Emergency India. In this chapter, I suggest that the supernatural took a very specific form in the Ramsay horror film in the 1980s, and a closer examination of its formal and narrative registers allows us to see the complex ways in which the genre as a whole dealt with questions of politics, violence, and political violence in this era. In this sense, the Ramsay horror film most snugly fits into the gender-genre-modernity triad that forms the bulwark of this book as a whole.

THE RAMSAY HORROR FILM: MONSTROUS MASALA

The supernatural in Hindi commercial cinema takes a decidedly excessive turn in the *masala* format of the Ramsay horror film; the array of appropriated tropes integrated into these films is nothing short of astonishing,[4] ranging from Mario Bava's saturated Gothic colors to stylistic devices pilfered from Hollywood slashers.[5] With miniscule budgets, an internal star system, recognizable motifs, iconography, and even props that traveled between films, the seven rambunctious Ramsay brothers certainly transformed the texture of horror cinema in South Asia. However, to read the Ramsay horror film as an audacious "first" in Indian cinema would be somewhat misleading; these films did not emerge ex nihilo as a fully formed genre.[6] While the Ramsay film's heady concoction of baroquely Gothic imagery and numerous citations from global horror films[7] was in many ways unique, it also drew a great deal from older cinematic formations, such as the Hindi Gothic films explored here in Chapter 1. And unlike the earlier decades when the supernatural emerged as a possibility only to be quelled at the end, commercial cinema in the 1970s and beyond provided a hospitable formal habitat for the excessive, the irrational, and the fantastic. However, some aspects of the older form sustained: even a cursory glance at the most famous Ramsay film titles would attest to the genre's obsession with haunted houses, especially the feudal *haveli*: *Purana Mandir* (*Old Temple*, 1984), *Haveli* (*Mansion*, 1985), *Tehkhana* (*Dungeon*, 1986), *Dak Bangla* (*Dak Bungalow*, 1987), *Purani Haveli* (*Old Mansion*, 1989), and so on. I hope to trace here both the continuities and the departures that reconfigure the supernatural in the Ramsay genre in the 1970s and 1980s.

The Gothic mutates into an outlandishly overblown avatar in the Ramsay horror film. The most notorious components of the genre include flimsy, often utterly inchoate plots punctuated by oddly placed song sequences and bizarre comic routines, horror set pieces involving burly monsters in old mansions, tacky prosthetic makeup, gratuitous exploitation of young female bodies, sexual violence and violence against women, patently fake blood and gore, and rudimentary special effects. Plots often[8] involve old curses or monsters that inhabit derelict feudal mansions in imprecise country locations, alerting us to the Gothic motifs that had already crystallized by this time; singing specters, too, make fleeting appearances in this otherwise transformed generic landscape. Modern descendants of the erstwhile feudal clans unwittingly arrive at the mansions to encounter the malefic forces that lurk within. Terrifying sightings and uncanny experiences plague the urban interlopers. Bloodbaths ensue and bodies pile up, before the collective efforts of the protagonists—usually aided by benevolent religious figures, icons, and discourses—finally destroy the monster and disable the curse in question.

This recursive textual universe is buttressed by inept performances and abysmal production values. It is, therefore, hardly surprising that the Ramsay horror film has received its share of scorn and derision over the years from the press and critics across multiple languages.[9] Indeed, the best evidence of its unacceptability—at least in certain quarters—has been its absence in scholarly studies of Indian cinema, until very recently. Simply put, the Ramsay film was too low-brow—too insistently and defiantly smutty and tawdry—to be the object of serious research and reflection.[10] Conversely, then, the genre implicitly signposts its other—the discursive universe of "good" cinema in this era.[11] It is also worthwhile to recall that genres of the fantastic—with their visceral, sensationalist pleasures—have been routinely disdained by bourgeois audiences since the early silent era; the excessive, potentially transgressive, "bazaar" energies of these genres have threatened certain sections while thrilling others since the beginning of cinema's bid for respectability.[12]

However, beyond questions of form and good taste, the Ramsay genre as a whole remains an important index of an especially turbulent period of India's history; its narrative and stylistic excesses and contortions are no less *symptomatic* than, for example, the suppression and disavowal of the supernatural in the 1950s and 1960s genre I explored in the last chapter. To begin with, a number of scholars have noted that the Ramsay film offers a privileged point of entry into the media ecology of the 1980s; examining where and how these films traveled allows us to engage with unexamined conduits of distribution and reception.[13] Second, the genre deserves consideration as a historically contingent formation—a genre that can be situated alongside and, I would argue, shares certain critical similarities with the mainstream Hindi film of the era. Third, and most important for my purposes, the Ramsay horror film offers a fecund terrain for interrogating the social and political imaginaries of the period.

Particularly relevant in this regard is the ideological incoherence of the Ramsay horror universe: random and often incommensurable—indeed irreconcilable—discourses jostle together within this generic domain in spite of significant formal and iconographic unities. And finally, the afterlife and repurposing of Ramsay horror in television demands that we reconceptualize notions of "good taste" and the ethos of the bourgeois living room that the Ramsays so successfully penetrated in the 1990s and beyond. Simply put, the standard narratives about the Ramsay horror film—its regressive politics, its unremitting reliance on sex and violence, its address to a largely lumpen urban male audience—come to be unsettled when we take a closer look at the entire Ramsay output; this is not to suggest that the Ramsay film does not deserve these readings, but to propose that a more complex picture emerges from a closer, more historically grounded scrutiny. I argue that in many ways, the Ramsay film congeals as a recalcitrant genre—one whose excesses are too great to be straitjacketed within neatly ordered theoretical edifices.

The challenge thrown up by the formation, then, is twofold: at first

FIGURE 2.1. Purani Haveli *poster. Used by permission of the National Film Archive of India.*

glance, the Ramsay film remains deceptively transparent in its politics and form; simultaneously, however, a more sustained examination compels us to abandon at least some of our initial assumptions. In this chapter, my attempt is to resist the temptation of "disciplining" the profligate pleasures of the Ramsay film; I am, on the contrary, interested in the chaotic and unpredictable predilections and trajectories of the genre, and in what these inconsistencies, incongruities, and detours might tell us about the political and public cultures of post-Emergency India. To that end, taking a cue from the Ramsay assembly line, I will dismantle the genre into component parts, in order to interrogate what each "element"—narrative preoccupations, song sequences, "sexy scenes," and so forth—might tell us about the genre as a whole. In other words, because the Ramsay film confronts us as an inchoate assemblage, I argue that deconstructing it into its most notoriously routine "attractions" enables us to uncover what tasks these elements undertook or performed in the 1970s and 1980s. It is also of considerable importance to me that the Ramsay film's popularity continues to thrive in multiple platforms of reception and that the meanings that accrete around these films continue to mutate. Whereas the Ramsay film signified a series of things in the 1970s and 1980s, the same body of films today provokes a different series of questions altogether. Breaking open the loose "system" that constitutes the Ramsay film allows for multiple points of entry into this otherwise fractious generic domain.

The astonishing story of F. U. Ramsay and his seven resourceful sons has been enthusiastically and affectionately documented in recent years:

> After years of apprenticeship, the sons of small-time film producer F. U. Ramsay persuade the patriarch to finance an all-out horror film. The result: *Do Gaz Zameen Ke Neeche* (*Beneath Two Yards of Earth*, Shyam and Tulsi Ramsay, 1972), a breakout hit that sets the style for Ramsay productions to come. Every few months over the next two decades, cast and crew alike would be packed into buses and transported to the outskirts of Bombay for filming. Here, brothers Shyam and Tulsi Ramsay would dispatch directorial duties; brother Kumar would write the scenes while brother Gangu would lens them; Kiran Ramsay was usually in charge of sound and Arjun in charge of production; meanwhile, Mother Ramsay would cook for everyone.[14]

The narrative is charming for its invocation of the organically cohesive joint-family business, but also interesting because it gives us a sense of why the final products look the way they do—the emphasis on writing "scenes" instead of fully articulated screenplays, for instance, is clearly visible in the randomness of plots and the sequences unfolding as a series of "attractions"—romantic song, followed by a comedy track and action sequences, interspersed with "horror" and sightings of the supernatural monster in question. Tulsi Ramsay explains the *masala* assemblage as a demand of the audiences through especially apposite gastronomic metaphors: "They (the audience) want a proper film, with proper songs . . . a dish is made . . . the audience wants everything . . . when we eat, we do not simply eat lentils and rice, lentils and rice (*dal chawal, dal chawal*), we also partake of poppadums, pickles . . . and vegetables too—that is enjoyable. Indian audiences want this."[15]

If the artisanal—fragmentarily manufactured—nature of production is to be noted,[16] equally important are the compressed temporalities of generic production and the trajectories through which the Ramsay film traveled at this time. Traversing working-class cinema halls in cities and speedily traveling into semi-urban and rural centers, the Ramsay horror film functions as an important and protean point of entry into Hindi cinema's murky conduits of production, distribution, and exhibition in the 1970s and 1980s.[17] Given the admirable productivity of the Ramsay brothers, we may surmise that the genre—once commercially viable—was quickly consolidated to maximize profits and speak most meaningfully to its target audience—non-metropolitan, non-bourgeois male spectators.[18]

Formal particularities of the genre and its modes of address further suggest that the ideal spectator of this cinema was male ("because ladies cannot watch so much *khoon kharaba* [murder and mayhem]"), a propensity not limited to horror at this time. Indeed, Tulsi Ramsay describes their target audiences thusly:

> Our first targets were the masses—by masses I mean the taxi drivers, those who drive rickshaws, lower middle classes, plus college-going girls and boys, this is my audience, in my estimation. . . . College kids would come and scream and shout, they would cling to each other in terror. All the masses. See, India is a vast country with so many small cities—our films ran in these small cities for 3 days—Friday, Saturday, Sunday—on Monday a different film would arrive . . . if the daughter-in-law (*bahu*) wearing lots of gold jewelry came in a Mercedes (car), she wouldn't be able to digest our films.[19]

To summarize, the Ramsay horror film was "non-mainstream" in several respects: it lacked the budget of the mainstream industrial product; it was distributed through smaller distribution companies and often enjoyed its longest runs in non-metropolitan centers; and it was classed and gendered in specific ways, both in terms of the representational domain and the target audiences.[20] In other words, it flourished within a political economy that was adjacent to, but not co-extensive with, the Hindi film industry at the time. I further argue that the Ramsay films are especially sensitive barometers of the political unrest of this era, a sensitivity that can be unpacked at both formal and narrative registers. The tenuously held-together generic mélange that the capacious edges of the Ramsay genre enfolds can be read as a telling symptom of the frayed and unraveling political fabric of the 1970s and 1980s. Therefore, first, we need a brief look at the context—both national and industrial—within which the Ramsay film comes to congeal as a genre.

THE 1970S AND 1980S IN AND OUT OF CINEMA

The 1970s were a time of significant political turmoil in India. This is the phase in India's history that witnessed the final unraveling of the Nehruvian consensus—a consensus that was, reductively put, erected on four rhetorical pillars: commitments to socialism, secularism, democracy, and a careful non-alignment in terms of foreign policy. From a shortage of food supplies to a war with Pakistan, from separatist movements in the northeast and Punjab to Jay Prakash Narayan's call for "total revolution" and the conflicts in Naxalbari and Telengana, the political fabric of India enters into utter disarray at this time. What emerges in the 1970s from this cacophony of strident protests and demands is the dismantling of the *negotiated* nature of Nehru's vision; the picture is one of rupture, and a general disintegration of social and political imaginaries. Nehru's success as the first prime minister—however understood—was foundationally tethered to his ability to hold together different interest groups; he was a remarkably canny juggler of the divisive agendas both within the Congress Party and without; for example, the instrumental, if uneasy, truce between agrarian and industrial elites. With Nehru's death, the scramble for succession, and Indira Gandhi's audacious consolidation of power, we note the re-splintering of these different interest groups. All of these processes would reach their dénouement with the declaration of Emergency and the subsequent suspension of democracy and civil liberties for a period of twenty-one months.

In her work on the Emergency, Emma Tarlo has shown that despite the existence of narratives both from proponents and detractors, the period remains shrouded in silence and "has somehow slipped through the net of academic disciplines."[21] Sifting through hundreds of government files and gathering testimonies from dozens of people, Tarlo excavates "chilling demonstration of how state abuses not only produce local worlds but also become re-worked within them."[22] For my purposes here, several strands of the Emergency narratives remain crucial. First, the matter of silence is complicated by the fact that Indira Gandhi came back to power in January 1980—an astonishingly swift recovery from the debacle of 1977. With the death of Sanjay Gandhi, "one of the most controversial stars"[23] of the event later that year, the Emergency's traumatic memories and legacies were quickly swept under the political carpet. Having been effaced from "official" memory, it was incumbent upon popular artifacts—fiction and film—to dismember and remember the Emergency in specific ways. Second, Indira Gandhi's confounding combination of irrational authoritarianism and crude populism—for example, the twenty-point program, which was announced even as forcible "voluntary" sterilizations were being carried out on hundreds of slum dwellers in Delhi[24]—generated a profound kind of uncertainty in the public culture of the time.

The combination of the state-supported violence and winsome homilies that created the discursive texture of this period would come to have considerable impact on how the popular Hindi film imagined the nation for at least the next decade. And this is why the "afterlives" of the Emergency do not exhaust themselves in the 1970s, but as Rajinder Dudrah and Priya Joshi have suggested, "the legacies of the Emergency are often inadvertent, occurring *despite* will and design to propel history otherwise" (emphasis in original).[25] The final trope of the Emergency that is especially relevant to my discussion here is also its most scandalous legacy: the forcible sterilization of the poor carried out in numerous health centers, camps, and hospitals, in dubious and arguably undemocratic ways. Tarlo and others have pondered the short- and long-term implications of this violent iteration of "family planning," so that terrain—though incredibly important—need not detain us here. What I want to underscore is the dovetailing of sex and violence—the concatenation of these terms, such that one becomes coterminous with the other—that would bequeath to India, apart from other traumas, also the most recognizable commercial cinema of this time. Bombay cinema's take *on* the 1970s, as Joshi has noted, had to be, of necessity, symbolic: "Bollywood's commentary on the 1970s, much as its commentary on other moments, is widely present, though it emerges indirectly through the use of highly elaborate symbols that displace the nation's political crisis and its public fantasies elsewhere."[26] It is precisely through formal contortions that the Ramsay genre refracts the discourses of the Emergency, as I argue below. But the industry, too, underwent seismic shifts at this time.

Madhava Prasad has written about a process of disassembly of the historically dominant Social genre at this juncture: "[W]ithin the ideological sphere, the film industry faced a challenge to its established aesthetic conventions and mode of production. It was able to survive the crisis by a strategy of internal segmentation . . . [which] produced three distinct aesthetic formations—the new cinema, the middle-class cinema and the populist cinema of mobilization."[27] Whereas Prasad reads the advent of Amitabh Bachchan as a specific kind of star, and the "Bachchan film" as almost entirely coextensive with populist cinema, I would like to suggest that the Ramsay horror film also participates in the discourses of a specific kind of populism that animate the nation's public spheres at this time, especially in its address to a specifically classed and gendered spectator.[28] It is critical to note that the genre of the *masala* film that dominated the 1980s—including and especially the Bachchan film—was also largely aimed primarily at male, working-class audiences, and elaborated an aesthetic of violent disenchantment. And, as Sangita Gopal has argued, the Ramsay film found a hospitable generic environment in the *masala* format: "[T]he reigning generic form—the *masala*—lacked the social form's integrative drive and was thus more accommodating of diverse cinematic material. Most Ramsay films were structurally *masala*—they had song-and-dance sequences, action fights, comedy routines, and family melodrama—while featuring curses, monsters, and gory slayings as major themes. In other words, horror was hatched as a unique form by being placed inside a more capacious genre."[29]

The media ecology within which the Ramsay horror film was spawned and thrived included the 1980s video boom, a time in which televisions and the VCR were at the height of their popularity. Attendance at movie theaters dropped alarmingly as middle-class audiences preferred to watch films—both Hindi and international—in the comfort of their living rooms.[30] Some segments of this audience simply watched television instead. As the middle classes retreated into the safety of domestic spaces, the commercial film registered this shift in profound ways. Any significant sampling of popular films from the 1980s would show that the *masala* film had morphed into the archetypal "bad object" at this time, relying ceaselessly on spectacular action and fights, blood and gore, sensationalism, and overblown melodrama. The reduction of women to two-dimensional sex objects was a predictable corollary of this formation, as any number of Bachchan films of the era would demonstrate. Not surprisingly, the number of women who attended movie theaters at this time also dropped significantly; women were simply not the target spectators of these films, and, as such, did much of their viewing within the safe spaces of the home. The Ramsay film flourished and circulated within this public domain that had come to be deeply masculinist, misogynist, and potentially violent.[31] The video boom also impacted the Ramsays in other ways: untrammeled video piracy ensured that a steady crop of international horror films became available to them as well as their audiences for the first time. For them, this meant a vast body of films that could now be mined as potential material for future films; for their audiences, the citational nature of the Ramsay film became a richer experience as the references and "borrowed material" became increasingly more recognizable. Additionally, pirated copies of many of their films were circulating illegally not only in individual homes, but also in video parlors that had begun to mushroom all over urban and semi-urban areas.[32] Whatever the loss in actual revenues, the Ramsay horror film was significantly popularized via this underground, illegitimate, and illegal video circuit in the 1980s.

The Ramsay horror films are also, unmistakably, trauma texts. The violence that characterized 1970s India continued to live on and haunt Indian popular films in predictable and unpredictable ways. Although the *masala* form as a whole registered the upheavals and disintegrative processes that began in that momentous decade, the status of *horror* is a special one in this context; it is perhaps no accident that the Ramsay genre is perceived to

FIGURE 2.2. *Posters of* Mahakaal, Bandh Darwaza, *and* Do Gaz Zameen Ke Neeche.

be Hindi cinema's first foray into horror proper. Horror, as Linnie Blake has argued, "is ideally positioned to expose the psychological, social and cultural ramifications of the ideologically expedient will to 'bind up the nation's wounds' that is promulgated by all aspects of the culture industry in post-traumatic contexts."[33] Even earlier, drawing on Walter Benjamin's conception of the *jetztzeit* (present time), Adam Lowenstein has argued that trauma texts

> invite us to recognize our connection to historical trauma across the axes of text, context, and spectatorship. They do so through the agency of an allegorical moment, situated at the unpredictable and often painful juncture where past and present collide. Each case reveals a different set of social and political variables that contribute to a jagged composite portrait of trauma's relation to cinematic representation, rather than a smooth, broadly thematic version of this relation that does not reckon with the intractable substance of history and culture.[34]

These insights are productive in unraveling the specific ways in which the Ramsay horror film registered the upheavals and terrors of the 1970s and 1980s. However, the cinematic archive is tricky in certain ways, because it ossifies as an "unmediated response to events as they were unfolding";[35] especially in the case of the Ramsay genre, the archive remains confounding, chaotic, and arguably "inchoate." As the most recognizable aspect of the Ramsay horror film is its assemblage of attractions, here I disassemble these in order to understand how the formation as a whole understood and articulated the horrific in its time. The Ramsay film is both a product *of* the 1970s and a commentary *on* that disturbing phase of Indian history; simply put, my aim here is to understand how these two registers dovetail with each other.

ROMANCING THE GOTHIC: THE FEUDAL AS MONSTROUS

As I noted in the introduction to this book, the complex legacies of colonialism and the startling iterations of modernity in the non-West have gained much theoretical traction in recent years. Scholars from humanities as well as social science disciplines have persuasively argued for different lenses that can illuminate the entangled, unfinished, contingent nature of modernity in India and elsewhere in the developing world. Theorists of Indian cinema have also expended considerable critical energy in elaborating the complicated ways in which the cinema—the poster child for industrial modernity in other contexts—comes to be imbricated with the non-modern or the feudal in South Asia. This transaction can be unpacked at various registers, including those of genre, style and representation, ideology, and discourse. Like the Gothic film of the earlier period, the Ramsay film, too, participates in this overdetermined transactional domain, albeit in very specific ways in the 1970s and 1980s. Indeed, one of the core concerns for almost every Ramsay horror film is to contend with the feudal: the films in question stage reckonings with the feudal in a manner that is both compulsive and deeply symptomatic of the political moment sketched above.

The genre's expressive grammar registers this complex universe through a series of Manichean binaries and signs: old versus new, urban versus rural, Western versus Indian, and so on. However, even in its reductive and garbled representational terrain, the genre does articulate the impossibility of purging the feudal, even as it doggedly attempts to concretize the modern. The Ramsay film's generic allegiances are best demonstrated by their faithful adherence to the basic codes of the Gothic, as it was configured in Hindi cinema. As mentioned above, to read the Ramsay horror film as a sudden onslaught that emerged out of a generic vacuum would be to miss the continuities that attend to the consolidation of the supernatural in Hindi cinema.[36] Earlier films such as *Mahal*, *Woh Kaun Thi?*, *Madhumati*, and *Kohraa* generated a specific template for the invocation of Gothic tropes in Hindi cinema, and the legacies of the earlier genre are palpable in, for example, the Ramsay film's obsessive return to the haunted feudal *haveli*.

Needless to say, what a haunted *haveli* symbolically represents undergoes massive transformations between the 1960s and the late 1970s. While the feudal had to be disavowed in crucial ways in the earlier films, it was also mourned as a richer and more gracious realm of history and experience. By the 1970s, the very notions of feudal power and privilege had come to be vilified in the larger, discursive terrain.[37] Unsurprisingly, the psychological complexity of a film such as *Mahal*—which connected the ruin of the *haveli* with the sepulchral decrepitude of protagonist Hari Shankar's mind—is largely absent in the Ramsay text.[38] If it was primarily the male hero who found himself imperiled within the confines of old mansions in the earlier genre, hordes of noisy youngsters descend on the *havelis* and are summarily killed by the monsters who lurk in subterranean dungeons and secret chambers in the Ramsay film—horrors in Ramsay films remain solidly corporeal. Whereas the victim (hero) of the older films found himself dangerously fascinated—indeed, psychologically entrapped—by the female ghost, the Ramsay victims encounter the monster exclusively as physical threat: they are either brutally killed, or they are rescued in the nick of time from the monster in question. Clearly, this is a very differently constructed generic domain. The most obvious differences between the two figurations of the Gothic have to do with style, in terms of music and the introduction of color cinematography: whereas the earlier films achieved their haunting atmospherics through a very deliberate use of high-contrast black-and-white cinematography, one of the most striking aspects of the Ramsay film is its outlandish use of saturated color—lurid reds and electric blues dominate a very differently configured grammar of style. So although the Ramsays ceaselessly use the iconography of the Gothic *haveli*, the introduction of color transforms, foundationally, the texture of the image and the world evoked in films such as *Do Gaz Zameen Ke Neeche* and *Darwaza* (*The Door*). Music is, likewise, used for a very different end: to signpost the modernity of the city slickers, a point I shall return to later in this chapter. In spite of these key differences, however, I would like to stress that the Ramsay film's compulsive return to the *haveli* and its inability to locate horror in any other site than the feudal ties it to the earlier Gothic genre in a compelling manner.

Beyond these transformations, the feudal dispensation in the Ramsay film congeals as a recasting of the very notion of monstrosity. And I would argue that the trope of the monstrous often crystallizes around the Ramsay film's fantasy of feudal excesses, just as it did in many of the earlier Gothic films. Several films include a frame story or prologue of events that unfolded in the past—often bracketed off from the contemporary instance of narration by the title sequence. Notably, most of these prologue sequences foreground the feudal *haveli* as the locus of evil and terror. For example, in

Darwaza, we enter into the diegetic world via a strange and disorienting series of images of the Gothic mansion's exterior and then its interiors, as a woman's disembodied voice weeps and curses Thakur Pratap Singh on the sound track. Soon after, from his deathbed confession, we learn that the *thakur*'s exploitation of his poor villagers and the murder of the virtuous Dharma had prompted the latter's mother to curse the *thakur*'s family and everyone who inhabits the feudal mansion. Pratap Singh apparently dies, regretting his past crimes, after sending his young son Suraj Singh (Anil Dhawan) to Bombay, far removed from the blighted portals of the *haveli*. However, an adult Suraj Singh continues to be haunted by nightmares featuring the *haveli* and the monster that lurks therein. Suraj must return to the scene of the crime, as it were, in order to lay the ghosts of the past to rest, both literally and figuratively. After a series of grisly deaths, Suraj and the people of the neighboring village finally come face to face with the monster inhabiting the *haveli*. *Darwaza* invokes the trope of feudal monstrosity in a literal sense—Thakur Pratap Singh himself, barely human and hideously disfigured, turns out to be the monster that haunts the *haveli* and preys on all those who enter there. The subaltern woman's curse comes to be literally embodied in the figure of the feudal lord, now turned monster, who can morph back into his human form only in death and via the power of divine intervention, here represented through the goddess Kali's trident.

In *Dak Bangla*, the opening titles roll over a mist-shrouded *haveli*, now converted into a guest house for travelers, with dramatic, if patently artificial, lightning splitting the image between English, Hindi, and Urdu iterations of the title. Following the title sequence, we witness the current manager of the *dak bangla* engaged in sex with a young woman. Hearing strange noises, they investigate, only to be attacked by a monster that resides in an underground dungeon chamber, or *tehkhana*, in the Ramsay lexicon. The manager is killed almost instantaneously, but the woman apparently dies of sheer terror, trying to escape from the *haveli*. The protracted and abortive escape sequence is shot with the *haveli* prominently in focus in the background, enforcing its dreadful agency in bringing about the unnatural deaths of the 'innocent' couple. In *Dak Bangla*, the monster is an adversary of the raja from the past, but his destruction at the conclusion is accompanied by the destruction of the entire mansion—it implodes as a symbol of a defunct and outmoded social and political formation. The raja's murdered daughter, reincarnated as the modern heroine Sapna (Aloka), can thus move on without being burdened by this history.

A particularly interesting variant of the prologue/frame story occurs in the aptly named *Haveli*: very little of the actual action in the film takes

FIGURE 2.3. *Thakur Pratap Singh as monster in* Darwaza. *Used by permission of the National Film Archive of India.*

place on this site, and yet the entire narrative revolves around an episode of heinous violence that once unfolded there. Much of the plot takes place in a modern luxury hotel in Goa, where Criminal Investigation Department officer Shyam (Marc Zuber) attempts to solve the mystery of a serial killer murdering a series of apparently random, innocent guests. The prologue in this film remains exceptionally disturbing and quite novel in the representational matrix of the Ramsay film: Keshu Ramsay uses a series of seemingly disconnected, negative images of a screaming face, exploding fireworks, a group of people holding someone captive, and so on, as a woman's distraught voice-over describes the appearance of the men who have raped her within the confines of the *haveli*. Following these bizarre opening frames is a series of traveling point of view (POV) shots—reminiscent of the opening of John Carpenter's 1978 slasher classic, *Halloween*—inside the *haveli*, as we share in an unknown character's visual exploration of the feudal mansion, which culminates in the horrible discovery of a partially disrobed female corpse hanging from the ceiling. The sequence remains espe-

FIGURE 2.4. Haveli *from the Ramsays'* Veerana.

cially disconcerting for us as spectators, because we remain confused about not only the violent assault but also the identity of the character in whose field of vision we participate. *Haveli* remains an especially compelling text in terms of its understanding of the feudal as monstrous, first, because it firmly situates the horrific within the mansion (which afterward disappears from the plot), and second, because as the plot reaches its dénouement, we come to realize that the serial murders are retribution for a crime—in this case gang rape that is prompted by the villains' sense of feudal privilege and entitlement over women's bodies.

The *haveli* in the Ramsay film, thus, often stands in for feudal excesses and for crimes, misdemeanors, and exploitative practices nurtured within the feudal dispensation. For my purposes, the use of the voice-over as a sound effect—such as those used in *Darwaza* and *Haveli*—is particularly telling; the voice-over not only anchors the monstrous within the spaces of the *haveli*, it also withholds the body from which the voice emanates from the spectator for a while, generating an affective terrain of suspense.[39] In beginning with the subaltern victim's voice recounting the tales of feudal exploitation, the Ramsay film would seem to condemn the practices engendered within the political economies that attend to the elite landed gentry of the nation's past. This assignation of blame would also seem to be an endorsement of modernity and of more egalitarian and less exploitative social and economic relations. However, matters are rarely this straightforward in supernatural films. Very much a part of the 1970s ethos, the Ramsay horror film refuses—or is unable—to espouse ideological coherence in any sustained manner.

A number of films of the genre overtly and covertly legitimize the feudal as well as the array of discourses that accrete around the dispensation. The Ramsay film accomplishes this sleight of hand through at least two distinct narrative and ideological maneuvers: first, casting the feudal monster/despot as malignant only when "wronged" by certain villainous agents of modernity, and second, disabling the very apparatus of modern law enforcement and the judiciary of the modern state.[40] As in the larger terrain of popular Hindi cinema at this time, the police appear repeatedly in the genre as bewildered, incompetent, and fundamentally unable to protect ordinary citizens against the wrath of the monster, whether human or supernatural. The Ramsay genre as a whole negotiates the general terrain of lawlessness, crime, and violence of Emergency India via these symbolic ruses and resolutions.

Haveli remains an excellent instantiation of this privileging of vigilante justice, "the toppling of the state from a position of symbolic value."[41] As described above, *Haveli* begins with a young woman's description of her rapists, morphing soon after into a murder mystery at the helm of which is Inspector Shyam. His chief suspect is Kumar Saxena[42] (Rakesh Roshan), who suspiciously lurks in proximity of the victims as the bodies pile up. In spite of the inspector's energetic efforts to uncover the identity of the killer, the murderous spree continues unabated. The police commissioner of Goa (Parikshit Shahani) also joins the investigative effort, reinforcing the haplessness of the police and the increasing symbolic powerlessness of the state. In terms of the hierarchy of knowledge, the spectator, too, is largely left in the dark, as glimpses of the killer provide only flashes of a terrifying mask that he wears over his face. In this sense, generically, *Haveli* is a hybrid: horror-cum-investigative-thriller, as well as a police procedural. It is only at the very end that the film discloses, retrospectively, its status as a revenge narrative. We learn that the entire plot has been an elaboration of a vendetta, a tale of retributional justice on behalf of the raped woman, Sudha (Farita Boyce). Sudha had been lured into the feudal *haveli* and repeatedly raped by Thakur Veer Singh (Mazhar Khan) and his cronies. Both of the leading men, Shyam and Kumar, are related to Sudha, the former having been her fiancée and the latter, her brother. Both men have followed the perpetrators to Goa in order to bring the *thakur* and his cronies to justice. Remarkably, the inspector dies after killing the *thakur* and confesses to all of the murders, which he had been supposedly investigating all along. *Haveli* ends with this narrative twist that entirely dismantles the modern state as the appropriate arbiter of justice. Not only is the legal apparatus rendered obsolete within the matrix of extra-legal vigilante justice sought by Kumar and Shyam, but the law enforcement official, in this instance, doubles as the vigilante—discrediting the authority of the judicial system as one that *can* dispense and ensure justice for all citizens. Thakur Veer Singh is killed as a figure of monstrous feudalism, but it is not the modern state that dispenses this punishment. The intermediary figure of the vigilante—police inspector gone rogue, a familiar type in many Hindi films of this era—is the only one able to lay the monster to rest.

Other Ramsay films endorsed traditional feudal authority as benign until provoked. In *Do Gaz Zameen Ke Neeche*, the *thakur*, aptly named Rajvansh (which literally translates as someone from an aristocratic bloodline and was played by Surender Kapoor), is a kind, just, and generous man who is swindled by his second wife, Anjali (Shobhna), her uncle (Satyen Kappu), and her lover, Anand (Imtiaz). Interestingly, he is also a scientist who spends hours in a laboratory observing bubbling substances in vats and beakers. First paralyzed from accidentally ingesting one of these concoctions, and then "murdered" by the villainous trio, Rajvansh returns as a terrifying corpse—a zombie.[43] What follows is a downright Shakespearean elaboration of ghostly sightings, bloodstains, guilt-induced madness, and finally, retribution. At closure, a triumphant (and very much alive) Rajvansh declares that it had all been a ruse to expose the greed and duplicity of Anjali and her men. This astonishingly detailed and elaborate performance of the supernatural had been made possible by a collaborative effort of the master and his many loyal servants, including a grave digger.

3D Saamri (1985) is an even more remarkable text in terms of the affirmation of non-modern discourses. In this film, the titular character Saamri (Anirudh Agarwal), named for the earlier dismembered and interred monster in *Purana Mandir*, reappears as the putative hero. In *Saamri*, his mastery of the dark arts and occult practices—Saamri's skills as a tantric, essentially—elevates him to the position of a local guru of sorts, who spends his time worshipping the goddess Kali and ridding people of evil demons and spirits. Saamri is a figure of a benign feudal patriarchy, despite his expertise in black magic. Because he is also immeasurably wealthy—owner of a massive *haveli* to start with—a motley group of scheming men, Takleefchand (Prem Chopra), Khanna (Gulshan Grover), and Professor Chatterjee (Amarnath Mukherjee), along with his nurse, Maria (Asha Sachdev), plot to murder him and divvy up the spoils among themselves. The echoes of *Do Gaz Zameen* are fairly obvious here, as the villainous quartet brutally murder the 135-year-old Saamri and toss his body into a lake. The rest of the drama, predictably, revolves around his revenge—his faithful servant Bhisham (Jack Gaud) reanimates his corpse in the secret cellar so Saamri can exact his terrible vengeance—but what is noteworthy is the very deliberate staging of the conflict between distinct clusters of signs: dark arts/tantra/feudal patriarchy versus mercantile interests/modernity/immorality/greed. As Valentina Vitali has noted, "[T]hat forms of an ostensibly 'traditional' lifestyle, narrativized in the films as a cluster of 'religious' practices and beliefs, should be disrupted by the arrival of speculative capital and other symptoms of what is taken to be modernity, is a recurring theme not only in the Ramsay brothers' and other Hindi or Indian cinemas, but also in the [horror] cinemas of other countries." But what remains unique in the genre is "the ways in which the iconography . . . was mobilized and made to register these preoccupations."[44] Thus, at the end of *Saamri*, his vendetta complete, Saamri returns "to the soil and darkness" and Anju (Aarthi Agarwal) and Sandeep (Rajan Sippy)—the "good modern" couple—inherit the fortune under the sign of his feudal benediction. A new order is perhaps established, but it does not, symbolically or otherwise, invalidate or supersede the old.[45]

The feudal order—with its untimely authoritarianisms and outmoded patriarchies—appears in the Ramsay film as complex (and often confounding) configurations of signs and discourses; while evil lurks behind *haveli* walls and remains secreted away in the anachronistic spaces of *khandhar*s (ruins) and *tehkhana*s (underground dungeons), its interment—or rather concealment in the present—is always temporary. Modernity's tools are often simply not robust enough to withstand or suppress the monsters of the feudal when they erupt. However, as I have shown here, modernity, too, provides a salubrious environment for the incubation of new kinds of monstrosities; the Ramsay film's expressive universe most tellingly articulates the hesitations and tangles that continue to determine public fantasies of the political in India.

DISCO-MODERNITY: YOUTH CULTURE AND THE RAMSAY FILM

Because the feudal and the modern, as distinct clusters of signs, must come to a ceremonial reckoning in almost every Ramsay film, it becomes somewhat necessary for the genre to delineate, as sharply as possible, what these signs are. Whereas the feudal can be easily constructed by following the shorthand of the older Gothic film—the crumbling, mist-swept *havelis*, creaking doors, massive portraits of dead *thakur*s, and so forth—the modern can only be concretized in the present, deploying signs of the contemporary. The Ramsay film expends considerable labor in rendering palpable what it understands as "the modern"; I suggest that the song sequence provides the ideal space for such an elaboration, because it allows the genre to gesture to its immediate context in a recognizable manner. The song sequence—traditionally Hindi cinema's favorite site for presenting romantic love and conjugating the couple[46]—thus performs multiple tasks in the Ramsay horror film.

Recall that music—specifically the ghost's siren song—was a primary conduit for generating affect in the older Gothic film. The specter's song was used by the genre to stage the progressive dismantling of the symbolic authority that accrued to the postcolonial hero. The Ramsay film, too, on occasion has used the ghostly song number, for example, Lata Mangeshkar's memorable rendition of "Sunsaan Raaton Mein" ("In Lonely Nights") in *Sannata* (*Silence*, 1981); in this film, the older idiom of the Gothic is repeated almost exactly, complete with a white-clad female wraith. But alongside these types of songs—and more common variants such as the romantic duet, picnic songs, and so on—what the Ramsay film consistently featured was disco. By disco, I mean both the Western musical form (itself a composite of different styles ranging from funk to salsa) from the 1970s and the space of the discotheque or nightclub that it gets its name from. Disco was not exclusive to the Ramsay film, of course, and a vast number of Hindi films from the 1980s feature disco music as well as the setting of the nightclub.[47] *Disco Dancer* (B. Subhash) was a colossal hit in 1982, cementing India's romance with the music and dance associated with the form and catapulting Mithun Chakraborty into a dancing superstar of the era. The Ramsay film's repeated and compulsive reliance on disco, however, adds a certain kind of piquancy to its use; in a certain sense, I suggest that before the Ramsay film could travel to the feudal *haveli*, it—almost inevitably, and sometimes symbolically—had to make a detour through disco.

In 1981, the pop album *Disco Deewane* featuring Biddu and Pakistani pop singer Nazia Hassan became a raging success among the youth in India, and in the same year, music director R. D. Burman masterfully used disco in such songs as "Dil Lena Khel Hai Dildar Ka" ("Stealing Hearts Is the Game of Lovers") and "Poochho Na Yaar Kya Hua" ("Ask Me What Has Happened to Me") in the film *Zamane Ko Dikhana Hai* (*We Will Show the World*, Nasir Hussain); as Geeta Dayal suggests, disco was very much part of the zeitgeist, and the 1980s were "a time in India when disco reigned supreme."[48] The overwhelming presence of disco in the Ramsay horror film can be at least partially credited to music director Bappi Lahiri—well known for popularizing disco in Bombay film—who composed for numerous Ramsay films, including *Aur Kaun?* (*Who Else?*), *Saboot* (*Evidence*), *Guest House*, *Dahshat* (*Terror*), *Haveli*, *3D Saamri*, *Dak Bangla*, and *Shaitani Ilaka* (*Demonic Area*). Interestingly, however, even those films that Lahiri did not compose for featured disco songs, such as the "superman" disco song in *Sannata* (with Helen performing in the nightclub) and the "Hello, Darling" number that opens *Telephone* (1985), both of which were scored by Rajesh Roshan. Beyond the matter of record sales—which are bolstered by the inclusion of popular musical forms, and disco undoubtedly was one at this time—the form signified and symbolized something in the generic domain that was considered an essential component of its *masala*.

The disco—both song and setting—can be genealogically traced to the "cabaret number," a performance sequence set in a hotel or club that typically featured the vamp, as Sangita Gopal has observed. As such, the cabaret song "visually conveyed the dangerous enticements of Western modernity—sex, alcohol, and half-naked women—or rather, conveyed these enticements as dangerous."[49] She also argues that in the 1970s, when Hindi cinema becomes more Westernized, "incorporating the youthful sexuality and bodily deportment of a global consumer culture," the heroine—who had earlier been enclosed within the space of the romantic duet—could gradually access more mobility and move into nightclubs and other performance spaces. In the Ramsay horror film, the disco certainly functions in a similar manner, standing in for a modern, urban, indeed global, consumer culture and its heady sensations. Although the heroine only occasionally dances in the discotheque or club, the policing of her body or sexuality is less of a burden for the Ramsay film, as the genre as a whole depended on a certain exploitation aesthetic. But more on this later.

For the Ramsay film, the disco song both underscores the youthful modernity of the protagonists—it is often the leading men who sing and dance with the vamp and backup dancers in this space—and acts as a portent for the imperilment of this domain. In several films of the genre, the disco song immediately precedes the journey to the haunted *haveli*, where the modernity/rationality of the primary characters is horrifically challenged and eventually dismantled. In *Hotel*, for example, there are two disco songs: the first, "Kaun Yeh Aaya Mehfil Mein" ("Who Is This Stranger"), features Sanjay (Prem Krishan), a spoiled young man who is sent to the town of Ballipuram to oversee the construction of his brother Vijay's (Rakesh Roshan) hotel. He is killed soon thereafter, not by a supernatural entity but by the group that forms the villainous core in the film. The second disco number, "Tere Jaisa Pyara Koi Nahin" ("No One Is as Lovable as You"), is performed by the vamp, Shabbo (Prema Narayan), to celebrate the titular hotel's inauguration. Even as Shabbo shakes and shimmies in a shiny outfit and thigh-high fetish boots, the film cuts away to show us clouds of smoke signaling the encroaching presence of supernatural agents. The standard-bearers of speculative capital, a "bad modernity" in the Ramsay lexicon, soon get their comeuppance, but simultaneously, the inhabitants of the entire hotel are terrorized as well. Similarly, the disco song in *Purana Mandir*,

"Main Hoon Akeli" ("I Am Alone"), signals the end of carefree dates between Suman (Aarthi Agarwal) and Sanjay (Mohnish Behl) before they are initially separated by the *thakur* (Pradeep Kumar) and thereafter threatened by the monster in the *haveli*. A frisson of anxiety accompanies the convulsive delirium of strobe lights, pounding beats, and the (often literal) gloss of the Ramsay disco song; they suggest the imminent arrival of horror. These songs operate as codas of sorts for modernity, before the horrific/supernatural takes over the proceedings; they spectacularly signal the end of one register and the transition to the next. In this sense, then, the disco song functions quite differently than the ghost song of the older Gothic film, in which the hero was ushered into the irrational and the supernatural via song in the *haveli*. Here, the disco number signposts, in a manner of speaking, the last outpost of the modern. Additionally, the disco song also underscores urban youth culture alongside other leisure activities (swimming, playing games, picnics, and so on) that Ramsay protagonists are seen to routinely indulge in before their fateful travels take them elsewhere.[50]

EN-GENDERING MONSTROSITY: SEX AND VIOLENCE IN THE RAMSAY FILM

Whereas historians chronicle the Emergency as a period most critically aligned to the suspension of democracy and the invalidation of the institutions of civil society (such as the muzzling of the press), the absolute and arbitrary power assumed by the state lives on somewhat differently in the popular imagination of South Asia. Undoubtedly, alongside the demolition of slums in the aid of urban "beautification" programs, one of the most egregious violations of human rights occurred under the aegis of a public health drive, the euphemistic discourse of "family planning." And as Emma Tarlo points out, this unthinkable violence on citizens was widespread in urban areas as well, and both official and apocryphal narratives suggest that at least some of the "gifts" bestowed on the urban and rural underclass as an incentive to curb procreation and "overpopulation" were as humble as radio sets. Drawing on Tarlo's research, Kartik Nair writes, "This coercion—the preferred term was 'motivation'—occurred in more than one way: Sometimes whole villages were rounded up and hauled to these camps; other times, men were offered 'gifts' in exchange for sterilization."[51] In other words, the very notion of sexuality—sexual relations, encounters, fecundity, parturition, and procreation—comes to be inscribed within a discursive field of violence and violation during the Emergency era and beyond.[52] In a contested public sphere transformed by violence and unrest, sex and sexualities become the most expressive tropes, real as well as imagined. The Ramsay horror film's presentation of sex must be situated within this overdetermined domain where the erotic and the violent are not simply twin engines for producing cinematic sensation but come to be mutually constitutive. Simply put, there is no sex without violence in the Ramsay film—sexuality is necessarily strange, unnatural, often non-consensual, and indeed monstrous within this generic universe. The imbrication of sex and violence provides the most notorious recipe for the Ramsay *masala*: in this generic terrain, I suggest, the terms cannot be disentangled. Ribald to the hilt, the Ramsay film embraced the fleshly and the corporeal with unrestrained, gleeful enthusiasm. If the monster's body was excessively visceral in one sense—horrifying, decomposing, slimy, or covered in fur—the heroine's body performed other, and no less important, tasks.

Interestingly, the Ramsay horror film is obsessed with fathers and female offspring; mothers are largely absent in the formation, a stunning reversal of Hindi film's typical family romance. Numerous films of the genre, notably *Purana Mandir*, *Purani Haveli*, *Veerana*, *Shaitani Ilaka*, and *Bandh Darwaza* (*Closed Door*), revolve around curses and horrors that haunt specifically female progeny of erstwhile feudal landlords. These modern young women unwittingly step back into the haunted portals of decrepit ancestral mansions, only to be preyed on by the monsters that lurk therein. Although this insistence on female subjectivities occupying the center of diegesis may seem somewhat at odds with the overall tenor and address of the genre, the narrative preoccupation makes perfect sense when we consider to what ends the female body is deployed in this context. The female body comes to be a site upon which multiple fantasies and anxieties are projected en masse in the Ramsay horror film. Although this type of deployment is hardly novel in cinema more generally, taking cues from numerous American slasher films, the Ramsay genre pitches its version of exploitation at a uniquely excessive, overwrought register.

Perhaps the most notorious ingredient of the Ramsay horror film is the consistent and gratuitous display of semi-nude female bodies, and the generation of erotic effects that teeter perilously on the edge of pornography.[53] The censor board's response was predictable—almost all Ramsay films carry A, or adult, certificates, attesting to their racy content and no doubt sharpening audience curiosity with regard to the same.[54] In the peak of its popularity in the 1980s, the Ramsay film was infamous for its bold and "sexy" grammar, especially when compared to the more staid mainstream Hindi film that remained—albeit grudgingly—more attentive toward the dictates of the censor board. Women in Ramsay films—young, attractive, and victims par excellence—cavort, writhe, and frolic in various states of undress, especially swimwear.[55] Although some of these displays are nestled within the less rigidly policed contours of the romantic song-sequence, innumerable instances of attempted rape and assault furnish the narrative motivation for the rest. In fact, rape is a staple of the Ramsay film, assaults that are enacted by human and supernatural agents alike.[56]

Almost any Ramsay horror film would provide examples of sexual assault and violence. Anita (Amita Nangia) in *Purani Haveli* is repeatedly threatened by Vikram, a spurned suitor, until he finally attacks her physically. Anita runs through the woods screaming in terror; Vikram catches up with her in a shallow river and manhandles her further, before she is finally rescued by her beau, Sunil (Deepak Parashar). The sequence is odiously lengthy, and audiences are invited to relish Anita's abject fear and distress. Unsurprisingly, the monster who lurks in the old *haveli* assaults Anita in the climax in a very similar manner, groping her as she screams in terror—the Ramsay heroine is besieged by sexual predators on all sides. Likewise, in *3D Saamri*, Khanna (Gulshan Grover) ties Anju on the bed and gags her, before proceeding to sexually assault her; she, too, is saved by her beau, Sandeep (Rajan Sippy), but not before being reduced to a state of helpless terror. As the Ramsays devised increasingly innovative ways of staging rape, heroines such as Nangia and Aarthi Agarwal became classic "scream queens": their terrified, high-pitched shrieking provides visceral thrills and dominates the aural universes of the Ramsay horror film, cementing, as it were, its smutty ill-repute. The spectator is specifically invited to contemplate hypersexualized female bodies being threatened and violated. In Emergency India, the Ramsay horror film most expressively apprehends the overarching concatenation between sex and violence.

The Ramsay film's inscription of gender and sexuality remained determinedly crass, prurient, and predictable. However, it also produced a number of female monsters who unsettle, at least to a degree, these easy generalizations. One of the most iconic Ramsay monsters is Jasmin (Jasmin) in *Veerana*. This film tells the story of Thakur Mahendra Pratap Singh (Kulbhushan Kharbanda), his clan, and his subjects, all of whom are threatened by a powerful witch (*chudail*), Nakita, who dwells in the wilderness nearby, along with a bevy of acolytes. Almost vanquished by the *thakur*'s brother (Vijayendra Ghatge), Nakita avenges herself by possessing Jasmin, the *thakur*'s young daughter. *Veerana* liberally cannibalizes *The Exorcist* (William Friedkin, 1973); numerous sequences involving the possessed child and terrifying witch whose head swivels 360 degrees are unapologetically lifted from the Hollywood hit. To these, *Veerana* adds local folkloric elements as demanded by the genre.

FIGURE 2.5. *Rape scene from* Purani Haveli.

In the consolidation of a typical generic terrain, the adult Jasmin, however, remains something of an aberration in the Ramsay universe. Beautiful, seductive, and lonely, she picks men up, seduces them, and summarily kills them when possessed by Nakita. Her father, the aging *thakur*, is aware of some deep malaise in his daughter but remains a largely ineffectual figure of feudal patriarchy. Jasmin/Nakita is able to penetrate and inhabit the feudal family with relative ease, violating its rules with impunity. When a psychiatrist is summoned and gets uncomfortably close to the truth of Jasmin's "strangeness," Nakita slays him easily—this time appearing as a vampire—in the wilderness the film is titled after. Undoubtedly, it is the trope of possession—the fact that the female body is overtaken by a vengeful, supernatural entity—that enables Jasmin to transgress gendered as well as cinematic imperatives. As Barbara Creed argues in her classic work on the monstrous feminine, "possession becomes the excuse for legitimizing a display of aberrant feminine behavior which is depicted as depraved, monstrous, abject—and perversely appealing."[57] Errant, undisciplined, and murderously promiscuous, Jasmin is allowed an unprecedented degree of liberty and license in *Veerana*. But the fact that her monstrous appetites and unspeakable urges flourish within the feudal home is, nonetheless, remarkable in this context.

The possessed Jasmin is monstrous and abject, but she is also desirable, and indeed irresistible to the men she preys on, including Hemant (Hemant Birje), the hero, who is able to escape her spell only fortuitously. As a figure of rampaging, predatory female sexuality, she is offset by Sahila (Sahila Chadha), the good daughter and Hemant's beloved. However, it is Jasmin—her sexuality and her splendid isolation—who dominates *Veerana*, a remarkable fact when we consider the larger generic predispositions of the Ramsay horror film. Jasmin consistently and defiantly violates every taboo and prohibition that underpin figures of acceptable femininity in

FIGURE 2.6. *Alluring Jasmin in* Veerana.

Hindi film and even the Ramsay film: despite the presence of feudal patriarchs, she remains unschooled and unintegrated into this hefty universe.

At the climax, with Nakita destroyed by the combined might of Shiva's trident and Hemant's fighting skills, Jasmin presumably returns to her earlier state of innocence. But notably, she is never punished or taken to task for the dreadful crimes she has committed or the forbidden pleasures she has enjoyed during her tenure as a possessed body. Horror is probably the only genre in Hindi film in which women can survive such transgressions.[58] The film ends with a didactic voice-over that extols the triumph of light over darkness and good over evil, as we look at a stock shot of the rising sun; the triangulated grid of desire that has been established among Hemant, Jasmin, and Sahila is elided altogether. The chaotic assemblage of the Ramsay film—perhaps inadvertently—opened up spaces for such aberrations to exist.

Shalaka/Lal Bai (Neelam Mehra) is a similarly malevolent figure in *Shaitani Ilaka*. Masquerading as the heroine Anju's (Sri Pradha) governess, she practices black magic that haunts her charge in nightmares. Lal Bai's grouse is, predictably, against Anju's feudal ancestors who had destroyed her master, a dark and evil power. She sustains him for years with virgin blood, until Anju comes of age, as she is the ultimate gift, and the sacrifice that will reanimate him for all eternity. Although not fetishistically presented like Jasmin, Lal Bai remains a formidable adversary throughout *Shaitani*

Ilaka—shape-shifting at will and a truly terrifying figure of demonic rage, she battles a whole host of young protagonists, even circumventing the strategies of a powerful *sadhu baba* (holy man) who comes to their aid. It is only the absolute divine power of goddess Kali—whose massive idol is a key feature of the film's mise-en-scène—that Anju is finally able to vanquish the dark forces unleashed by Lal Bai.

Even the good women—dutiful wives and virginal daughters—willfully violate codes of sexual conduct in the Ramsay film. *Bandh Darwaza* is virtually a catalog of wayward, aberrant, unruly feminine behavior. Lajo (Bina), the *thakur*'s (Vijayendra Ghatge) wife, willingly submits to the seduction of Nevla (Anirudh Agarwal), the monstrous vampire, in order to procreate. Nevla is both monstrous and clearly potent, and the seduction sequence relays the combination of Lajo's fear and desire with remarkable candor. Lajo's subsequent repentance betrays the truth of her desire for Nevla's hyperbolic sexuality. Later in the film, Bhanu (Anita Sareen), yet another wife, similarly succumbs to Nevla's advances—in keeping with the Dracula narrative that the film liberally plunders. In one critical sequence, Bhanu writhes on the bed, orgasmically replaying her union with Nevla, as her hapless husband, Anand (Satish Kaul), looks on in horrified impotence; thereafter, she willingly goes to Nevla, in spite of Anand's concerned entreaties. The most complex figuration of female desire is, however, reserved for Kamya (Kunika), the daughter Nevla had sired with Lajo but who grows up in the *thakur*'s home as his own child. Interested in the black arts, and always assertive of her sexual needs, Kamya's union with Nevla perversely extends the Ramsay film's obsession with fathers and daughters. The song "Main Ek Chingari Thi" ("I Was a Spark") articulates the twisted and convoluted affective domain of Kamya's desire, disgust, and despair in this incestuous, perverse melodrama; the shot of Kamya lying on top of Nevla's glass-topped coffin—in a profoundly intimate communion with father/lover/monster—is, indeed, one of the bleakest in the Ramsay genre. Kamya's transgressions are too great to be overlooked, however, and Nevla eventually brutally murders her by tossing her against giant phallic spikes, symbolically reinforcing his right to penetrate her body. As her distraught "other" father—the victimized *thakur*—discovers her impaled corpse, the Ramsay film's grotesque idiom of gendered violence reaches a suitably melodramatic climax.

The inscription of gender and sexuality in the Ramsay horror film, and the libidinal excesses of the genre as a whole, remain deceptive in their recursive simplicity. Largely peddling sex and violence—crude objectification of female bodies combined with sexual violence against women—the Ramsay film also, on occasion, provides startling figures of female monstrosity and feminine desire that trouble theoretical edifices considerably. Moreover, the sexual unruliness that animates the Ramsay film is not limited to female figures; the genre is simultaneously shot through with queerness and non-heteronormative energies that demand closer scrutiny.[59]

LAUGHING IT OFF: QUEERNESS AND THE COMEDY TRACK

In a recent article, Aditi Sen has argued that the Ramsay horror film is far more conservative than the progeny it spawned in the 1980s—filmmakers such as Harinam Singh, Kanti Shah, and Joginder remain far more subversive in their inscription of non-mainstream sexualities and sexual deviances than the more sedate Ramsays, who "did not consciously subvert mainstream values. Their films were 'safe' as order was always restored in the end, and good succeeded over evil."[60] I have no quibble with the transgressive potentialities lurking within the sex-horror films of the post-Ramsay mediascape, but to overlook the queerness of the Ramsay film would be a disservice to the sexual politics of the genre as well as the tasks it undertook at the time. Queerness and sexual perversions abound in the Ramsay film—including, but not limited to, rape, incest, necrophilia, and a range of other non-mainstream sexual behaviors and non-heterosexual proclivities. Harry Benshoff has argued that the monsters from Universal's classic horror films from the 1930s—*Dracula*, *Frankenstein*, *Bride of Frankenstein*, the denizens of the *Old Dark House*, and so on—remain decidedly queer because the makers and producers managed to imbue their own sensibilities as sexual outsiders into the characters and films in question.[61] By contrast, the Ramsay monsters do remain aggressively heterosexual.

However, as I have explored here, the sexual registers of the Ramsay film are far from self-evident. Decidedly queer characters and non-heteronormative impulses are usually nestled within the awkwardly situated comedy track. In *Purani Haveli*, Mangu (Satish Shah), the hero's comic sidekick, boards the bus that the protagonists are traveling in, in drag, wearing a *burqa*. Attired thusly, he immediately arouses the curiosity and desire of the Pathan bus driver, Sher Khan (Raj Kishore). This interest is represented and communicated via decidedly off-color jokes and double entendre—involving "big and small fish" in one instance, for example—even after Mangu's gender is revealed, and it continues for the rest of the film. Similarly, Hitcock (Satish Shah) shares several queer moments with the manager of a strange guest house (Rajendra Nath) in *Veerana*, on one occasion inviting him into the bathroom "because his soap has slipped away." In *Hotel*, what starts off as a straight seduction of a Hyderabadi begum (a Muslim woman of high rank) by Popatlal (Rajendra Nath) goes horribly awry when her husband ingests the love potion intended for her. Thereafter, the husband, Nawab Arshad Ali (Mehmood), determinedly pursues Popatlal, much to his alarm and the begum's distress. The manner in which many of these moments are framed within the absurd comedy tracks make them more homophobic than anything else, but it is important to note that queerness is the *primary* comic modality of the Ramsay film—and as crude and tasteless as these jokes are, they could only make appearances within a formation that inhabited the underbelly of popular culture. Strange and colorful characters, quite literally "foreign bodies," also populate these comedy tracks. Changez Khan (Jagdeep) is an outlandishly attired, anarchic cook in *3D Saamri*; Hitcock, who wants to make horror films in *Veerana*, is a similarly strange vision; Mangu and Kala Gangu in *Purani Haveli* are the long-lost identical twins of the typical *masala* potboiler. In other words, these are all bodies and figures from other worlds and textual terrains that the commodious Ramsay genre makes room for, if only in the awkwardly inserted comedy track.

Although these queer figures—they are not quite characters in the strictest sense—and moments remain fleeting in the Ramsay film, their recursivity in a vast number of texts attests to the non-bourgeois ethos harnessed by the genre. Tucked within comic subplots that remain prosthetic at best, they nonetheless buttress the overall non-normative, indeed, transgressive effects of the Ramsay horror genre as a whole. In fact, pushing this argument a step further, I would suggest that the comic subplot of the Ramsay genre also queers it *formally* in a way that is unique. Despite the capacious contours of the *masala* form, the comedy track of the Ramsay film meanders wildly afield. *Purana Mandir*, for instance, includes a protracted spoof of *Sholay* that takes up considerable screen time but contributes virtually nothing to the plot of the film; *Purani Haveli* veers off into a lengthy digression about Mangu and his twin brother, Kala Gangu (also played by Satish Shah), a *dacoit* (armed robber), and pays homage to the dacoit-film genre that was popular during the era. In other words, the queerness of the Ramsay film can be unpacked at multiple registers and manifests as a range of formal eccentricities as well.

Alongside horror, sexuality was undoubtedly the unique selling point (USP) of the Ramsay horror film. The genre combined sex and violence in a delirious cocktail that not only pushed the envelope in terms of representational limits, but in tightly braiding the two, also captured something of the affective energies of Emergency India. The braiding of sex, violence, and sexual deviance in the Ramsay film was both implacable and efficacious for the audiences and sensibilities it was trying to cater to in the 1980s, a fact that made its survival difficult when the socio-political moment of the 1970s and 1980s slowly gave way to a different dispensation altogether.

BRAND RAMSAY: TELEVISION AND BEYOND

The advent of economic liberalization in the early 1990s changed the mediascape in India rather dramatically. The introduction of cable and satellite television and Bombay cinema's transition into what we understand as "Bollywood" were two of the pivotal events of the era. Cable and satellite TV introduced Indian viewers to hundreds of global channels seemingly overnight, and simultaneously, Bollywood went aggressively global, thematically as well as in the audiences it was trying to woo. The euphoric mantra of consumption and globality that animated the broader public culture meant that Hindi cinema's target spectator was no longer working class or exclusively male; in this period, Hindi cinema's address largely turned toward the urban, affluent, or aspirational middle-class consumer of all genders. Although the excessive *masala* form continued to survive, the focus of the mainstream Hindi film perceptibly shifted to big-budget romances and family melodramas. While I explore these shifts in greater detail in Chapter 4, they were also of tremendous consequence for the Ramsay horror film.

The processes of industrial streamlining and corporatization meant that production values improved considerably, and the shoddiness of the Ramsay horror universe was no longer appealing to audiences. Undoubtedly, multiple factors contributed to the demise of the Ramsay film genre, not least of which was the end of the collaboration between brothers Shyam and Tulsi, and *Bandh Darwaza* (1990) would be their last major commercial success. Thereafter the Ramsays regrouped, realigned, and concentrated on television instead of film, and astonishingly, they made the transition from second-run movie houses and grimy, provincial video parlors to middle-class living rooms with relative ease. Starting in the 1990s, the Ramsay film morphed into a television series called *Zee Horror Show* and then *Anhonee* (*Impossible*), each of which was enormously popular and ran for a considerable length of time (1993–2000). The televisual afterlife of the Ramsay horror film and its success upends our basic assumptions about what made the Ramsay horror film successful in the first place—how did a low-budget, trashy, non-bourgeois generic formation find a hospitable habitat in television, which is considered to be the most middle class of media?

As hundreds of satellite television channels broadcast content from around the globe into Indian homes, the Ramsays—always adept at makeovers—found a less stringently policed mediascape in which they could unleash their low-budget monsters. Unlike the cinema, satellite television channels did not have to undergo censorship in the same way, and this provided an apposite moment for the Ramsay genre to travel to a different media platform; in Shyam Ramsay's own words, "[W]e realised that other than the front-benchers (a section of the audience that was anyway disappearing with the rise of the multiplexes) even the middle-class family could be Ramsay-friendly."[62] One might imagine that given the "middle-class" ethos of television, the Ramsays gentrified their content. This assumption does not hold up, however, if we look closely at the particulars of the television show. For example, an early story titled *Aafat* (*Trouble*) quite closely follows the template of the Ramsay horror film. In this show—each horror tale was broken up into multiple half-hour episodes—three older businessmen (Goga Kapoor, Feroz Irani, and Rana Jung Bahadur) travel to an ancestral *haveli* that is faithfully looked after by Gangua (Mushtaq Khan) and his young, nubile daughter, Mayuri (Mayuri). The debauched trio sends the old retainer on an errand in order to brutally gang-rape Mayuri, who dies as a result. Although Gangua is unable to protest this injustice—or even articulate it aloud—Mayuri's ghost extracts a terrible vengeance on the perpetrators. The thematic resonances with a vast number of Ramsay films are, of course, unmistakable. But even more remarkably, the rape sequence remains lengthy and graphic, at least by contemporary standards of Indian television. Likewise, the "revenge" segment is shockingly gory, featuring, among other bloody deeds, a post-mortem sequence shot in extreme close-ups with appropriate sound effects, such as the noise of an electric saw drilling into a skull. In other words, the Ramsay horror genre did not have to fundamentally transform itself in order to travel into Indian living rooms; rather, the liberties and licenses that satellite television brought in its wake created yet another salubrious media habitat within which the formation could flourish anew. The startling, non-theatrical afterlives of the Ramsay horror genre—in grimy video parlors, sanitized middle-class abodes, and now in the far-flung corners of the Internet—remind us of the monsters they created in the 1980s. Like those creatures who refused to stay dead, the Ramsay genre continues to haunt in the era of new media.

The Ramsay narrative, as I trace it here, is one of considerable resilience. Although the older Ramsay films have been reincarnated in the global circulation of cult, trash, and exploitation cinemas in recent years, the formation has struggled to reinvent itself in the post-liberalization industrial landscape. The commercial failure of such films as *Aatma* (*Soul*, Deepak Ramsay, 2006), *Ghutan* (*Suffocation*, Shyam Ramsay, 2007), *Bachao* (*Save Me*, Shyam Ramsay, 2010), and most recently, *Neighbours* (Shyam Ramsay,

2014) attests to the fact that the Ramsay genre is unable to find traction in the vastly altered media ecology of the new millennium. The recent films display a certain amount of confusion regarding current cinematic tastes, and it appears as though the Ramsay horror genre can only circulate as an exemplar of kitschy camp, a quaintly tacky artifact of a past that current Bollywood is quick to disavow.

My basic task in this chapter has been to dismantle the complex formal and ideological universe generated by the Ramsay horror film in the 1970s and 1980s. Complexity, in this context, is not a carefully worked-out system of relations between component parts but a mélange of signs and discourses that do not necessarily hold together in any meaningful way. I contend that the fundamentally "attractional" format of the Ramsay horror genre accounts, at least partially, for its popularity in post-Emergency India; in its chaotic assemblage of convulsive, overwrought sensations and pleasures, the Ramsay film inscribed, in its own way, the turbulence of its times. To that end, I have dismantled the genre into its most enduring component parts in order to uncover some of the ways in which each of these engaged the public cultures and public fantasies of that era. But as Bollywood moves toward a more integrated global cinema, this formal disarray can no longer find foothold in millennial India.

The Ramsays, however, continue to produce media—both film and television—and in a typically astute manner, have made several "snake serials" for television in recent years. *Nagin* (*Snake*, date unavailable) on Zee TV and *Neeli Aankhen* (*Blue Eyes*, 2008) on Sahara One were both based on the legends of the supernatural, shape-shifting serpent, one of the most enduring mythic-folk formations in South Asia. The continuities—of themes, preoccupations, and audiences—between the erstwhile Ramsay horror film and the snake genre are numerous, and I turn to this formation in the next chapter.

CHAPTER THREE

Ravishing Reptiles

MAGIC, *MASALA*, AND THE HINDI "SNAKE FILM"

The reasons why the monstrous-feminine horrifies her audience are quite different from the reasons why the male monster horrifies his audience.

—BARBARA CREED, *THE MONSTROUS-FEMININE: FILM, FEMINISM, PSYCHOANALYSIS*

WHILE GOTHIC MODALITIES CONTINUED TO APPEAR in fits and starts over the 1970s, it was the baroque *masala* film of the era that eventually provided a hospitable gestational domain for the supernatural. The Ramsay horror film, as I argued in the last chapter, is a telling example of these tendencies. In terms of stars, style, and affect, the *masala* form of the 1970s is replete with excess and irrationality; and, unlike the Social's tortured attempts to ultimately affirm the "scientific," it suffers no internal torment for allowing the fantastic to emerge and consolidate. Indeed, many of the *masala*'s most profligate charms hinge on a certain romance with the fantastic through plot, character, or dénouement. It is worth reiterating that the Social's repressive rationality had something to do with the larger philosophical tenor of the immediate postcolonial period, and when the *masala* film dislodged it as the dominant generic formation in Hindi cinema in the 1970s, many attendant discourses were swept aside in tandem. Aided by the introduction of color technology, the "modern-popular" of Nehruvian reformist cinema had already given way to a delirium of escapism in the 1960s; the *masala* was simply the logical climax to this process of disassembly. The relationship between sociopolitical transformation and the cinema is far from indexical, especially because the commercial form operates within entrenched circuits of production and consumption; however, I argue that specific generic clusters do provide a privileged window into a rapidly changing public culture of the 1970s and 1980s. This chapter investigates one of the most interesting generic constellations in Hindi cinema—the snake film. Although the formula has been popular in specific historical moments and remains instantly recognizable to viewers and fans of Hindi cinema, it has puzzlingly languished in obscurity with regard to scholarly exegesis; thus, the spirit of the present inquiry is, at least partially, recuperative.[1]

Before moving on to the films in question, however, it is important to note that, the complexities of the *masala* notwithstanding, the snake film does not operate in Hindi cinema as a stable or robust generic form; its status is more of a film cycle, which gathered around itself specific resonances in the 1970s and 1980s. In her work on American film cycles, Amanda Ann Klein points out several important distinctions between genres and cycles:

> Like film genres, film cycles are a series of films associated with each other through shared images, characters, settings, plots, or themes. However, while film genres are primarily defined by the repetition of key images (their semantics) and themes (their syntax), film cycles are primarily defined by how they are used (their pragmatics). In other words, the formation and longevity of film cycles are a direct result of their immediate financial viability as well as the public discourses circulating around them. . . . Because they are so dependent on audience desires, film cycles are also subject to defined time constraints: most film cycles are financially viable only for five to ten years. After that point, a cycle must be updated or altered in order to continue to earn profit.[2]

Although the Hindi film industry has its own internal logic of determining hits, flops, and commercial viability of certain kinds of films—stars, for example, play an important role in these determinations—in terms of a temporally circumscribed formation as well as popularity, Klein's description snugly fits the snake film. The two major texts I discuss in this chapter were made exactly a decade apart, and thereafter, the cycle disappeared from Hindi cinema's A-budget circuit altogether. A recent bid to resuscitate the snake film was not successful, as I discuss later in this chapter.

The serpent has enjoyed a long and considerably illustrious career in Indian cinema. Beginning with Mandakini Phalke's charming victory over the papier-mâché demon-snake Kalia in *Kalia Mardan* (*The Banishment of Kalia*, 1919), the snake has operated as a potent recursive trope across film genres. Phalke's film also reminds us that Indian cinema's expressive possibilities have always been aligned to the magical and the miraculous; film's constitutive allegiance with modern technology does not imply disenchantment in this context, as scholars who work on the devotional and mythological genres have repeatedly demonstrated. In this chapter, I make a distinction between what I call the "snake film" and films with snakes in them; here, I am not considering films with snakes as important characters, such as the remarkable *Doodh Ka Karz* (*The Debt of Milk*, Ashok Gaekwad, 1990), but something slightly different. The snake film does not draw much of its narrative or iconographic energies from the globally legible "creature-feature"; its moorings, instead, are more solidly South Asian.[3] Films involving bands of snake charmers had been prevalent for years, but the cycle that centered on shape-shifting, supernatural reptiles congeals as a formation proper in the 1970s and 1980s in films such as *Milap* (*Union*, 1972), *Nagin* (*Female Snake*, 1976), *Nagina* (*Female Snake*, 1986), *Nache Nagin Gali Gali* (*The Serpent Dances Everywhere*, 1989), and *Sheshnaag* (*Lord of the Snakes*, 1990), most of which were commercially successful.[4]

The figure of the supernatural serpent garners much of its affective resonance in South Asian culture from its robust presence in epic, mythic, and folk traditions—oral, written, visual, and performative.[5] From Shiva's sinuous companions to Vishnu's celestial ride, serpents are everywhere in Indian—and especially Hindu and Buddhist—narratives. Snakes are considered phallic symbols signifying procreation and fertility, and they are also objects of veneration and ritual worship in many parts of India, no doubt needing to be propitiated additionally for their potentially lethal venom.[6] Amy Allocco, for example, has shown how reverence is considerably tempered with fear and ambivalence when it comes to snake worship in South India, both historically and in more recent times.[7] Classic Orientalist tropes insistently imagine the snake charmer and his basket of deadly, swaying reptiles as the most emblematic figure of South Asia. From Kaa in Rudyard Kipling's *The Jungle Book* to Lord Voldermort's pet snake Nagini in the *Harry Potter* films, the association between India and the snake is both unrelenting and unavoidable.

In a certain sense, the commercial Hindi film draws on this array of sources, as well as on the visual cultures of South Asia, particularly calendar and bazaar art, and even local comic-book iconography. Tracing the story of these influences and intertextual cross-pollination would make a fascinating project; it is, however, beyond the purview of the current inquiry. Here, I interrogate the story of the snake film from the other end: that is, I look at the snake film's generative power—its ability to create and disseminate modern-day myths that are no less effective for their contemporaneity. I argue that the snake film is both aligned to and departs from the basic imperatives of the *masala* form in critical ways. I also hope to demonstrate that unlike commonplace perceptions, the cycle is in fact far from homogeneous and transforms quite radically over the course of its relatively short life as an "A" cycle in Bombay cinema. In particular, I focus on three distinct moments in the trajectory of the snake film to map the shifting contours of public and political culture in India; in each of these moments, the formation registers larger transformations in a manner that emphasizes its overall plasticity. Finally, I suggest that the snake film harnesses a curious paradox: on the one hand, it resists "Bollywoodization" in a fundamental sense; its basic ingredients as well as its address make it a defiantly anachronistic formation that cannot be reconciled with Hindi cinema's current bid for globality, or its transnational aspirations. However, simultaneously, it has found new habitats and audiences in the era of digital media. But first, a word on the protagonists: the reptiles themselves.

In the wake of the important work done by Gilles Deleuze, Jacques Derrida, John Berger, and Donna Haraway, among many others, the field of animal studies has gained considerable traction in humanities disciplines, including film studies, in recent years. At first glance, the snake film appears to be precisely the kind of cluster that could benefit from a conversation with this posthumanist turn. The critical exploration of non-human others as meaningful participants in cinematic texts—cyborgs, inanimate objects, plants, the environment, and so forth—has also turned the spotlight on animals, both domestic and feral. From Balthazar to Bambi, animals both real and animated are being subjected to critical revaluation by film scholars from a number of perspectives. The bulwark of this philosophical terrain is its commitment to decenter the human from its position of primacy and power, and in doing so re-conceptualize the nature of coexistence of different life forms. Indeed, for scholars who work on film, this de-anthropocentrism implies a reconsideration of the cinematic medium itself. For Anat Pick, for example, the "creatureliness" of cinema "effectively means abandoning the distinctions of—and more importantly the narrative conventions attached to—the identity and hierarchy of species. The result is the absorption of the human figure within the leveled plane of the photographed world."[8]

Undergirded by specifically Western philosophical ideas, animal studies is foundationally preoccupied with *separation* between the human and the animal, and the legacies and violence that this difference and hierarchical ordering of the world has generated historically. And herein one encounters a theoretical impasse when attempting to read something like the snake film through the lens of posthumanism/animal studies. The creature-protagonists of the snake film inhabit a quasi-mythic universe that is constitutively infused with fantastic possibilities, where the boundaries of the human and the non-human are not only fragile and indeterminate, but also, in a certain sense, irrelevant. In the introduction of their anthology on animals in South Asian texts, Fabrizio M. Ferrari and Thomas Dähnhardt grapple with precisely this mode of incommensurability when they write:

> Mastering "the animal" is . . . an ontological necessity in Western (and Westernized) societies. In other words, as suggested by Derrida (2008:102)—the animal is not just reified but, made into a taboo, an object that is "at once religiously excluded, kept in silence, reduced to silence, consecrated, and sacrificed, branded a forbidden or just plain branded" . . .
>
> In South Asia the individualization of the human being and the otherization of the "animal other" are less definite. The construction of the body is more flexible. Bodies are porus [*sic*] entities in which the essence of beings moves temporarily into. Transmigration, possession, embodiment, reincarnation, descent are not mystical concepts related to an infantile projection or a secret, supreme condition of the mind. What in South Asia is ordinary reality, in Western culture has been relegated to fairy tales, is derogatively labeled "folklore" and explained as allegory.[9]

The snakes in the Hindi snake film are magical creatures that are never fully human nor fully reptilian; this indeterminacy furnishes the basic coordinates of the cycle as a whole. The spaces and temporalities they traverse and inhabit are, likewise, shot through with fantastic potentialities.[10] The snake film is an intractably enchanted narrative and formal terrain, where the animal—in this case, the reptile—is, if anything, nobler and more heroic than the human *others*. When Hindi film uses the animal in a less fantastical manner, as Rachel Dwyer has shown, it is most often anthropomorphized to perform a series of human and melodramatic tasks.[11] And it is important to note that in its insistent elevation of reptiles into heroes, and in its equally formulaic presentation of humans as violent and potentially harmful, the snake film does indeed take for granted a certain kind of posthuman ethos, but it constellates in Hindi cinema as a magical formation that cannot be easily herded into familiar theoretical enclosures. My close readings of the films in question will highlight and clarify this specific form of privileging the non-human in greater detail.

MYTH, MAGIC, AND *MASALA*: DEFINING THE "SNAKE FILM"

It is difficult to trace the origins of the snake film not merely because it sprawls across multiple-language cinemas and industries, but especially because its basic energies can be traced back to the earliest mythologicals and fantasy films.[12] However, as mentioned above, in Hindi film the cycle gathers momentum at a specific historical juncture—in the 1970s. In many ways, the snake film is a curious formation that straddles a whole array of contradictions, caught as it was within the tensions and transformations that attended to form, industry, and nation at this time.[13] Often set in bucolic, nonspecific rural locations, the cycle crafts for itself a "pastoral *masala*" that is peculiarly its own.

The Hindi snake film has, over the years, generated an elaborate series of myths surrounding snakes and their magical, often quasi-divine powers. Indeed, so influential are these discourses that *they* now inform larger cultural understandings about snakes in South Asia. In this sense, the snake film is a formation that is constitutively cinema and pop-culture driven; although mythology and folklore have certainly informed the snake film, the form has now consolidated as an autonomous formation altogether, whereby its connection to these other textual modes is heavily mediated by the conventions of the popular film. Juwen Zhang's formulation of what he calls "filmic folklore" is particularly relevant in this context. Zhang defines filmic folklore as

> an imagined folklore that exists only in films, and is a folklore or folklore-like performance that is represented, created, or hybridized in fictional film. . . . Filmic folklore imposes or reinforces certain stereotypes (ideologies), and signifies certain meanings identified and consumed (as "the truth") by a certain group of people. The folklore in filmic folklore may appear as a scene, an action, an event, or a storyline (plot), and in verbal or non-verbal form.[14]

The Hindi snake film spawns a robust body of filmic folklore that continues to have considerable resonance in the popular culture of South Asia.[15] In terms of generic tropes, magic, and the miraculous powers of the *ichchadhari nag* and *nagin* (shape-shifting male and female snake, respectively)—literally the ability to transmogrify into any form they desire, especially into humans—form core thematic preoccupations, buttressed by a nonspecific, even inchoate assemblage of Hindu mythology and folklore. Despite the snake film's chaotic inscription of myths, however, the dissemination of certain ideologies is not without considerable political import.[16] A certain *filmi* (pertaining to the ethos of Hindi popular cinema) form of kitschy, "pop-religiousness" undergirds the snake film, which is informed by a whole plethora of fictions, images, and textual regimes—classical, folk, written, oral, and performative. The filmic *nag* (male snake) and *nagin* (female snake) are semi- (or sometimes completely) divine entities themselves, forming, as it were, the *dharmik* (ethical) core of the narratives. Attendant tropes include the *nagmani* (jewel) and assorted figures of good and bad snake charmers, tantrics, fakirs, and sages. The love story between the snake couple is often the narrative lynchpin against which the action unfolds. In many of the films in question, the central struggle comes to be between "good" and "bad" practitioners of magic. The snakes, typically, are beleaguered, melodramatic protagonists, besieged by humans with less than honorable intentions—the personifications of *adharma* (unethical behavior).

Arguably, it is no coincidence that formations like *Nagraj* comic books (or even *Amar Chitra Katha* comics), snake films, and the "mythological film," which had become somewhat moribund in the 1950s and 1960s, enjoyed resurgence in the 1970s and 1980s. It is instructive to recall that *Jai Santoshi Maa* (*Hail Santoshi Maa*) was one of the highest-grossing films of 1975, alongside *Sholay* (*Flames*) and *Deewar* (*The Wall*), much to the bewilderment of certain stolidly middle-class critics. Hindutva's canny retailing of a simply packaged Hinduism is certainly one of the imaginative engines that propel the visibility as well as the popularity of these and other similar artifacts of the era.[17] As Geeta Kapur notes in her seminal work on the mythological,

> the rising tide of nationalism encourages myths and legends as indeed all aspects of tradition *to surface*, to literally come up front and take on new or newly adapted forms in the various arts. The tradition thus shows itself (and I am talking primarily of the visual and performing arts), seeking beholders, native and foreign, who have hitherto turned away from it in ignorance or embarrassment.[18]

Regarding the snake film, one can discern a gradual hardening of religious discourses over the years—the later films from the 1980s and 1990s tend to be suffused with a kind of strident religiosity that is quite distinct from the folksiness of earlier films such as *Nagin*. Films like *Sheshnaag* or *Nache Nagin Gali Gali*, for example, are deeply indebted to the televised versions of *Ramayan* and *Mahabharat*, especially concerning mise-en-scène, texture, and the use of special effects; *Sheshnaag*'s layered narrative structure precisely illuminates how the snake film grafts snake mythology (and mythic energies more generally) onto the basic template of the Hindi film melodrama.[19] Like many other Hindi films, *Sheshnaag* banks on a certain kind of audience competence in unraveling the mythic nuances of event, plot, and character. Furthermore, as a classic snake film, it combines familiar mythic and folk narratives with the magical possibilities harnessed by special effects in order to—almost literally—dazzle its audience.[20]

In many respects, the snake film—and the *masala* film more generally—is akin to what Tom Gunning has famously called a "cinema of attractions." What sets this cycle apart is its insistence on presenting spectacle *as such*, largely unencumbered by the tug of causal momentum. Whether during elaborately choreographed song sequences or scenes of special-effect transformations, the snake film "addresses and holds the spectator, emphasizing the act of display."[21] This tendency toward a frontal solicitation of the spectator's attention is strongest in situations when the supernatural event unfolds on-screen. Although the narratives of the snake film absorb older textual and performative traditions, its fantastical visual syntax depends on the harnessing of modern cinematic technologies. As the focus on magic and supernatural transformation would imply, the cycle as a whole demands a certain deployment of cinematic "tricks," but of the most rudimentary kind—stop-motion cinematography, clunky dissolves, and inept superimpositions constitute the bulk of technological wizardry. For example, in *Sheshnaag*, as Bhanu the *nagin* confronts Aghori the evil tantric[22] in a customarily spectacular song-and-dance number, "O Mere Dushman" ("Oh, My Enemy"), her spiralling reptilian rage is conveyed through the use of arguably primitive cinematic tools: colored lights/filters, smoke machines, fast motion, and split screens. In several sequences, the magical serpents emit flames from their mouths or bolts of what looks like electricity from their bodies—shoddy effects that were clearly added on during postproduction. The climax of *Sheshnaag* involves the collapse of a patently fake, papier-mâché temple and a similarly flimsy (if sizable) Shiv-lingam being hurled at his enemies by Aghori.[23] Other films of the cycle simply used "snake vestments," makeup, or colored contact lenses to communicate the supernatural shift from human to reptilian modes of being. Thus, in terms of visual texture, too, the snake film mimics the fantasy film and the mythological, which, Phalke's early sophistication notwithstanding, relied on similarly crude special effects to render visible the divine miracles performed by gods and goddesses on-screen.[24]

I would argue that the snake film's generative power in terms of creating a unique combination of narrative/visual syntax depended on braid-

FIGURE 3.1. *Champa dancing in* Sheshnaag.

ing filmic folklore with special-effects spectacles, at a moment when more advanced technological feats were simply unavailable or prohibitively expensive. The lamentably "down-market" production values of these films constitute the cycle's overall status as the quintessential "bad object" of Hindi commercial cinema, and that accounts for its enduring popularity as an object of camp veneration in recent years, a development I return to later in this chapter.[25] The magic of the snake film—its persistent enchantment in the wake of its demise as a viable formation—depends precisely on this cluster of effects and discourses, all of which remain tethered to a sense of what is past, regressive, and primitive.

The reliance on folk tales, myths, and unsophisticated special effects would seem to imply an equally artless spectator, which brings us to the public consumption of Hindi cinema in the 1970s and 1980s. I concern myself here with the mode of address that this cinema typifies, rather than the complicated idea of empirical viewership; although it is certainly possible—and quite likely—that real viewers remained largely dubious about the shoddily performed miracles,[26] the cycle as a whole does not invite this sort of skepticism.[27] In this period, the snake film labors to render its magic as convincingly as possible to a community of spectators able and willing to suspend disbelief. In other words, the cycle as a whole remains obdurately enchanted.[28]

As I have noted in Chapter 2, following massive industrial, cultural, and historical shifts, certainly, a vast majority of commercial films made in the period clearly targeted the urban (usually male) underclass. The flight of elite and middle-class audiences from the theaters in this period furnishes some of the basic generic preoccupations of the snake film—such as its non-metropolitan ethos and texture, for example—and propels its inevitable demotion to B movie circuits. However, the snake film's reliance on the thematic of feminine power coupled with its continued popularity in regional cinemas, on television, and now the Internet complicates this well-ordered reading of a specifically classed and gendered viewership. However, it is undeniable that in certain aspects, the snake film works perfectly in tandem with the blood-and-guts action-adventure *masala* film that typifies the era. Beyond action and magic, though, the singularly defining feature of the formation is its use of music and dance.

"TAN DOLE MERA MAN DOLE": MUSIC, DANCE, AND THE EROTIC

The most viscerally thrilling, affectively charged, and enduringly popular syntactic features of the snake film are music and dancing. Of course the song-and-dance sequence remains the *masala* film's most recognizable feature even today, and in the period under discussion, commercial films without song sequences were practically nonexistent. However, despite this ubiquity, I would argue that the song-and-dance sequence is *peculiarly* potent in the snake-film cycle as a whole. The performance sequence is pivotal to my understanding of the supernatural more generally in this book; as I have shown in the earlier chapters, it is often in the song sequence that these genres most tellingly enact the vicissitudes of the historical moment within which they are embedded.

Recall, for example, that the Gothic film staged a (temporary) dismantling of the Five Year Plan hero via the siren song of the female "ghost"; the final rehabilitation of the masculine citizen is concomitantly accomplished via speech and dialogue, not music. The Ramsay horror film, similarly, uses the disco/nightclub song to signpost the modernity of the youthful protagonists, before these vectors of class and belonging are unsettled in/by the feudal *haveli*; rape sequences additionally operate as "set pieces" in lieu of songs in that specific generic domain. In other words, the supernatural almost always manifests *formally* via or in relation to the performance sequence. The performance sequence, in other words, is sine qua non for the presentation and elaboration of the supernatural in the Hindi film; when the performance sequence undergoes radical transformation—or is removed entirely, as I explore in the final chapter of this book—the supernatural, too, follows suit. However, if the performance sequence operates somewhat distinctly in supernatural genres, then it simultaneously also tethers these films securely to the industrial aesthetic of the period—its most recognizable and familiar attraction in the 1970s and 1980s. Unsurprisingly, the attraction format of the *masala* is pushed to its limit in the song-and-dance sequence in the snake film, simultaneously signposting the supernatural as well as its deep kinship with the modality through which the integrative drive of the Social was upstaged by the centrifugal tendencies of the new form.

However, to reiterate, the salience of the song-and-dance sequence is occasioned by the particularities of the snake film as a cycle: in both music and dance, the mythos of the magical reptile crystallizes visually in such sequences. In other words, the song sequences—which sometimes remain tenuously connected to the narrative—become excellent spaces where the specifically *serpentine erotic* can find elaboration. Magically liberated from the straitjacket of causality, the human-reptile fantasy finds its most pleasurable articulation in these moments of narrative suspension.

Songs featuring the wind instrument, or *been*, that snake charmers carry in South Asia dominates the aural universe of these films; indeed, the characteristically high-pitched wailing of the *been* provides the constitutive acoustic tone and texture for the cycle as a whole—it is what makes the snake film most authentic, most "Indian," and most charmingly homespun. Unsurprisingly, even today, practicing snake charmers in South Asia often perform tunes from hit films like *Nagin* and *Nagina* to entertain audiences, and presumably, their reptilian colleagues. A feedback loop of instant recognition and recall are key aspects of public performance here, much like bands perform "covers" of more successful or famous performers in the West. Startlingly, however, the music of the *been* in film is actually produced by the clavioline, a European instrument, whose introduction to Hindi cinema was a matter of technological experimentation with acoustic quality by music director Kalyanji Virji Shah.[29] With the clavioline's dulcet tones accompanying Lata Mangeshkar's voice in *Nagin*'s popular song, "Tan Dole Mera Man Dole" ("My Body Sways, as Does My Heart"), the "authentic" sound of the filmic snake charmer was born! This, too, attests to the fecundity and mythmaking potentialities harnessed by the snake film as a formation. The sound on film does not actually replicate the sound of the native instrument but nonetheless "appears" to do so with absolute conviction. It is this hybridizing/assembling capacity of the cycle—in narrative or thematic sources, and in stylistic features such as sound design—that makes the snake film an especially efficacious habitat for the invention of traditions and their perpetuation.

Alongside music, dance is a key generic attraction of the snake film. It is productive to recall that spaces of dance can often be liberatory in Hindi film; women can (temporarily) escape the disciplinary regimes of the patriarchal home and hearth in such sequences:

> Dance space in Bollywood perhaps is constructed as outside, as independent (perhaps threatening) to the male nationalist project, which . . . has its drawbacks in that it reiterates and demarcates gender stereotypes. However, it may also have its advantages. The dancer's body always already remains an outsider. Dance space remains removed from "real" life using several tactics. It is heightened in its theatricality and emotionality. It is understood as risqué, as stepping beyond what is acceptable in "real" life. The dancer and dance space are removed from the State project that is male in its nature. . . . Since dance space is believed to be unreal but desired, it is possible to play with issues of sexual freedom by displaying more than what is allowed in the narrative, by donning alleged masks of "performance" that in fact reveal very real desires, lifestyles and aspirations.[30]

The "snake dance" remains a constitutive element of the formation; spectacularly choreographed interruptions that not only allow women, but also men (actor Jeetendra, most frequently) to transcend the strictures and prohibitions that undergird Hindi film's ideological universe. Like music, the dance-form in the snake film is a delirious mishmash: classical mudras like *sharpashirsha* (the snake's hood) and *nagabandha* (snakes twining) from *Bharatanatyam* are paired with Hindi cinema's penchant for frenzied hip and torso movements, which have very little in common with these older traditions.[31] It is in these dance sequences that the protagonists' serpentine characteristics find clearest expression. Although the idiom itself—very much a pre-Bollywood entity—now languishes in relative obscurity, the dance associated with the snake film has taken on a life of its own. For example, the "snake/nagin dance" can find its way into films that have nothing at all to do with snakes—e.g., in *Qaidi* (*Prisoner*, 1984), which includes it presumably only to showcase actor Jeetendra's dancing skills; it appears as a comic interlude in *Bride and Prejudice* (2004); and even Waheeda Rehman's energetic rendition of the snake dance in *Guide* (1965) remains strangely disconnected from the rest of the narrative. Dance schools all over the globe teach students the "snake dance" from Hindi film, just as they teach non-specific forms of belly dancing. On social networking and micro-blogging sites such as Twitter and Facebook, one can find an array of videos of laypeople performing the snake dance under the hashtag "#Nagin."[32] Undoubtedly, the classical roots of the dance form accounts for some of its motility, but Hindi cinema provides a certain charge and affect to it.

The erotic energy of these dances perhaps also draws from earlier Orientalist film extravaganzas such as Fritz Lang's *The Indian Tomb* (1959), in which a nearly naked Debra Paget performs a remarkably lengthy dance

FIGURE 3.2. *Nag and Nagin dancing and cavorting in* Nagin. *Used by permission of the National Film Archive of India.*

to mollify a patently artificial snake and a snake goddess. Either way, the female snake and her seductive dance remain highly eroticized and spectacular set pieces in these films, also because these song-and-dance sequences stand in for ritualized mating sequences of the reptiles in question. In other words, much that would be beyond the permissible in terms of Hindi cinema's visual syntax comes to be possible because of the constant slippage between signifiers—human and reptile.[33]

In the 1976 film *Nagin*, for example, the song "Tere Sang Pyar Main" ("I Will Not Stop Loving You") is a barely veiled simulation of heterosexual copulation, with Jeetendra and Reena Roy in minimalist "snake" costumes slithering over each other with unabashed ardor and considerable physical flexibility—in one startling shot, Jeetendra (as the *nag*, he has no name), hanging upside down from a tree, slides down the entire length of Roy's body in a bravura performance of both desire and dexterity.[34] The film is careful to show us a moment of transmogrification just before the song commences, to ensure that the spectator reads the following sequence as involving specifically magical, "non-human" creatures. The pair sinuously writhe, frolic, and embrace in a variety of natural locations—meadows, waterfalls, and the like, endowing the landscape itself with a kind of voluptuousness, in stark contrast with the sterile bedrooms of the "humans" we encounter later in the film. The presence of Vijay (Sunil Dutt) as the diegetic voyeur who witnesses their love-play only heightens the erotic intensity of this song sequence, as our gaze is often mediated through his. Additionally, the song takes on tragic resonances because the very next time we hear it, the *nag* is brutally murdered by a group of thoughtless, ignorant, urban men. It is this act of senseless violence that provokes the *nagin*'s revenge and provides the basic fulcrum for the rest of the narrative.

In *Nagina*, as Rajni is forced into her "snake form" by the *been*-toting Bhairavnath (Amrish Puri), her moment of reluctant transformation is simultaneously a moment of sexual transgression and ecstasy:

> The Sapera and his acolytes begin playing their *beens* (instruments)[,] the tune played by all snake charmers in India. The Nagina rushes indoor[s], her body framed against a wall. She writhes, rolls and gyrates in a frenzy of orgiastic arousal. She holds her husband's picture to her breasts, as she rolls on the bed, her body heaving with the transformative pleasure of being a snake. Her face is repeatedly framed with the lattice of the bed—the source and site of pleasure—and her eyes are gleaming with a snake-like coldness mixed in with an animalistic gleam.
>
> Both animal and human, her sexuality and violence, now cohabiting, she runs to the cupboard and takes out a white mujra dress (for a dance performed by a courtesan). Meanwhile the Sapera and his acolytes play their *beens* with increased force and agitation, waiting for the Nagina to appear. She does so in spectacular style, arms raised above her head, she runs down the curving staircase in the main hall, a staple architectural feature of Hindi movies (reifying the class structure of the actors in patently uncomplicated terms). Running between the Sapera (and the acolytes) and around them, she begins to dance for them in the traditional mujra fashion, alternately sexual and shy in her movements.[35]

The fact that Rajni's snake outfit approximates the costume of a courtesan is, of course, no accident. In this moment of the film, she is violating

FIGURE 3.3. *Rajni performs the snake dance in* Nagina.

multiple taboos of the feudal patriarchy she is wedded to, a point I shall return to presently.[36] Here, it is worth reiterating that the song-and-dance sequence in the snake film is a potent terrain that allows for sexual expressivity of a kind that was uncommon in Hindi cinema of the period, barring the occasional nightclub sequence where the figure of the vamp showcased her dancing skills. The snake-dance sequence is yet another reminder of how the fantastical energies of the snake film make it an unruly aberration of sorts in the history of Hindi film.

REVENGE OF THE REPTILE: *NAGIN*

The carefully orchestrated image of the benign and benevolent state came to an abrupt end with the declaration of the Emergency in 1975.

In Hindi popular cinema, Amitabh Bachchan—psychologically scarred and physically wounded—lay bleeding to death in the arms of grieving mothers and distraught buddies. As the *masala* form became baroquely melodramatic, sex, violence, and violent sexualities proliferated on-screen; the "avenging woman" and "rape-revenge" films, for example, are two of the most iconic generic products of the 1980s. Indeed, there is something single-mindedly orgiastic about violence in the *masala* film, an excess that can be productively read as a barometer of those troubled times:

> Even if it is debatable that the state of emergency is the origin of the crisis of legitimacy of the Indian state, at the very least we can speculate that it did set into motion contestations between power and authority that have pressed upon a more thorough exploration of hegemony, citizenship, community, nationalism, and democracy in India. In short, discussions of violence have to consider how films replete with avenging women, gangsters, a brutal police force, and vigilante closures stage some of the most volatile struggles over representations that shape our public and private fantasies of national, communal, regional, and sexual identities.[37]

It is within this new hyper-violent *masala* idiom that a film such as *Nagin* becomes meaningful. *Nagin*'s audacious gesture—and it is an astonishingly brave film in many respects—is to graft onto the basic contours of the *masala* film the folklore of the supernatural snake. In fact, *Nagin* is very much a predecessor to the "avenging woman" film of the next decade, insofar as the vendetta-seeking snake can also magically transform into her feminine form at will.

The plot of *Nagin* is deceptively simple. Vijay is a professor who studies the legend of the *nag* and *nagin* and has searched for years for the shape-shifting reptiles. His efforts are finally rewarded when he saves the *nag* from a hungry bird of prey and is able to witness the *nag* and *nagin* as they magically shift between their human and reptilian avatars. Excited by his discovery, he writes to his city friends (played by Kabir Bedi, Feroz Khan, Sanjay Khan, Vinod Mehra, and Anil Dhawan), who initially dismiss his story as fanciful. When they actually witness the miraculous powers of the serpents in the forest, one of them shoots and kills the *nag*, and the *nagin* only just escapes with the *nagmani*, the jewel. The identity of the murderers is reflected in the dying *nag*'s eyes, which is a recurrent trope in the folklore generated by Bombay cinema. What follows is a carnage of sorts, as the *nagin* goes on a killing spree to avenge the death of her lover. She manages to kill all five perpetrators before finally being vanquished by Vijay and then dies, impaled on iron spikes.

Far from being a "B" film, *Nagin* boasts an extensive star cast, including a range of "A"-list stars such as Sunil Dutt, Rekha, and Mumtaz. In fact, it is a quintessential "multi-starrer" of the era, with a protracted action-adventure-sex-violence recipe that makes it a prototypical 1970s film.[38] But despite its pedestrian revenge plot, I would argue that it remains exceptional in terms of its inscription of gender and sexuality. First, it is important to note that the 1970s were, in fact, a period when Hindi cinema took a decidedly masculinist turn; the avenging-women films do not appear until the following decade. The fact that the protagonist is a strong, aggressive, female subject pitted against the strength and ingenuity of *six* men is itself somewhat exceptional. Second, as mentioned above, Reena Roy as the *nagin* is unabashed in her sexuality—unlike the simpering wives and girlfriends who also populate the film, she embodies a kind of feral sexuality that remains remarkable in its directness. Furthermore, the *nagin* has sex with three of the five male adversaries before killing them, transgressing, at least momentarily, Hindi cinema's proscription against promiscuity. Of course, the film is able to stage these unconventional—and highly eroticized—encounters because the female protagonist is not *really* a woman. The *nagin* is, after all, a snake, and thus her "animal instincts" remain dominant and can be allowed elaboration.

However, and this is where *Nagin* is extremely interesting as a text, in many instances she masquerades as the "good" women in order to accomplish her task. She first seduces and then kills Rajesh (Vinod Mehra) while masquerading as his fiancée, Rita (Yogeeta Bali). Similarly, when she administers the kiss of death on Raj (Feroz Khan), she appears to him as his girlfriend, Rajkumari (Mumtaz). Certain instabilities are allowed to gather around female identities and notions of acceptable gendered behavior: thus, women who "appear to be" disarmingly domestic hide behind their unthreatening exteriors venomous possibilities—*Nagin* allows such deliciously transgressive potentialities to emerge and develop.[39] Because the *nagin* can transmogrify into anyone at will, the film stages a vertiginous series of doublings and slippages between the domestic "good" women and the rampaging, monstrous reptile. The *nagin* also discards her "snake attire" early on, and in subsequent sequences appears in a range of highly stylish 1970s outfits, reinforcing the playful dichotomy between essence and appearance.

As feminist critics across disciplines have argued, masquerade allows for at least a temporary suspension of otherwise stringently policed gendered

FIGURE 3.4. *Sunita and the human* nagin *fight in* Nagin.

roles and behavior. The pleasures of stardom, doubling, and spectatorial knowledge come together marvelously in these subterfuge sequences of *Nagin*, because *we* know who the seductress is, even as the hapless heroes remain blissfully unaware of their impending demise. In a particularly risky sequence, the film stages a hand-to-hand combat between two of its most popular female stars: Sunita (Rekha) and the *nagin* come to blows in an extended action sequence with high angle shots, weapons, and sound effects, of the kind strictly reserved for male leads in Hindi cinema. *Nagin* is too much a product of commercial imperative to be a feminist text, and I am not trying to suggest otherwise. However, the fact that the spectator, in fact, identifies with the *nagin* and her quest for justice, and not the imperiled humans, in spite of wives, mothers, children, and lovers featuring prominently as characters, makes it extraordinary. In other words, Hindi cinema's melodramatic imperatives are somewhat unusually deployed in much of the film.

Again, the subversion of gender norms is constitutively enabled by the fact that the woman is not in fact human and her voracious appetites—for sex and violence—are attributable to her "natural" animal instincts. Nonetheless, I would argue, we glimpse something unusual here. In the snake film, the aggression and rampaging sexuality of the female snake would seem to imply different ideological stakes than those traditionally associated with the commercial form, a reading not borne out by the conclusion of *Nagin* when the female snake dies, impaled on iron spikes, and regretting her thirst for revenge.[40] However, it is also critical to note that *Nagin* appeared in a time of flux—before the neo-conservative ethos of the 1980s and 1990s had found robust foothold in Bombay cinema. Subsequent snake films would feature female protagonists of a very different ilk.

FROM SEXY SERPENT TO DEMURE DAUGHTER-IN-LAW: THE TRANSFORMATION OF THE SNAKE FILM

The commercial cinema's ideological propensities become more obvious in the later incarnation of snake films—baroque family melodramas that feature reptilian interlopers. Here, the snake functions as an agent of threat from without and (temporarily) jeopardizes the perpetuation of the Hindu feudal family. The ur-text in this iteration of the cycle is *Nagina*, the actress Sridevi's colossal hit from 1986. What is remarkable about *Nagina*—and other texts of the kind—is not so much the power of the female snake but the absolute, inviolable sacrality of the Hindu marriage and the patriarchal feudal family.

Nagina's plot revolves around Rajiv (Rishi Kapoor), the sole heir to feudal property who falls in love with Rajni (Sridevi), a mysterious woman with a shadowy past. Rajiv's mother (Sushma Seth, who remains unnamed as the maternal figure and the chatelaine of the mammoth mansion) is initially resistant to accept the match but relents after she meets the eminently suitable Rajni. The couple's integration into the feudal family remains peaceful, until the evil tantric, Bhairavnath, arrives to disclose the secret of Rajni's origins—she is a *nagin* who has returned to seek vengeance for her serpent lover's death. The complicated backstory involves an incident in Rajiv's childhood when he had been bitten by the *nag* who was subsequently forced by Bhairavnath to retract the poison and thus died; in effect Bhairavnath had placed the soul of the snake into child Rajiv's dead body; in other words, the *nag* dies in Rajiv's place. After discovering Rajni's true identity and fearing for her son's life, Rajiv's mother seeks Bhairavnath's aid. However, the climax reveals that, in fact, Bhairavnath is the villain, and he wants the *nagmani*; Rajni was acting to protect her husband and family's interests all along. The mother is killed during the fight between Bhairavnath and the couple, and she dies regretting her mistrust of Rajni. Bhairavnath dies, too, but not before ridding Rajni of the "curse" of her serpentine avatar.

Nagina, the second-most-successful film of the year 1986, is a very different film from *Nagin*, made just a decade earlier. Rajiv's initial encounters with Rajni in the ruins of the abandoned mansion retain the uncanny energies of the Gothic film; much like the ghostly beloveds who haunted the heroes in that earlier formation, Rajiv, too, is completely besotted by Rajni's mysterious ways and her plaintive song, "Bhuli Bisri Ek Kahani" ("I Recall a Forgotten Story").[41] However, the ghostly intensity of the romance is decisively defanged by the monumental institution of the Hindu marriage. Once married to the scion of the feudal family, Rajni values her

FIGURE 3.5. Nagina *poster of Rajni with her mother-in-law. Used by permission of the National Film Archive of India.*

sasural (conjugal home), *suhaag* (marriage), and *khandaan* (feudal clan) above all else, and she certainly displays no interest whatsoever in the ontological potentialities inherent in her supernatural powers. Needless to say, the expressive/performative/transgressive possibilities that inhere to the idea of conjugality between a human and a reptile are glossed over with considerable rhetorical dexterity.[42] Rejecting her reptilian roots and allegiances—in a telling sequence following her marriage, she even cremates the long-preserved corpse of the *nag*, her former mate—Rajni literally and figuratively morphs from serpentine seductress into the good Hindu wife. The monstrous, indeed feral, feminine is thus rendered charmingly domestic. Also tellingly, Rajiv's role comes to be relatively marginal after the wedding, as *saas* (mother-in-law) and *bahu* (daughter-in-law) negotiate their differences, much like familiar characters in popular television serials.[43] Again, it is important to remain cognizant of the eclectic source materials the snake film draws from—cinematic and televised mythologicals, devotionals, and fantasy film, as well as the feudal family romance.

Although *Nagina* incorporates many of the prototypical pleasures of the formation—most famously, the protracted snake-dance sequence when Rajni battles a whole host of villainous snake charmers to the tune of "Main Teri Dushman, Dushman Tu Mera" ("You Are My Enemy and I Am Yours"), it is not a film *about* the monstrous feminine. Likewise, the affective pleasures of song-and-dance sequences cannot be fully accounted for via ideological analysis alone. It must be acknowledged that Sridevi—palms cupped as the cobra's hood, blue eyes blazing—is a formidable figure of serpentine rage as she performs Hindi cinema's most iconic snake dance. However, even in this song sequence, when we see the serpent aggressively confronting masculine power/knowledge represented by the tantric, it is her place as wife/daughter-in-law that she energetically defends; predictably, the sequence ends with Rajiv slapping Rajni for her indiscreet "performance." The film remains solidly invested in the perpetuation of the feudal—wealth, family, sexual arrangements, and so on—and Rajiv's (intermittent) embodiment of a certain "progressive" worldview does little to alleviate this foundational commitment.[44]

Let us consider, for example, the twin engines of the *masala* film: sex and violence. Unlike the fetishized garments of the snake protagonist in *Nagin*, Rajni is always clad in traditional clothes—*sindoor*, *mangalsutra*, and *sari* firmly proclaiming her status as the idealized Hindu wife.[45] These signifiers of chaste femininity do not mean that Sridevi as the female star is not sexualized, of course, but it is important to note that we are invited to gaze upon a distinct constellation of visual signs here.[46] In *Nagina*, we never actually see Rajni transforming into a snake; what the film offers us by way of miraculous shape-shifting is a series of superimpositions. The image of the snake is briefly superimposed on medium close-ups of Rajni's face, before the next shot shows us the reptile. In other words, the "action" sequences are actually performed by the reptiles and not Rajni in her human form. A particularly remarkable fight ensues between her and a male snake that Bhairavnath sends to kill Rajiv when he lies incapacitated in the hospital: in this instance, too, all we are offered in Sridevi's person are contact-lens-aided blue eyes before the superimposed snake takes over the proceedings and engages its opponent in an energetic battle. Similarly, in the climactic fight sequence when Bhairavnath demands the *nagmani* from her and then attacks after being refused, Rajiv has to come to Rajni's rescue. She is very much a passive spectator as the men fight it out, more in keeping with Hindi cinema's designation of appropriately gendered behavior. Unsurprisingly, both the evil tantric and the meddling mother-in-law die at the closure of *Nagina*, and with Rajni's reptilian soul purged—a blessing from the remorseful Bhairavnath—the heterosexual couple and the sacrality of the Hindu marriage come to be satisfyingly restored. With Rajni now shorn of her supernatural powers, the feudal bloodline can continue unsullied.

No doubt, the political moment of the mid-1980s also has something to do with the spaces that Rajni must occupy and defend. Although equations between political imaginaries and mass-cultural forms like cinema are extremely complex, *Nagina* certainly registers a shift in the mythography and cosmology advocated by the snake film. *Nagina* remains unmistakably a *Hindu* film, by which I mean to designate more than the religious identities of primary characters. The mise-en-scène of *Nagina* is cluttered with specifically Hindu iconography: there are not one, but *two* temples dedicated to the family's *kuldevata* (patron deity), Shiva; Rajni's worthiness as a daughter-in-law is buttressed by her deep faith; and when Bhairavnath is finally vanquished, Shiva's trident plays a prominent part. As mentioned above, the snake film draws on the energies of the mythological in important ways; its reliance on the miraculous and the supernatural more or less necessitates, to some degree, an affirmation of the divine. However, I would argue that over the course of the 1980s and into the 1990s, "religion" in the snake film transforms into a more definite form of religiosity; the imprecise inscription of random "folk" signifiers gives way to a theological/philosophical universe that is considerably more definitive and thus less inclusive.

The snake film is very much an artifact of the past, a formation solidly tethered to Hindi cinema's pre-Bollywood incarnation from the 1970s and 1980s. The "traditions" espoused by the cycle are enthusiastically invented and recycled by Hindi film; they find their way into regional cinemas as well.[47] As a syntactical form that is constitutively dependent on a certain kind of technological finesse—in terms of plausibly rendering miracles on screen—the snake film astonishes us with the degree of credulity it demands from its spectators. Perhaps because it so transparently acknowledges the undertow of enchantment, it has to be consigned to the past in a certain sense. Its attractions—song and dance, myth-folklore, sex, violence, and melodrama—are ingredients of the kind of cinema that would make contemporary Bollywood shudder in embarrassment, unless presented as a highly self-conscious camp aesthetic. In keeping with its retrograde energies, it addressed a spectator who has also been largely abandoned by contemporary cinema. In the next section, I interrogate the "untimeliness" of the snake film in the current historical moment.

SNAKE VENGEANCE AND THE GLOBAL FILMSCAPE: THE CURIOUS STORY OF *HISSS*

The most recent iteration of the snake film, *Hisss* (2010), was made by Hollywood director Jennifer Lynch and much publicized as a transnational collaboration between Bollywood and Hollywood talent. Let us

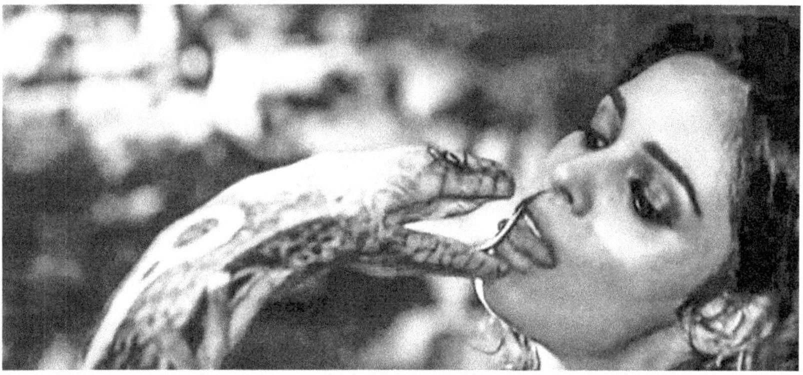

FIGURE 3.6. *Mallika Sherawat's snake woman kisses male snake in* Hisss.

note that it is precisely this type of international visibility that Bollywood endlessly aspires to, and concomitantly, the project received significant attention in print and electronic media. *Hisss* takes the basic template and even the syntax of the snake film and transforms it into something virtually unrecognizable. In its most important reconstructive gesture, it does away almost entirely with music and dancing, which, as I describe above, are constitutive attractions of the cycle. The narrative arc, however, includes some standard elements: George States (Jeff Doucette), a cancer-ridden American man, believes in the restorative powers of the *nagmani*. He comes to India and imprisons the male snake in a tank. The female snake—played by Bollywood star Mallika Sherawat—is forced to venture out into civilization in her human form. She then kills everyone who stands in the way of her being united with her lover. Alongside basic narrative features, *Hisss* very much relies on the floridly Orientalist erotica/exotica associated with tourism films on India; the film includes an array of gratuitous images of temples, chanting priests, lush forests, and above all, endless shots of a slithering, semi-nude Sherawat.

Hisss is a curious film because it remained mired in controversy, and in its attempt to transnationalize an arguably local formation, it alienated global and local audiences alike. Control over the film was allegedly wrested away from Lynch at postproduction, and she completely disowned the finished product once it was released.[48] Although the director washed her hands of the film, star Sherawat aggressively promoted *Hisss* in India and Cannes, often appearing draped in small and large snakes.

At these promotional events, Sherawat insisted that the film's unique selling point is its digital technology and the spectacle of a woman transforming into a snake and back in front of our eyes—again, the spectator being privileged to witness the moment of miraculous transformation. Sherawat makes an important point in this regard, because the older snake film has often been criticized for its reliance on crude special effects; its magic was, without a doubt, shoddily performed. In the age of digital manipulation and computer-generated imagery (CGI), a form like the snake film *could* get a much-needed digital makeover on the global stage. The planetary popularity of fantasy franchises such as *The Lord of the Rings*, *Twilight*, and *Harry Potter* is testament to the fact that audiences worldwide have embraced the cinematic supernatural in an unprecedented way in recent years. Thus, one can see the economic logic behind the resurrection of an old and moribund generic form that has been banished to B and C circuits in recent years. But *Hisss* remained a colossal flop, and moreover, some viewers found the film so deeply unsettling that it merits scrutiny; something was clearly lost in translation.

Hisss has more in common with *Anaconda* (Luis Llosa, 1997) than *Nagina*, and therein, I would argue, lies the problem. The snake film relies on a different kind of magic than the plenitude promised and delivered by virtuoso performances of digital technology. In its robust ties to older genres, like the mythological and the fantasy film, the snake film is a curiously rooted beast—it is difficult to disentangle it from its industrial and social context and give it unanchored transnational currency. This is not to make an essentialist argument about local genres, but to try to understand how a film such as *Hisss* allows us a point of entry into the discourses that surround the concept of "transnational cinemas." Is there something about the snake film that resists easy co-optation into the global market of images? Recall that filmic folklore gathers momentum from repetition and intertextual resonance—perhaps this is why it is somewhat challenging to uncouple the snake film from the fabric of texts to which it has historically been tethered. Reviewers speculated that Indian audiences rejected the film because it had too much blood and nudity for Bollywood, and one of them called it "abominable and loathsome";[49] indeed *Hisss* is a remarkably visceral, corporeal film that includes all sorts of bodily fluids and several shots of Sherawat mating with a giant snake in quasi-pornographic detail—not for the squeamish or faint of heart. Indeed, Julia Kristeva, Barbara Creed, and Linda Williams's conceptualization of bodily abjection, body horror, and pornographic elaboration are literalized in this film, as it unleashes a "frenzy of the visible" on unsuspecting audiences. Isabel Cristina Pinedo points out that "[p]orn and horror are obsessed with the transgression of bodily boundaries. Both are concerned with the devouring orifice, but whereas pornography is concerned with the phallic penetration and secretions of sexually coded orifices like the mouth (gaping in ecstasy or pain), vagina, and anus, horror is more concerned with the creation of openings where there were none before."[50] For the snake film, traditionally, fluidity, bodily transgressions, indeterminacy, and metamorphosis are occasioned by the serpent's supernatural powers, which remain ineffable and therefore enchanting; *Hisss*, however, insists on the "gross palpability of the flesh,"[51] especially—but not exclusively—in regard to its female protagonist, and in the process disables the magical and the metaphysical altogether.

I would argue that the reason for the film's failure is the generic short-circuit between creature-features like *Anaconda* and snake films like *Nagin*. There is an incommensurability of filmic discourse here, a misrecognition, if you will, between two different kinds of syntax: if the snake film used cinema's expressive possibilities to *gesture* toward a range of affect and abomination—the trope of bestiality, for example, which is invoked even in a conservative film such as *Nagina*—*Hisss* misses the point entirely and renders everything in excruciating, literal detail. Blood, vomit, brains, semen, bodily wastes, and so forth are all presented via a crude naturalism that becomes absurd within the generic form *Hisss* tries to inhabit. The film embodies a curious paradox: in trying to render the supernatural and the miraculous so basic to the snake film in a more sophisticated manner, it demystifies—indeed disqualifies—magic and fantasy altogether. In sprucing up the Hindi snake film, its hip, global upmarket avatar fails because, far from being the powerful, pagan goddess, the *nagin* here is reduced to a defanged, abject sex object.[52]

The snake film is an extraordinary formation in Indian cinema. Its impressively hybrid contours enclose the commercial form's disregard for realist narration, its penchant for excess and its attempts to address a community of the credulous who were presumably less familiar with better special effects. At a time when the commercial cinema surrendered completely to masculine interests—both in terms of content and spectatorial engagement—the snake film featured imprudent, supernatural, semi-divine female creatures as protagonists. As a cycle that flourished in the troubled decades of the 1970s and 1980s, it remained remarkably sensitive to larger socio-political transformations of the era, some of which it registered formally and in narrative terms. Unsurprisingly, in Bombay cinema's triumphant march to global visibility, the snake film—marginal even in its heyday—has been relegated to almost complete obscurity. This invisibility is echoed by scholarly discourses that have thus far failed to engage with the form altogether. However, the snake film is enjoying a somewhat unexpected rebirth: as excellent instantiations of camp aesthetics, many of these texts have been exhumed by cult-movie fans on the Internet, a phenomenon to which I turn as a coda.

REPTILES REBOOT: CAMP AND THE AFTERLIFE OF THE SNAKE FILM

Despite the failure of *Hisss*, and what that narrative tells us about the anachronistic tenor of the snake film, in recent years it is enjoying an astonishing—indeed quasi-magical—afterlife on the Internet. That the Internet has revolutionized how films are made, distributed, and received needs no elaboration in the current dispensation. Furthermore, the web has come to be an enabler for many other things vis-à-vis film, not least of which is a new kind of cinephilia. A search for Bollywood brings up thousands of blogs, and not all of these are geared toward new releases or contemporary stars, although those form the bulk of online data. A certain kind of enthusiasm for the many pasts of Hindi film is also visible online, and it is in this domain that the snake film is enjoying a rebirth of sorts.

Scholars of Indian cinema often find themselves dismayed when asked about the inherent "campiness" of the popular form; they contend that to use the term "camp" willy-nilly to account for all of the formation's particularities does a deep disservice to its complex histories, aesthetics, and industrial trajectories. However, occasionally, the idea of camp does provide a valuable theoretical template for how popular Indian film is being received globally in the era of new media and media convergence. The snake film's online avatar is one such instance when camp is the dominant modality through which these films are being watched, written about, and discussed.

In her seminal essay on camp, Susan Sontag defined it as "the exaggerated, the fantastic, the passionate, and the naïve." This definition of what constitutes "pure camp" snugly fits the snake film, with its penchant for the overblown and the outlandish, and in its sincere insistence on creating a synthetic universe of pure illusion, myth, pleasure, and fantasy; indeed, from this perspective, the snake film is a perfect camp artifact—all of Hindi cinema's most flamboyantly excessive tendencies are manifest within its generic contours. The *masala* film in general has found a passionate fan-following online, and the snake film's new visibility must be understood within this larger celebration of all things *filmi*.

Although the cycle encloses within itself much that can be perceived as campy, what makes the online ferment around it extraordinary is the new audiences it has garnered in the era of media convergence. If the formation addressed a largely credulous, non-metropolitan, but *specifically* South Asian spectator in the 1970s and 1980s, it now enjoys a far more diverse global audience—the unintended spectatorship that the explosion of digital media has made possible. Aided by Bombay cinema's planetary visibility, and coupled with the wide availability of the films themselves online and on DVD, the snake film has come to be a staple on blogs created by non-native viewers and fans of Indian cinema.[53] This is not to surrender to any kind of essentialist notions of "native spectatorship" or resurrect the weary bugbear of "cultural appropriation," but to suggest that this new type of engagement is separated from the original production-reception context in both spatial and temporal terms. Let us recall that it is precisely this kind of distance and detachment that Sontag characterizes as a key aspect of the humor that accompanies the camp sensibility. Concomitantly, the snake film is subjected to gentle derision as well as greeted with considerable bemusement, and amusement, for its "strangeness" in blogs such as these. This, for example, is how *Nagin*'s first vengeful murder is described in the *MemsaabStory* review:

> There is a bunch of stuff about him fixing his killers in his eyes and sending the images to Reena, and he expires tragically. It doesn't take Reena long to dispose of Kiran (it seems to me that the friends get knocked off in order of their star status). She wakes him that same night and tells him that she is a simple snake charmer who was held captive by the snake, and that she's grateful to him for saving her. Being the flirt (at best) that he is, he takes advantage, leading her by the hand into his room and locking the door. He realizes when he sees their reflection in the mirror that—oops!—he's not holding a snake charmer's hand, but it is too late.[54]

Sometimes the humorous tone of the reviews is a byproduct of the fact that the DVDs available for purchase have either lamentably poor subtitles or none at all, and the reviewers have no familiarity with the Hindi language. This is arguably an entirely different terrain of reception than the ones these films circulated within in the 1970s and 1980s. The following, for example, is the first paragraph of Beth Watkins's review of *Sheshnaag*, which she allegedly watched entirely without subtitles:

> I am pretty certain I missed at least a third of what was going on in an average scene in *Sheshnaag*. Based on what I could understand, however, I'm not sure that detracted from my enjoyment of this eyes-a-bulgin' scenery-chompin' tale of two good snake-people, one very, *very* evil villain, and the people who get mixed up in their conflict. Pesky details like *why* the people are involved in the good/

evil conflict will be glossed over, partly because I do not have any concept of some of them and partly because they probably don't matter much.[55]

The snake film, then, finds itself adrift on the vast uncharted frontier of the Internet, where it is encountered as a different meaning-making system than the discourses it was embedded within in Hindi cinema's pre-Bollywood days.[56] Ironically, of course, it is Bollywood's global popularity that has brought these other, older formations to light. Barring a few exceptions, the robust mythic scaffolding that undergirded the cycle in its local context has fallen away in this new online habitat; it stands somewhat disenchanted here. What fans and bloggers seem to find pleasurable are precisely those components of the popular form for which the sloughed-off pasts of Hindi cinema have come to be notorious: excessive and florid melodrama, unbridled and unembarrassed kitsch, unlikely/fantastical scenarios, and tacky special effects—the "so-bad-it's-good" mantra of camp.[57] In this newfound appeal to an unlikely and unintended viewership, the snake film remains a bedfellow of the low-budget horror film, which I have previously explored. Whereas the Ramsays successfully transitioned into cable television, horror cinema took on new guises following economic liberalization. I turn to this new post-liberalization moment in the next chapter.

CHAPTER FOUR

Present Imperfect

BOLLYWOOD AND THE GHOSTS OF NEOLIBERALISM

They have copied the successful Ramsay formula and upgraded it with good music, star cast and promotions. Vikram Bhatt's Raaz *was a super-duper hit, but if you see it carefully, it has all the masala of a Ramsay film.*

—"SHYAM RAMSAY: PEOPLE SAY THE GHOSTS IN MY FILMS WERE NOT SCARY," *REDIFF*

SOME OF THE FOUNDATIONAL THEMES OF THIS BOOK focus on the contortions of Indian modernity and the modes through which genres of the supernatural register, and indeed, refract these complexities in form and narrative. That modernity in South Asia—and the non-West more generally—confounds, complicates, and unsettles standard definitions of the term and has been at the core of my engagement with Hindi film. The Ramsay horror film, as I suggest in Chapter 2, provides a hospitable generic ecosystem where post-Emergency discourses found elaboration in several startling ways. The snake-film cycle that I explored in the last chapter is fundamentally dependent on a certain deployment of cinematic technologies but remains intractably enchanted as a formation. Here, I investigate another pivotal moment of this emergent narrative—the reformulation of the horror film in the wake of economic liberalization in the early 1990s.

In the overwrought climax of Vikram Bhatt's 2008 horror film *1920*, the struggle between good and evil is—quite literally—waged over the body of the heroine, Lisa (Adah Sharma). Lisa, the Anglo-Indian wife of the Hindu protagonist, Arjun Singh Rathod (Rajneesh Duggal), is possessed by a wrathful evil spirit that haunts the mansion that Arjun has been commissioned to restore and transform into a luxury hotel. Because Lisa is Roman

FIGURE 4.1. *Exorcism in* 1920.

Catholic and deeply faithful, the first attempt to exorcize the spirit is made by Father Thomas (Raj Zutshi), in a series of scenes that are clearly reminiscent of William Friedkin's classic, *The Exorcist* (1973). The spirit, however, proves to be too wily for the priest, who is dispensed with fairly quickly. What follows is a protracted sequence of "Hindu exorcism" that Arjun must perform in order to save his beloved's life. Even after being battered and buffeted by the superhumanly strong, monstrous Lisa, Arjun channels the remnants of his strength to invoke his favorite deity, Hanuman. Previously in the narrative, Arjun had rejected his Hinduism because it acted as an impediment to his union with Lisa; at the hour of crisis, however, it is not simply the god or a vague invocation of Hinduism, but scripture—the sacred words of the *Hanuman Chalisa*—that successfully rids Lisa of the spirit that had pushed her to the brink of destruction.

Several aspects of this climax sequence are noteworthy. First and most visibly, in spite of Lisa's own faith, Father Thomas remains a well-meaning but ineffectual agent of the divine; Christianity is rendered obsolete through his bumbling attempts to exorcize the evil spirit, which is able to manipulate his weakness with ease. Second, Arjun's chanting of Sanskrit scripture from memory establishes the superiority of not only Hinduism, but a certain form of strident religiosity.[1] Finally, and for my purposes, most saliently, the visual presentation of this momentous event:

Arjun physically embraces Lisa to literally pour the sacred incantation into her ear, even as she (or, more accurately, the spirit possessing her) shrieks, struggles, attacks, and attempts to escape his implacable grip. The sequence remains memorable precisely because it combines the invocation of the divine with a great deal of physical violence and a thundering sound track. The spectator is supposed to read this moment as a devoted husband's desperate, last-ditch attempt to save his wife's soul, but I would argue that the sequence appears to us as precisely what it is: an assault. The *Hanuman Chalisa* must physically penetrate Lisa's unruly, possessed, female body in order for it to be purged of evil, and perhaps of her own "inferior" religious beliefs as well. All of this also transpires within the immense splendor of an English manor house, invoking, as it were, a specific kind of history.

Unsurprisingly, scholars have read this sequence as indicative of Bollywood's more general capitulation to Hindutva, a process that began well before the millennial turn.[2] And certainly, much has changed for the Hindi horror film since the Ramsay horror monster had to be vanquished with Gitas, Korans, Bibles, and assorted religious talismans ranging from the trident to the crucifix. However, to read this moment—or the ones that came before—as simply a transparent expression of an easily identifiable ideology may be something of an oversimplification. Although scholars and critics have in recent years turned to the "Bollywoodization" of horror to demonstrate the transformations that have attended the genre since the 1990s, my aim here is to explore the reverse of this proposition: Is there anything that remains unchanged in Hindi horror cinema *despite* its upward mobility and recent gentrification?

Throughout this book, I have traced certain tropes—such as the singing female ghost/specter, or motifs of feudalism or non-capitalist ideologies—that consistently haunt the genres of the supernatural in popular cinema. In this sense, the supernatural most compellingly inscribes the scandalous deviances of Indian modernity. Has the horror film finally broken completely free of those legacies in recent years? Does anything—formal or philosophical—from the older Hindi commercial film continue to haunt these contemporary texts? Or, as Shyam Ramsay audaciously contends in the epigraph above, has Bollywood simply "upgraded" old tropes to secure new audiences in the wake of liberalization? In the innovation/accommodation dyad—the breaks and continuities in the figuration of the supernatural that I have been mapping throughout this book—the decade of the 1990s constellates as an important juncture. And, as before, the dyad tells us something about the historically contingent dovetailing of cinema and modernity in India.

Before addressing these questions, however, a few key events that impacted public cultures in India must be underscored. Processes of economic liberalization had been underway for several years before India formally opened its economy to the global market under intense pressure from entities such as the World Bank and the International Monetary Fund in 1991. And alongside a growing and increasingly more assertive middle class and the explosion of commodities that came to define globalization in India, the Hindi commercial film mutated into what we understand as Bollywood proper.

THE LIBERALIZING MOMENT

Scholars across the humanities as well as the social sciences have explored the watershed moment of the early 1990s from an array of perspectives. Here, I will briefly summarize those aspects of the transition that are especially pertinent to the transformation of the Hindi horror film. Beyond purely economic reforms such as the progressive devaluation of a teetering rupee and the state's abandonment of protectionist policies that enabled the arrival of global competition, the discursive impact of this moment is of considerable significance. Although it is tempting to read this moment as an absolute break in the cultural sphere, here, too, certain complications persist; nevertheless, this moment *registered* as a profoundly transformative one both socially and culturally. A shift in the economic structure did not *produce* cultural shifts; indeed, they were mutually constitutive within the same discursive domain that had been congealing over time. The idea of the middle class, so central to any discussion of capitalism, allows us to explore this imbrication of economy and culture in particularly productive ways. For my purposes, the emergent middle class remains especially important also because it would become the protagonist and addressee of a specific kind of cinema.

Most scholars contend that the "expanding middle class"—as much the target of an ascendant consumerist ethos as the commodities themselves—came into its own, in a manner of speaking, in this juncture;[3] I refer to an increased visibility in the *literal* sense here:

> The new Indian middle class represents a specific social category that has emerged in the context of economic policies of liberalization that were initiated in India in the 1990s. This social group refers to a culturally constructed category. The boundaries of this middle class are defined by practices of consumption associated with newly available consumer goods in liberalising India. Advertising and

> media images have contributed to the creation of this image of the liberalising middle class as a social group that has transcended the limits of state protection and austerity associated with Nehruvian and Gandhian visions of the Indian nation. The new middle class is a social group that embodies a cultural standard associated with the globalising Indian nation. The consumption of commodities such as cell-phones, colour televisions, washing machines and cars forms some of the status markers that distinguish this social group.[4]

This putative middle class had to be conjured up in a commodity world; its consumer "image" had to be "unshackled" from the thrift that characterized the Nehruvian mode, and a new formation of promise and aspiration had to be carefully imagined at this crucial moment. In a similar vein, William Mazzarella has shown that this new middle class did not consolidate overnight; it had been gestating within the mass consumerism that began in the 1980s or even earlier.[5] The shift from a developmentalist to a consumer dispensation was neither abrupt nor without contradictions that had to be actively managed and negotiated.[6] Like Leela Fernandes, Mazzarella contends that, aided by the rapid spread of commercial television in the 1980s, it was the advertising industry that helped consolidate this vision of a middle class straining against the stagnation and torpor that the planned economy allegedly fostered. However, in envisaging this "new notion of collectivity" and communicating with it as such, older discourses could not be jettisoned altogether. In generating what Mazzarella calls the "commodity image," advertisers had to invent a new kind of address that could tether the old citizen to the new consumer; the bugbear of pleasure/consumption had to be creatively reconciled with a new notion of public service.[7] In these explorations of that arguably pivotal moment of Indian history, the narrative that emerges combines an epochal break with persisting continuities: a new universe of commodities that had been forged over a decade or longer; an inhabitant and an addressee of this domain—the middle-class citizen-consumer—who had concomitantly congealed over time in the same discursive crucible; and a medium—television—that had been around for a while but was now poised for a dramatic makeover.

The advent of first commercial and then satellite television in conjunction with policies of economic liberalization was yet another node in the crystallization of the consumer discourse in this moment. Perhaps nothing was more emblematic of the inertia and apathy of the planned economy—and the planning ethos, more generally—than the state-controlled television: Doordarshan; partially, this characterization was an effect of its inextricability with statist imperatives and programs, until commercial programming began in the mid-1980s. Arvind Rajagopal describes the inefficacious functioning of state-run television:

> [I]t might be said that Doordarshan offered a mirror to the state's official aspect, presenting it as it wished to be seen. In practice, this meant that the political party and the leaders in power at any given time were presented making speeches, cutting ribbons, presiding over parades, and deliberating at meetings. The purely self-referential character of broadcasting was confirmed by the negligence shown to the issue of viewership.[8]

It was not simply its official aspect, but the obdurately *officious* and ceremonial nature of the programming that ensured that viewership remained limited.[9] By the time satellite television exploded on the scene, bringing a dizzying range of television channels to Indian living rooms, Doordarshan had already been rhetorically consigned to a certain kind of past; dubbed as irrelevant, sclerotic, and immeasurably dull, state-controlled television quickly became symbolic of regulations and control as such, a lamentably outmoded relic of the planning structure and the image that India was keen to shed. Conservatives may have blustered at the "invasion" and corrosion of cultural values implied by Music Television (MTV) and such imported shows as *Baywatch*, but the urban Indian youth and the middle class finally found themselves addressed by a medium that was in keeping with the euphoric, aspirational—indeed, transformative—tenor of this historical juncture. But television had also played a critical role in the consolidation of yet another discursive domain: the rise of Hindu nationalism.

Although Hindu nationalism of several persuasions had been part and parcel of the political tapestry since well before national independence, the most recent—and robust—version of it gathered momentum in the 1980s, in tandem with the other shifts outlined above. Unsurprisingly, the climactic Babri Masjid incident—when militant Hindu devotees demolished a medieval mosque in Ayodhya, triggering bloody riots across the nation—coincided almost serendipitously with this phase of economic reform; the mobilization of a new kind of *Hindu* consumer was successfully underway. Hindutva (Hindu-ness, in this context denoting a specific political configuration) would come to be a critical piece of the jigsaw that constituted the moment of the early to late 1990s.

Indeed, as such scholars as Arvind Rajagopal and Purnima Mankekar have argued,[10] the concatenation between the energies of economic reform and Hindutva were unmistakable in envisaging a new kind of nation altogether, such that "[e]ach tells the story of the other, ideology that of the economy, and the economy that of ideology."[11] Interestingly, the marriage between Hindutva and economic reform was being consummated, as it were, in an era when the ruling Congress Party's fortunes were in decline; in this context, it hardly mattered that the first steps toward liberalization had been undertaken by Rajiv Gandhi in the 1980s:

> Two streams of discourse, on economic liberalization and "Hinduness," came to prominence in close succession in the mid-1980s, each reinforcing the resurgent rhetoric of the other, while also periodically clashing in their laissez-faire and communitarian resonances. With the prying loose of voters from the Congress Party's decades-old hegemony on the one hand, and the efforts of businesses to secure dominance with market liberalization still nascent on the other, voters and consumers both became subject to intense recruitment. Communal mobilization occurred at the nexus between these strategies which were united in their technologies of communication and in their credo of opening out to the world.[12]

It was the Bharatiya Janata Party (BJP) and its ragtag group of militant Hindu outfits, collectively called the Sangh Parivar, that were able to effectively mobilize the Hindu consumer and reconfigure the public sphere in a certain sense. It is important to understand the mutually constitutive nature of economic reform and Hindutva, because they *could* seem to share a dialectical relation, a mutually antagonistic relationship in a somewhat reductive schema.[13] The religiosity that Hindutva espoused—and continues to disseminate—is a specific series of ideas that cannot be pried loose from late capitalism in India. In turn, a certain moment in the trajectory of capitalism cannot be accessed critically without taking into account the scaffolding that Hindutva provided. Bombay cinema becomes what we now know as Bollywood within this socio-cultural context of shifts and uncertainties, and, indeed, "Bollywoodization" is a constitutive thread in the tapestry of this moment. A new kind of supernatural horror would emerge only at the interface of all of these entangled developments.

FROM HINDI CINEMA TO BOLLYWOOD

Bollywood today is much more than the Hindi film industry.[14] Connected to myriad other commercial and media domains of music, television, fashion, art, architecture, tourism, and even cuisine, it enfolds within its capacious contours an altogether different logic of cultural production than that of Bombay cinema in pre-liberalization days. As Ashish Rajadhyaksha has noted,

> Bollywood is *not* the Indian film industry, or at least not the film industry alone. Bollywood admittedly occupies a space analogous to the film industry, but might best be seen as a more diffuse cultural conglomeration involving a range of distribution and consumption activities from websites to music cassettes, from cable to radio. If so, the film industry itself—determined here solely in terms of its box office turnover and sales of print and music rights, all that actually comes back to the producer—can by definition constitute only a part, and perhaps even an *alarmingly small* part, of the overall culture industry that is currently being created and marketed.[15]

But Bombay cinema's transmogrification into the hydra-headed, globally ubiquitous "Bollywood" did not happen overnight. As the idea of India underwent critical changes and realignments in the early 1990s, the film industry in Bombay was experiencing its own mutative phase. Although it would not be recognized as an industry proper until 1998, economic liberalization had set in motion a ripple effect that enabled Hindi commercial cinema to accrue a symbolic status that was previously denied to it by the largely dismissive developmentalist state; briefly put, the industry has shared a notoriously fraught relationship with the postcolonial state over issues ranging from taxation to censorship since independence.[16] This relationship would itself undergo certain key changes following economic liberalization, as the state's overall attitude toward the industry thawed considerably. Tejaswini Ganti notes that alongside the "invasion" implied by satellite television, and with the increased presence of Hollywood films in this period, "Hindi films took on the value of cultural authenticity and Indian-ness."[17] Although the neo-nationalism of the Hindi film meant something specific for domestic audiences within a rapidly changing mediascape, its Bollywoodization hinged on garnering a new kind of spectator—the diasporic citizen.[18] As virtually every study of Bollywood cinema notes, it was in this phase of reform that the overseas Indian became a part of what Aswin Punathambekar has called the "global Indian family." Films such as *Diwale Dulhania Le Jayenge* (*The Brave-Hearted Will Take the Bride*, 1995) and *Kabhi Khushi Kabhi Gham* (*Sometimes Joy, Sometimes Sorrow*, 2001) did not simply include characters who are situated overseas but are texts that specifically addressed the non-resident Indian (NRI) market: "[I]n this new imagination of a global Indian family, belonging is defined in terms of one's willingness and cultural competence to participate in

India's integration into a global economy and the consumerist vision of the nation that undergirds this transition."[19] If the Hindi film melodrama becomes increasingly more conservative in what constituted "Indian culture" at this time—the films mentioned above are obsessed, indeed besotted, with notions of nation-ness and cultural citizenship—the horror film embarks on a somewhat different trajectory and veers closer to its Hollywood counterpart in an unprecedented manner. But this generic transformation was enabled by yet another development in the arena of exhibition: the development of the urban multiplex theater.

Critics of media have long contended that spaces of exhibition are far from value neutral, and that sites of consumption inform the nature of the product consumed. The multiplex theater in India is a relatively recent phenomenon,[20] and one that was foundational to the rapid urbanization that liberalization did not create but certainly helped intensify and sharpen. Multiplex theaters in India imply something grander than their more pedestrian cousins in the West. Most often nestled within the glittering new shopping malls that have come to occupy a special position within the consumerist ethos of post-liberalization India, multiplexes are, simultaneously, sites of aspiration and consumption;[21] in the first few years of its existence, "[t]he very *form* of the multiplex . . . excited both audiences and commentators, it symbolized for them the dream of development in which they were eagerly participating."[22] The multiplex's location within the new shopping mall impacts the status of film itself: jostling against a dizzying range of products, images, and sensations, cinema in this setting comes to be a commodity within a range of other, equally seductive, consumables, vying for the consumer's disposable income. A second aspect of the multiplex is its exclusivity: its sleek sanitized interiors, "[c]lean, shiny, climate-controlled, and technologically state-of-the-art" ensure that though "India's elite might feel perfectly at home here, the multiplex remains an object of awe and wonder for the country's growing middle classes."[23] Indeed, multiplexes are reception spaces where the wealthy can watch films in splendid isolation from the chaotic material realities of India. However, the multiplex has also been generative in terms of film genre, form, and grammar; in fact, the "multiplex film" is a new type of Hindi film in which formal experimentation "seem[s] to run far ahead of [its] content," and sound design is often intricate, sophisticated, and as important as the image. The multiplex phenomenon has also ushered in generic differentiation in an unprecedented manner; romantic or sex comedies, sci-fi films, and thrillers are often advertised as such, in marked departure from the portmanteau nature of the *masala* film. What Sangita Gopal calls "New Horror" is a testament to all of the transformations sketched above; it comes of age within the social and industrial landscape enabled by the multiplex boom.

HABITATIONS OF MODERNITY: FROM *HAVELI* TO HIGH-RISE

In Chapter 1, I argued that the topos of the feudal *haveli* facilitates the encounters between dissonant temporalities in the Gothic ghost film. It is within the inward-looking contours of the *haveli* that the FYP hero must come face to face with that which has been repressed and rendered invisible in the 1950s and 1960s. The Ramsay horror extravaganza in the 1980s, similarly, compels its protagonists to return to the feudal mansion where terrible secrets and terrifying demons remain buried, often literally in dungeons and adjacent ruins. The abode of the ghost, monster, or evil spirit is of critical importance to horror in general,[24] but for Hindi film in particular, spatial geographies determine a whole array of attendant discourses of genre, history, ideology, and so on.

The Hindi horror film's journey from grimy video halls and small-town theaters to the air-conditioned and exclusive splendor of the urban multiplex is necessarily accompanied by processes of sanitization and rationalization.[25] The "Bollywoodization" of horror inaugurates an era of formal streamlining, as well as purging the genre of the embarrassing excess that characterized so much of the Ramsay output. As horror gets a Bollywood facelift, it also gets shorn of the smut and anarchic bawdiness that was the hallmark of its existence in the B and C circuits. The very first casualty was the song sequence: Ram Gopal Varma, who, in many ways, initiated the new horror boom[26] with such films as *Raat* (*Night*, 1992), *Kaun?* (*Who Is It?*, 1999), *Bhoot* (*Ghost*, 2003), and *Phoonk* (*The Spell*, 2008), jettisons songs altogether, preferring instead a dense sound track that retains an atmospheric tautness more in line with the international horror formations of Hollywood, Japanese, or Korean cinema.[27] Of course, given the genre's newfound respectability and box-office returns, several East Asian horror films have been remade in Bollywood in recent years, including *Naina* (*Eyes*, 2005) and *Click* (2010), which appropriated almost entirely the plots of *The Eye* (2002) and *Shutter* (2004), respectively. Such other recent films as *13 B* (2009), *404 Error Not Found* (2011), and *Horror Story* (2013) are not remakes, but they do effortlessly replicate the "international look" and feel of globally circulating horror films, a problematic I turn to in the final chapter of this book.[28] Generous budgets secured with corporate financing and the extensive use of technology and CGI enable sleeker films with much higher production values than the Ramsay film could manage or even aspire to. The chunkiness that was part and parcel of on-screen special effects has given way to a competent performance of cinematic and digital technologies that ensures a new kind of plenitude and immersive experience for audiences.

The "new" horror film is perfectly tailored for new exhibition venues as well as its new audience: the confident cosmopolitanism of India's post-liberalization urban middle class now occupies the narrative core of much of this cinema. This new horror is both *about* and *for* this demographic, which had shunned the genre in earlier incarnations for its obvious lacks and failures. Understandably, the moldy old *haveli* with its creaking doors and odd inhabitants must give way to some other space where fear can dwell and specters haunt—Bollywood horror's most preferred current domicile is the swanky, upmarket apartment nestled in the upper floors of the expensive, exclusive high-rise building. Indeed, scholars such as Gopal and Bishnupriya Ghosh[29] have commented on how the new horror film is not simply situated in, but *obsessed* with the urban apartment and its commodities:

> In its efforts to elicit the supernatural, the horror camera meticulously details the chic interiors that define a middle-class utopia. The repeated zooms on cars, elevators, windows, doors, stairwells, furniture, appliances, and even kitchen utensils construct a mobile catalog of desirable objects. The inventory on display may not equal that of the classic Bollywood interior, which was regally sumptuous, but it is much more *real*. Here technology plays a big part, cameras like the Steadicam, close-ups, pan shots, and the innovative use of sound give us a much better sense of the actual presence of things. Further, the repeated representations of humans interacting with objects—people using cell-phones, clicking on remotes, opening and locking doors, getting in and out of elevators, stir-frying food, driving to and fro to work—suggest a lifestyle that is inseparable from its commodities. We see, then, that the domestic interior and the sum of its possessions function as the central figure in New Horror.[30]

Whereas Gopal stresses the commoditized interior as a perfect setting for the middle-class protagonists of new horror to inhabit, Ghosh argues that it is precisely these pristine and sanitized interiors—wrested away from the chaos and strife that remains endemic to the implied urban surroundings—that generates the sense of the "unhomely" and sets the stage for the entry of spectral interlopers: "[B]eyond the accretion of these material traces in the spanking new flats . . . there are disjointed secretions of *something else* in those films where the flats are haunted—and therefore not free for effortless habitation. In other words, an embodied sense of something else unsettles the aspiration to become elite."[31] For Ghosh, the horrific in this cinema is the "problem of recalcitrant squatters who *return* in spectral form to haunt the new residents of spanking new apartments in globalizing India." Subaltern life-worlds in the form of smudges and traces begin to intrude into the flats that promise separation and distance from a certain kind of exterior, from "the squatter or the evicted whose furtive presence registers on surveillance technologies (motion detectors, alarms, CCTV) mounted to secure property."[32] For Gopal, the political stakes of this cinema are somewhat different: the horrific unsettles something more basic to narrative cinema and a figure that Hindi cinema has traditionally labored to consolidate—the modern conjugal, nuclear couple, only to reconjugate it at closure; quite radically, she suggests that the new horror film's ideological task is not simply to represent the modern, nucleated couple, but the "journey into the realm of the supernatural . . . *produces* the couple as the basic unit of capitalist reproduction" (emphasis mine). The new Bollywood horror film, in a certain sense, then, affirms, concretizes, and *makes possible the modern* in its most recent iteration.

I find these arguments especially valuable when we consider what the new Bollywood horror sets out to achieve, as well as the meanings and resonances it actively disavows. However, one of the most challenging aspects of generic differentiation aided by the multiplex boom and the relative ease of access to digital technologies is that there is currently more than one kind of horror film, and some of them elude available theoretical matrices altogether. My contention in this chapter is that if new horror participates in the discourses of consumer capitalism, it *simultaneously* registers the attendant anxieties and ambivalences of the modern and even the postmodern dispensation. My aim is to extend and complicate Gopal and Ghosh's arguments in order to interrogate the precise strategies through which the complexities and vicissitudes of late capitalism are indexed in the genre. Here I suggest that though the feudal is extracted from the filial in the 1990s, it does not disappear altogether. Indeed, even as horror becomes more technologically competent—referencing a shinier, more global India—it continues to interrogate this gloss through narrative and content. In this sense, horror, now a properly industrial formation, enjoys an ideal vantage point to mount immanent critiques of the contemporary in a different way.

Hindi cinema's vexed relationship to the modern has been at the core of my engagement with the supernatural throughout this book. Once Bollywoodized, and produced under the aegis of a properly capitalized industrial system, Hindi horror does seem more aligned with international products. Trimmed of such "irrationalities" as song sequences, based on screenplays that reinforce the linearity and coherence of narrative, and aided by the careful and competent deployment of technology, almost nothing of the unruly *masala* form seems to have survived in the new genre. However, as we have seen in the other chapters, pre- or anti-capitalist modalities can appear and persist in the Hindi film in startling new guises. This is not to suggest that these films endorse the feudal or non-modern as disarmingly as the Ramsay text did, but rather to argue that film genres such as horror—themselves temporally circumscribed by industrial imperatives—reflexively render late capitalism as a fissured, contradictory, and contested terrain in spaces like South Asia.

Consider, for example, the much-cited *Vaastu Shastra* (*Vaastu Science*, Saurabh Narang, 2004), which Ram Gopal Varma produced and which bears all the hallmarks of his style. Jhilmil Rao (Sushmita Sen), who is a medical doctor, and her writer-husband Viraag (J. D. Chakravarthy) move into a sprawling bungalow in the wilderness to escape the strife of metropolitan existence. They are accompanied by their young son, Rohan (Ahsaas Channa), and Jhilmil's sister, Radz (Piya Rai Chowdhary), a college student. Soon after, Rohan claims to have made new friends, Manish and Jyoti, who remain invisible to the adults. The child's increasingly bizarre behavior alerts them to the presence of something else within their new home and environment. Quite unusually for Hindi horror cinema, the evil that imperils the new home and family remains unvanquished at the end.

Vaastu expends considerable time and narrative energy establishing the modern worldviews of the couple and their family. Although they move away from the city, the couple brings their modern metropolitan ideology to the wilderness. The family's non-traditional living arrangements are underscored by the presence of Radz, who is included in the family unit, and the fact that Jhil is the professional breadwinner, with Viraag staying at home writing and serving as the primary caregiver to Rohan. Soon after the family moves into the new home, we become privy to the unorthodox domestic arrangements when Jhil and Radz leave for the hospital and college, respectively, while Viraag is left at home to cook, clean, and look after the child. We are expected to note the liberal and liberated politics of

FIGURE 4.2. *House seen by/through the haunted tree in* Vaastu Shastra.

the family via these expository sequences. Elsewhere, I have argued that in *Vaastu*, the child Rohan is used strategically in order to mount a stringent critique of the discourses of neo-liberal modernity that the couple embodies, for the film makes apparent Viraag's inability to provide the child with the company he clearly needs.[33] In a key sequence, Rohan unsuccessfully tries to draw Viraag's attention to his ball that mysteriously gets suspended in mid-air. The mise-en-scène, particularly the blocking of the actors, alerts the spectator to Rohan's plight, because for much of the scene he remains in the foreground trying to make sense of the haunted ball while Viraag is placed in the deep background, with his back facing his son and the audience. In other words, the placement of actors in space demonstrates Viraag's inattention, as his child encounters supernatural forces in plain sight.

Whereas Viraag seems oblivious to his son's loneliness, Jhil's guilt over abandoning her child for her profession is immediately apparent—an early indication of the film's allegiances—as she frantically searches for Rohan as soon as she comes home from work and eventually locates him in the ramshackle shed. It is instructive to note the length of time the adults in the film spend hunting for an elusive Rohan; the implication is that the child would not be missing in the first place, if properly looked after. The very next day, Viraag finds him gone once again and finally finds him talking to his invisible friends, Manish and Jyoti, under the banyan tree that is the repository of malefic forces in the film. The fact that the family is increasingly besieged is largely conveyed through the efficacious use of modern technology. The film deploys a cornucopia of stylistic techniques to alert viewers to the evil that resides in the new home. Some of the most effective devices used are crane shots that simulate the point of view of the dead/dreadful tree; the audience is optically aligned with the tree during these "looks" at the hapless abode, via bird's-eye-view shots that dwarf the home and render it vulnerable. The cinematography, more generally, is absolutely crucial in generating terror in *Vaastu*: a restless, mobile camera constantly "stalks" the characters, while weird, canted frames render spaces and people out of kilter. The sound track combines ominous music with a plethora of disturbing noises, including, inexplicably, the loud buzzing of insects and high-pitched sounds of children giggling. All of these sonic components coalesce to create the disturbing aural universe of the film, a perfect foil for the unsettling visuals. As noted by Roy Choudhury, Gopal, and Ghosh, style in new horror goes a long way in establishing the sense of *unheimlich* that pervades the new homes.[34]

Alongside spectral presences, cinematography and mise-en-scène also underscore critical absences in the film. It is the absence of humans—extended family members—that propels the family into crisis; the film implies that it is the non-traditional familial situation to which Rohan falls victim. It effectively mounts a strong critique of late or consumer capitalism—of the modern nuclear family, of the modern companionate conjugal couple, and even modern parenting. Rohan—and by extension the rest of the family—is haunted by big empty spaces; there is so much space between characters in their luxurious new home that Manish, Jyoti, and the other undead are easily able to inhabit it. The uncanny, the unhomely, very easily erupts into domestic space that is left empty and unattended. Nucleated spaces, *Vaastu* suggests, are vulnerable spaces. It is the lack of "real" people that forces Rohan to befriend the spectral children; his far-too-modern parents create the situation that eventually imperils him.

The first climax of the film involves Radz's tryst with her boyfriend, which eventually leads to her brutal death. Echoing countless American slasher films, Radz seems to be punished for her promiscuity, but we never see exactly how she is killed; part of the punishment meted out to sexually active teens in films such as *Halloween* or *Friday the 13th* is the deliberation and relish with which they are brutalized by the killer. *Vaastu* spares us this spectacle. After Radz's boyfriend, Murli (Purab Kohli), disappears in the middle of their sexual encounter, Radz walks downstairs to look for him in what she perceives to be a game of erotic hide-and-seek. Something horrific accosts her soon after, but her terrified look off-screen is all we are privy to. An abrupt, disjointed cut transitions us into the next sequence, as Jhil, Viraag, and Rohan return home after an evening out. Jhil—to her utter horror—discovers Murli's mutilated corpse on Radz's bed and her sister's body strung up on the banyan tree. On the final day, Jhil leaves Rohan at home with Viraag, creating the necessary condition for the climactic series of attacks. She will become the target of ghostly assault upon her return.

The madman who had been uttering garbled warnings from the very beginning of the film manages to draw Jhil's attention at her hospital on this day, but his explanation of the haunted home and murderous tree and their wicked inhabitants remains as incomplete and incoherent as Rohan's understanding of the ghosts' angry energy. This incoherence that lies at the very heart of *Vaastu* lays bare its political propensities—we never quite find out what transpired in the site of the home. Our knowledge of past events and past violence—arguably crucial to our understanding of any horror film that invokes past events—remains vague; we have only intimations and the inchoate ramblings of a madman and a terrified child. In other words, the foundational reason for the hauntings remains unarticulated, decidedly unclear, indeed, incomprehensible. It is in resonance with this informational vacuum that Viraag's final attack on Jhil becomes meaningful—the fact that we do not have to be told what the horrific "something else" is.

When Jhil rushes back to the house, she is finally confronted by the monumental canker that has been slowly but surely eating away at her home—a crowd of silent, angry undead, including Rukma (Rasika Joshi), Radz, and, worse, her now (un)dead husband, Viraag. Finally, the empty space of the home is full of bodies and energies that it has seemed to lack from the beginning. Viraag's attack on Jhil is immediate, horrific, and inexplicable. He throttles her repeatedly and flings her across the room in a display of profound rage. We viewers do not echo Jhil's astonishment at this instance because we realize that the film has come full circle—the dénouement is a decisive blow to the discourses that Jhil has so confidently inhabited so far. Viraag's emasculation and impotence finally boil over, perfectly in keeping with the film's overall logic.

Vaastu finally makes its ideological allegiances obvious: it is a cautionary tale about being or becoming too modern. Wealth, education, and bourgeois discourses of individualism, consumption, and coupledom can be endorsed only up to a point: for instance, when traditional gender roles are subverted, the family taps into a fountainhead of rage that requires no naming or explanation. At the closure, Jhil—the confident, articulate, professional woman—is rendered completely silent and on the verge of psychological implosion. *Vaastu Shastra* is a particularly interesting case to think through the limits of Gopal's and even Ghosh's theoretical edifices. Importantly, the modern couple cannot be conjugated in this instance; perhaps their new bungalow has to be evacuated so that the spectral others can now populate it again and in greater numbers. It is instructive to note

FIGURE 4.3. *Jhil discovers Viraag transformed into a zombie in* Vaastu Shastra.

that the most horrific instance of violence in the film is enacted by the male partner on the female. This breaks apart the circle that encloses the conjugal couple as the most emblematic unit of capitalist modernity; Viraag's murderous assault on Jhil is an attack on more than this particular marriage or family.[35]

Vaastu is not the only contemporary horror film that neither takes place in an urban apartment nor is able to affirm or consolidate the modern conjugal couple. In fact, a whole host of recent films especially foreground the couple as besieged from both without and within—an institution on the verge of collapse, if not obsolescence. Notable examples include *Hawa* (*The Wind*, Guddu Dhanoa, 2003), in which Sanjana (Tabu), an independent single mother, is repeatedly raped by an aggressive invisible entity when she moves into a new bungalow in the woods of Himachal Pradesh. She is already divorced at the beginning of the film and is struggling to manage a failing business alongside parenting duties. That her desire for autonomy is perfectly offset by the increasing viciousness of the assaults goes without saying; in a particularly odious instance, she is raped in full view of her terrified children.[36]

In the even more recent *Aatma* (*Soul*, Suparn Verma, 2013), an ugly custody battle between Maya (Bipasha Basu) and Abhay (Nwazuddin Siddiqui) rages on even after his death in a car wreck. *Aatma* has all the trappings of Ghosh's "flat cinema," especially the luxurious high-rise apartment chock full of electronic gadgets and other commodities. CCTV cameras and other surveilling screens register ghostly disturbances as electronic failures or distortions; giant flat-screen televisions adorn well-appointed, color-coordinated bedrooms; the kitchen is "modular" and an important site for spectral disturbances. However, the modern conjugal couple is de-

FIGURE 4.4. Hawa *poster. Used by permission of the National Film Archive of India.*

composing from within. The daughter, Niya (Doyel), largely oblivious to the violence and abuse that had characterized the relationship, falls prey to the doting ghost's murderous attachment. In *Aatma* the couple is not only disintegrating but is a pathological and haunted institution from the very beginning. The only way to save Niya—thus ensuring the possibility of a future—is for Maya to sacrifice her own life at the end. The very possibility of modern heterosexual marriage and the nuclear family comes to be disabled as Niya must grow up in yet another adoptive, dismembered home.

Mainstream formations like genre films routinely imperil constructs such as the home and family in order to finally legitimize them; and, as Robin Wood and many others have argued, to restore normalcy is an important ideological function of genre films in general and horror films in particular.[37] My argument here is not to suggest that Bollywood horror radically provides an alternative to the couple or the nucleated family, or that recent Bollywood horror does not endorse or reify certain discourses of the modern—this, after all, is its basic task as a formation that is forever aspiring to global currency and relevance. However, it is important to interrogate what lurks within Bollywood's insistent presentism and euphoric embrace of all things contemporary. This includes technological competence: even as new horror screens itself as a state-of-the-art form, it narratively negotiates the price that such technophilia exacts on the social. I have suggested that the undertow of other allegiances informs these films;

horror, more so perhaps than any other genre in contemporary Bollywood, indexes the ambivalent and messy modalities of consumer capitalism in India. In the next section, I turn to a different kind of Bollywood horror—the period piece, or films in which specific kinds of pasts and historical temporalities are deployed in the generation of fear and anxiety.

HISTORY AS HORROR: ROMANCING THE COLONIAL IN THE FILMS OF VIKRAM BHATT

Filmmaker Vikram Bhatt is considered to be Ram Gopal Varma's counterpart in "rescuing" horror from the smutty pits of the B and C circuits. Unlike Varma, however, Bhatt's allegiances to the older Hindi film format remain fairly clear. He uses song sequences and heterosexual romance in ways that are traditionally associated with Hindi cinema—when people fall in love, they sing to one another in bucolic, natural landscapes; because love stories form the core of most of these narratives, they also enable an interrogation of the romantic or conjugal couple as a figure.[38] In a startling echo of the Ramsay discourse,[39] Bhatt contends that pure horror would not work in India, because, "for us it's more important to have a more wholesome story . . . a man-woman relationship, or other relationships, and horror being part of that larger story." His target audience—or the figure of the audience he imagines—is the heterosexual couple: "in my mind, there's a couple who's watching the film. There's a girl who is easily scared and a boy who is pretending not to be scared. And I make a film for them. They are in my mind when I'm making the movie, when I'm mixing a film, when I'm scoring a film." His films boast major stars, scenic locations, sumptuous music, and lavish production values—horror's "facelift" has undoubtedly been largely enabled by Bhatt's own aesthetic propensities; his films are as much "Bollywood" as horror, in a manner of speaking. Indeed, the question of a cosmetic makeover is critical for this cinema's relationship to its own genealogy, as I discuss below. I would suggest that Vikram Bhatt's canny rehabilitation of horror is a classic instance of old wine being served in particularly attractive new bottles, an idea that gets obscured when we read the current phase of horror as a radical break with what has come before.[40]

Certainly, films such as *Raaz* (*The Secret*), *1920*, *1920 Evil Returns*, *Shaapit* (*The Accursed Ones*), and *Haunted 3D* look and feel very different from, say, the shoddiness that the Ramsay film has come to be synonymous with. At the same time, however, the *nature* of horror—of what defines the horrific, spectral, ghostly, monstrous, and so on—remains uncannily similar.

For example, in *Raaz*, a corpse is physically buried in the vicinity of the bungalow that it haunts. In *Shaapit*, a 350-year-old curse plagues a set of young lovers in the present. Recall that in the Ramsay film, the monster had to physically inhabit the ruined *haveli*, and curses were a basic fulcrum for narrative propulsion in such films as *Purani Haveli*. While steadfastly updating/upgrading the genre, Bhatt's oeuvre is clearly indebted to older forms of supernatural in Hindi cinema.[41] Also, as I hope to demonstrate below, traces of the Gothic inhabit his work more easily than that of his contemporaries.

But the past is recycled in Bhatt's cinema in more complex ways as well. Many of his most successful films are period pieces—set in the historical past. Of these, here I will discuss *1920*, with which I began this chapter, and *Haunted 3D*, both of which mobilize a certain vision of India's colonial history. Why, one might ask, is the period piece necessary as a temporal contortion? What *work* might it enable the genre to do? For Vikram Bhatt's cinema in particular, one response can readily be furnished: a certain kind of temporal tourism that is pure visual design is offered for consumption in these films; "The trappings of the past serve as an occasion to expose the limitations of the present."[42] In other words, the spectator can gaze at a set of images, objects, signs—all of which collectively *appear to* re-present the past, but this is "a vision of 'history' as a country where only feelings reside, not socio-political conflicts."[43] A specific form of modern—even postmodern—nostalgia colors these images in digitized sepia;[44] as Svetlana Boym reminds us, "nostalgia is not 'antimodern'; it is not necessarily opposed to modernity."[45] Here, too, the past becomes a series of purely ornamental signs that are intensely pleasurable. The fetishization of the "past" lies precisely in generation of visual pleasure—warmly lit images of stone mansions, massive crystal chandeliers, "period costumes," bric-a-brac, ornate furniture, old photographs, grand pianos, and the like conjure up the past only as a series of visually consumable objects.[46] The "colonial" is thus reduced to an assemblage of locations and commodities, carefully packaged for audience consumption, much like Switzerland and Kashmir are in a different kind of Hindi film. I use the word "image" here in a specific sense—to gesture toward thinness and the two-dimensionality of the world represented; this is precisely what Fredric Jameson describes as a universe "of flatness of depthlessness, a new kind of superficiality in the most literal sense," in postmodern cultural artifacts.[47] As such, this historical fantasy—or fantasy of the historical, perhaps—has no real historicity or depth. Indeed, the fantasy is sustainable only insofar as the very question of historicity is kept at bay. The gaze invited is that of a tourist whose look skims over objects but never really dwells on the profilmic. If the Ramsay film appropriated motifs and themes wildly from Western horror and created an inchoate assemblage of visual signs, Bhatt's historical horror is, in a certain sense, no different. The settings and objects that generate the "past" in this new cinema is a similarly bastardized collection of *things* that have no tangible referents, such as repeated shots of the horse-drawn carriages in these films that come from sources as far-flung as Robert Wise's classic horror film *The Haunting* (1963), any number of Hammer Films adaptations of Dracula, and scandalously, even from a Ramsay film or two. These "images" of the past are also foundationally contemporary, in that they are *produced* through modern digital technologies; only a competent performance of technology renders this "old" world visible.

It is important to note that taking this sort of liberty is hardly remarkable for the Hindi film—old and new films continue to flout standards of verisimilitude in generating specific *cinematic* universes—after all, vagueness of time and place has always aided Bombay cinema in speaking to the broadest swath of audiences. The difference, however, is that the new kind of film—especially what is called the multiplex film—is lauded for its success in generating a sense of the real; the effectiveness of the new horror format shares an indexical relationship with this newfound realism.[48] Vikram Bhatt's cinema, though, feels no such obligation to conjure up any recognizable life-worlds; it markets a different sort of fantasy altogether. The historical horror film is unmoored from the real in both spatial and temporal terms. Spatially, the films reject Ghosh's contemporary urban flats in favor of a return to the *haveli*, which now appears as either an actual manor house or a colonial bungalow.

Settings are rarely neutral for genres of the supernatural; the site of horror determines what kind of fears and anxieties may find a hospitable habitat therein. The surprising inclusion of colonial architectural edifices has specific consequences for Bollywood horror as well. In the first chapter of this book, I argued that when the male citizen-subject leaves the modern city behind to enter the haunted ramparts of the feudal *haveli*, attendant discourses are also left behind. The interior of the *haveli* is domicile to a different temporal domain. In the historical horror film, because the contemporary is rejected wholesale, fears and anxieties, too, must come from a different location.

Haunted 3D is a particularly interesting example of the genre because the film moves back and forth between the past and present not via flashbacks, as is common, but through time travel. Rehan (Mimoh) comes to a hill station (Ooty, one of Bhatt's favorite filming locations) to sell his father's massive colonial bungalow, appropriately called "Glen Manor."[49] Although fearful locals warn him of the "*shaitan*" (the devil) who resides

FIGURE 4.5. *Rehan finds Meera's portrait in* Haunted 3D.

within, Rehan is determined to seal the deal for his father's real-estate empire. Interestingly, Rehan does not simply encounter a ghost inside Glen Manor, but instead an entire historical narrative must be reckoned with and put to rest. Ameliorating past wrongs is a standard trope for horror; restless spirits are often freed when injustices done to them in the past are set right in the present. Rehan's problem, however, is more complex. From an old letter, he learns of the tragic circumstances that befell Meera (Tia Bajpai), who was raped by her music teacher, Professor Iyer (Arif Zakaria), back in 1936. There are two separate twists in this otherwise commonplace scenario: first, when Iyer initially assaults Meera, she struggles and accidentally kills him with a heavy candleholder. The "rape" is committed later by the lustful, evil spirit of Iyer, when Meera is left alone and defenseless at Glen Manor. Second, after repeated assaults, Meera hangs herself and Iyer keeps her spirit imprisoned in the manor—so the atrocities and suffering continue even after Meera's suicide, and the only way Rehan can set her free is if he can stop the event from occurring in 1936.

Predictably, Rehan falls in love with Meera (as specter/spirit, since she's already dead when he meets her)—in fact, quite interestingly, the film shows Rehan masochistically identifying with the rape and sexual torture—and he must save her by traveling to the past, a gambit that allows *Haunted 3D* to morph into a nostalgia film proper, a pastiche of colonial tropes that range from lace gloves to dainty parasols and other assorted signs of the Raj. Why Meera's Indian family should inhabit a world so obviously "foreign" (complete with an ayah named Margaret, who is also brutally killed) is a question the film prefers not to answer. Jameson describes the nostalgia film as one that "does not reinvent a picture of the past in its lived totality; rather, by reinventing the feel and shape of characteristic art objects of an older period . . . it seeks to reawaken a sense of the past associated with those objects," and *Haunted 3D* as well as the other films mentioned here fit these parameters perfectly.

After failing to thwart Professor Iyer from assaulting Meera in the past on multiple occasions, Rehan finally manages to rid her of the demonic force only after he is helped by a Sufi mystic.[50] The action-packed climax features a protracted physical battle with Iyer on the ruins of an abandoned village, which makes extensive use of digital and 3D technologies. Once saved, Meera must live her life out in her temporal domain, as Rehan returns to his own. Glen Manor is finally rid of her screams and of ghosts. Unlike the haunted hero in the postcolonial Gothic, Rehan's own subjectivity remains firmly grounded in the present, even as he is able to regress into a specific moment in history. However, once back in Glen Manor, he finds a letter that Meera wrote to him about the trajectory her life took after Rehan rescued her from her tragic destiny. Meera married someone else and had a son she named Rehan, because he had bestowed on her the "gift of life." Now, this is a considerably complex figuration of temporalities—precisely what Bliss Cua Lim calls immiscible temporalities—because when Rehan re-enters his present, its past has already been altered—he can remember this past and his love for Meera, but he has no other way of accessing it. Thus, in scrambling temporal linearity, layering asynchronous temporal modes atop each other, and positing the possibility of other/alternative temporal trajectories, *Haunted 3D* posits multiple presents and futures as well. In *Ghosts of My Life*, Mark Fisher argues that temporal disjointedness and anachrony are, in fact, part and parcel of the cultural imaginaries of the twenty-first century: "[T]he 'jumbling up of time,' the montaging of earlier eras, has ceased to be worthy of comment; it is now so prevalent that it is no longer even noticed."[51] It is precisely what he calls a "refurbishing" of an imagined past, a "formal nostalgia"[52] that Bhatt's cinema insistently foregrounds.

Consider, for example, *1920*, which does not feature the temporal contortions of *Haunted 3D*, but through its mobilization of history invokes real events in outlandishly unreal spaces. As mentioned above, *1920* tells the story of Arjun Singh and his wife, Lisa, who move to a palatial mansion that Arjun has been employed to turn into a luxury hotel. In diegetic terms, the mansion is set in India, but Bhatt uses several locations in Yorkshire, including Allerton Castle, Bolton Priory, Bolton Abbey, and Ripley Castle, to bring his vision of 1920 to life. In this oddly fractured engagement with history, it appears that colonial India can only be imaged by returning to the past/spaces of the Metropole. Even more puzzling is

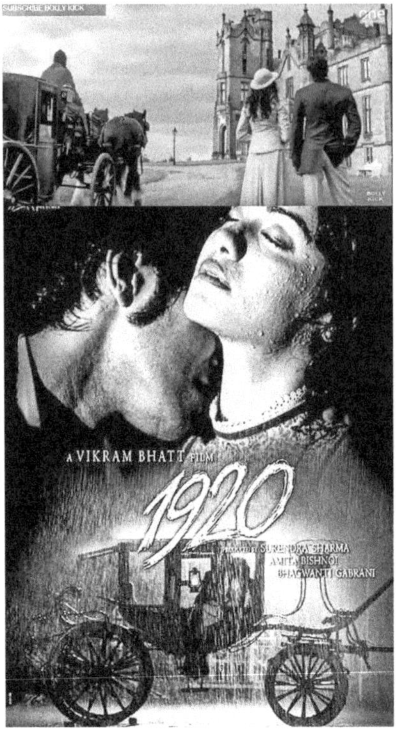

FIGURE 4.6. *Poster and* haveli *from* 1920.

the fact that the malefic ghost (Mohankant, played by Indraneil Sengupta) who possesses the Anglo-Indian Lisa is the spirit of a soldier who had betrayed his comrades in the uprising of 1857! He is, quite literally, a specter of history who returns as a reminder of the mutiny as betrayal. He wants Lisa because she is the reincarnation of Gayatri (Anjori Alagh), the woman who had seduced and then betrayed him to his enemies and thus caused his death. The tangled strands of love, memory, and multiple betrayals are typical of Bhatt's imaginary of horror—the past becomes a designer backdrop against which tortured lovers haunt and are haunted. Crimes and misdemeanors are specifically sexual in nature and brave young men routinely rescue imperiled damsels. The female body is simultaneously sexualized and subjected to considerable amounts of violence. Heterosexual couples sometimes manage to survive these tribulations, but only just. The question of whether this survival signals a ringing endorsement of capitalist modernity is complicated, as I hope to have demonstrated, by the other narrative, ideological, and stylistic propensities of the films in question.

Why the present remains a constant point of reference and yet clearly insufficient for this cinema is a critical question to ask. Drawing on Jacques Lacan's clinical work, Jameson suggests that this sort of nostalgia is a symptom of "cultural schizophrenia," wherein the very experience of temporality comes to be radically fractured:

> For Lacan, the experience of temporality, human time, past, present, memory . . . this existential or experiential feeling of time itself—is also an effect of language. It is because language has a past and a future, because the sentence moves in time, that we can have what seems to us a concrete or lived experience of time. But since the schizophrenic does not know language articulation in that way, he or she does not have our experience of temporal continuity either, but is condemned to live a perpetual present with which the various moments of his or her Past have little connection and for which there is no conceivable future on the horizon. In other words, schizophrenic experience is an experience of isolated, disconnected, discontinuous material signifiers which fail to link up into a coherent sequence.[53]

Jameson remains suspicious of postmodern art precisely because by foreclosing real historicity, it forecloses any possibility of action—collective or otherwise—in the present and the future. Despite an apparently inexhaustible appetite for commoditizing the past, this type of cultural production is symptomatic of a society that "has little by little begun to lose its capacity to retain its own past, has begun to live in a perpetual present and in a perpetual change that obliterates traditions of the kind which all earlier social formations have had in one way or another to preserve."[54] With its fraught relationship to an imperfect present and an equally opportunistic mobilization of a past disemboweled of substance, the Bollywood horror film should elicit similar apprehensions.

The present—as a dense, heightened, and utterly mediatized domain—appears repeatedly as diegetic content in more recent, "millennial" Hindi horror films. In the next chapter, I focus on generic novelties like the "zom-com," the creature-feature, the "horrex film," and the found-footage film in order to explore Bollywood's romance with the supernatural in the era of new media and media convergence.

CHAPTER FIVE

The Planetary Paranormal

MILLENNIAL MYTHOS AND THE DISASSEMBLY OF THE "HINDI FILM"

Luv: India has ghosts and spirits. Where did these zombies come from?
Hardik: Globalization! These foreigners have done us in! First they brought HIV, now zombie!

—CONVERSATION IN *GO GOA GONE* (2013)

SOME OF THE MOST STARTLING IMAGES FROM OMAR ALI Khan's 2007 film *Zibahkhana* (*Hell's Ground*) include a maniacal Sufi-mystic-cum-hitchhiker, hordes of bloodthirsty rustic zombies shambling along a country path, and, most famously, Burqaman—a burqa-clad, mace-wielding, corpse-chopping, killer-in-drag, chasing a young woman through the woods. Publicized as Pakistan's first "gore" and "extreme horror" film, *Zibahkhana* is certainly an astonishing text from a film culture stifled by decades of brutal censorship policies, and therefore one that has long shied away from producing anything remotely close to horror.[1] The film also engages in a flamboyant dialogue with global horror, especially American slasher movies from the 1970s and 1980s. From the basic narrative device of a van full of teenagers who stray into unknown territory and thus their doom, to the macabre and grisly decorations of Burqaman's lair and the very idea of a silent, masked killer, *Zibahkhana*'s plot and mise-en-scène remain obviously indebted to American horror films in general and *Texas Chainsaw Massacre* (Tobe Hooper, 1974) in particular.[2] As one amused reviewer put it, "If Leatherface, Freddy Krueger, Michael Myers, Norman Bates and the guy who knows what you did last summer got together for a Friday the 13th party in Islamabad, *Zibahkhana* would be the result."[3] However, beyond the density of allusions and clichés—both local and international, which jostle for the viewer's recognition—what sets this film apart from its Bollywood contemporaries is its deeply political content. As Ali Khan, Ali Nobil Ahmad, and Gwendolyn Kirk have argued, the film's politics are far from simple, ranging from critiques of class or the rural-urban divide to religion, gender, and state-sponsored violence.[4] Kirk finally posits that the film's central political gesture is its presentation of the Pakistani past: "[I]t is neither zombies nor serial killers, nor demented Sufis that terrify the viewer but rather, an illusive and traumatic past, which, when disturbed by the teenagers, emerges in violent, nostalgic encounters."[5] From festering class antagonisms that steadily punctuate the narrative to the gendered violence implied by Burqaman, it is undeniable that *Zibahkhana*'s crowded, allusive, and recognizably "global" texture does not rob it of its solid moorings in Pakistani history, culture, and politics.

Zibahkhana remains a singularly audacious experiment with horror in South Asian film; neighboring Bollywood has, so far, been unable (or unwilling) to venture into similar cinematic or political zones—a refusal that is, of course, deeply political in itself. Most of this book focuses on the particular ways in which Hindi commercial cinema has inscribed the supernatural over the last seven decades or so. But alongside this narrative, I have also traced how the formation has imbibed, engaged with, and spoken back to global cinemas. Whether the Gothic films in the 1950s, the Ramsay output in the 1980s, or Bollywood's slick, new horror in the era of liberalization, the labor that Hindi film has historically expended in adapting, repurposing, and provincializing global genres has been of considerable importance to this inquiry. In the new millennium, the fantastic and the supernatural become global obsessions. Both *The Lord of the Rings* (2001–2003) and the *Harry Potter* series (2001–2011) went on to become gargantuan global hits, followed closely by the *Twilight* phenomenon (2008–2012) and *Game of Thrones* (2011–present) a few years later. The popularity of the source material, and Hollywood's canny marketing and monumental distribution networks notwithstanding, it is difficult to overlook the decisive millennial turn toward fantasy genres. Unsurprisingly, the Bollywood industry aggressively embraced millennial trends and discourses, buoyed by the corporate reorganization and restructuring that came in the wake of economic liberalization in the 1990s. Although the processes of reorganization began in the 1990s, it is only in the new millennium that Hollywood studios—Disney, Fox, Viacom, and Warner Brothers, among others—have begun to function as local film-producing (or co-producing) entities in an industry that has historically functioned along feudal and kinship networks.[6] A different industrial ecology, inaugurated in the earlier decade, has congealed as a fully functional system in the 2000s.

But beyond purely industrial imperatives, Bollywood in the new millennium continued the process of generic streamlining that was enabled by the multiplex phenomenon discussed in some detail in the last chapter. Although the traditional *masala* film has been variously revamped and repackaged in recent years, the genres of the supernatural transmuted almost entirely to inhabit multiple globally legible formats. For example, Vikram Bhatt, whose horror films I discuss in Chapter 4, has always incorporated music, stars, and sets/locations in fairly traditional ways; in 2013, he co-wrote and produced *Horror Story*—a film not only devoid of songs, but also one that was shot on a single set of a dilapidated hotel with unknown actors. Beyond individual filmmakers experimenting with form, a slew of generic novelties appeared on the cinematic horizon: from "zom-coms" to found-footage films and creature-features, Hindi film audiences are now being introduced to a dizzying range of largely unfamiliar generic products. My intention here is not to provide a taxonomy of new genres—indeed, some of these films remain singular experiments with generic material—but to interrogate emergent formations and the modalities through which these concatenate with the contemporary global, digital dispensation.

Before proceeding to the millennial supernatural in particular, it is useful to recall that Indian cinema's relationship to global generic forms—and especially Hollywood—has been complex and promiscuous historically, as I discussed in the introduction. However, the "uniqueness" of Hindi cinema (or even Indian cinema) is subject to specific pressures in given historical moments; the new millennium presented a set of challenges to the Hindi film industry wherein the sameness/difference, derivativeness/autonomy question has to be posed afresh. As Madhava Prasad notes, even the moniker "Bollywood" "seems to at once mock the thing it names and celebrate its difference."[7] Moreover, Bollywood's global preeminence in recent years has been critically dependent on marketing and leveraging this difference overseas:

> The successful commodification of Indian cinema as Bollywood in the international market is based on the idea of an unchanging essence that distinguishes it from Hollywood. It cannot have a history or its history can only be a narrative of the spontaneous repetition of its innate predilection to sing and dance and cry. This agonistic relation to Hollywood is definitive. . . .
>
> At a time when Indian cinema is far more diverse than it has ever been in the past, "Bollywood" is an attempt to hold on to the idea of an essence of Indian cinema. Indian cinema's marketability is

becoming a matter of Indianness, which is its Bollywoodness. Bollywood keeps alive a sense of continuity amidst change.[8]

However, this story, too, has been mutating in interesting ways in the 2000s. A number of scholars have recently noted that part of Bollywood's present diversity includes an aesthetic modality that is critically dependent on "making a sustained effort to break once and for all with this 'Indian' style and its artifices. Their efforts are increasingly inspired by Hollywood and Asian cinema . . . , and the net effect of it all is still too early to gauge. But this does not look like Bollywood."[9] This remarkably not-like-Bollywood impetus dominates supernatural films in recent years, and these are the subject of this chapter.

The first decade of the new millennium presented a watershed moment when Hindi film had to renegotiate its relationship with globally circulating genres. Instead of what Prasad calls "genre mixing," what we see now is precisely the reverse: the desire for "genre distillation"—to sift out of the heaving assemblage that is the *masala*-form generic tropes and constellations that are shorn of the local in any recognizable way.[10] The lip-synched song sequence has historically crystallized as "the ultimate index of popular Indian cinema's alterity and cultural intelligibility: the reason for its inability to 'cross-over' to Euro-American audiences."[11] Fittingly, as the most emblematic marker of Bollywood's otherness globally, the song sequence has come to be the first casualty of formal compromise, but as I argue below, a more complex process of formal rationalization—even sanitization—is underway in contemporary Bollywood. And nowhere is this emergent tendency more visible than in the genres of the supernatural, formations that have long resisted this type of formal disciplining.

The millennial supernatural—what I shall call the "planetary paranormal"—is precisely the kind of Hindi film that seeks to be anything but. Beyond language—and even that has increasingly become a pidgin "Hinglish," the lingua franca of urban, middle-class youth in India—there is little of the erstwhile commercial form in this new kind of product. Since the processes of economic liberalization began in the 1990s, the Hindi film has responded to, negotiated, and embodied globality in a number of different ways. The current moment is an especially charged one in this larger aspirational narrative of "becoming" more global, and perhaps differently global than, for example, the non-resident Indian (NRI) film in the 1990s represented. An increasing number of Hindi films now replicate the look and feel of "international" cinema, however understood.[12] Interestingly, unlike other genres, such as family melodramas, horror films are not as widely distributed overseas; domestic audiences remain the primary addressees of this kind of cinema. Nevertheless, the genres of the supernatural, and especially horror, have responded in recent years with a degree of identification with planetary forms that remains unprecedented. If, as Prasad points out above, establishing the "autonomy" of Indian cinema has long been the Holy Grail for a certain kind of critic, viewer, or filmmaker, the current moment witnesses an upending of that discursive domain altogether. The millennial supernatural film is "Hindi film" only insofar as its immediate context determines, and that, too, with a degree of sheepishness and reluctance that is unmistakable; Bollywood horror's current bid for globality eschews wholesale its former eccentricities. The ideological significance of this un-coupling is the core problematic for this chapter.

MODERN, MILLENNIAL, PLANETARY

In tandem with its formal un-becoming, Bollywood's obsessive reflexivity has garnered considerable scholarly attention in recent years; its "commodification as a fetish object"[13] in the global arena has been unmistakable as well as unrelenting. From *Om Shanti Om*'s (Farah Khan, 2007) delirious camp, pastiche, and nostalgia to *Dabanng*'s (*Fearless*, 2010) muscular repackaging of the baroque *masala* idiom, Bollywood today is a well-oiled, self-mythologizing machine, untiringly churning out films that narcissistically gaze upon the inner workings of texts, industry, and audiences; Bollywood, as Bhaskar Sarkar notes, is constantly being "potentiated, performed, and rendered palpable all around us."[14] This self-reflexive turn—endemic to global media in general in the era of digital media and media convergence—is also Bollywood's ticket to global visibility. Only a specific kind of formal grammar and generic mélange, however, is highlighted thusly, pointing to its increasing contemporary obsolescence.[15] If the *masala* film is already relegated to Bollywood's embarrassing, less-than-global past, its audiences—the working-class masses, in the industry's perception—are simply conjured away. The millennial supernatural film, at least in some guises that I discuss here, feels little obligation to formulate an inclusive mode of address.

Bollywood today simultaneously flaunts and celebrates its difference while exhibiting considerable anxiety about the "standard" of its products in the global market.[16] A peculiar combination of defiance and apprehension seems to color its self-perception. The millennial supernatural film, among some other genres, seems to respond to the latter half of the paradox: I suggest that these films are a particularly telling instantiation of Hindi cinema's most recent bid for global legibility, currency, and acceptance. The enterprise smacks of more than a little desperation, no doubt, but then again, schizophrenia is by definition an untenable subject position. In what follows, I argue that this kind of formal capitulation also necessitates other modalities of compromise. Especially when it comes to the new forms of the supernatural film, there is much more at stake than ghostly song sequences and abandoned audience demographics.

What sets this avatar of Bollywood apart from even the 1990s formation is, of course, the explosion of digital media cultures in India. By digital media cultures, I mean more than a general understanding of the production and consumption of media. I am gesturing toward an entire universe of activities and affects that are aligned to and enabled by the digital media, from cellular phones, touch screens, and gadgets, to images produced in/by them, to fan videos, video games, social media, networked communities, and most conspicuously, the Internet. In the new millennium, the penetration of digital media has transformed life-worlds in South Asia irrevocably, and the cinema is no exception. Although regular access to the Internet still remains limited to a relatively small number of people,[17] other forms of sharing data are widespread, especially via mobile networks. New conduits and sites of circulation, exchange, and participation are constantly emerging alongside new logics of production and consumption of digital media and information. This, as Henry Jenkins has argued, is the essence of convergence culture:

> The flow of content across multiple media platforms, the cooperation between multiple media industries, and the migratory behavior of who will go almost anywhere in search of entertainment experiences they want. Convergence is a word that manages to describe technological, industrial, cultural and social changes depending on who's speaking and what they think they are talking about.[18]

Even though the worlds of new media and the emergence of convergence culture do not look alike everywhere, it is undeniable that broadly speaking, the digital has radically transformed private lives and public culture in India virtually beyond recognition over the last two decades or so.[19] So pervasive are these shifts that the boundaries between lived worlds, bodies, and technology are no longer easily discernible.[20]

The millennial supernatural is, likewise, constitutively informed by digital media cultures; as Shaunak Sen pithily puts it, "[t]he contemporary digital moment has produced a new order of the uncanny."[21] Bollywood's engagement with the millennial moment necessitates this to some extent, but the cinema of the supernatural is not necessarily predictable in formal or ideological terms, as I hope to demonstrate in this chapter. In the era of new media and media convergence, as mentioned above, a new kind of reflexivity and self-consciousness governs Bollywood's output, and here, too, it remains in conversation with global cinemas, many of which have taken similar turns in recent years. Undoubtedly, the cinema's status as a "dying" or "superseded" technology in the digital era has something to do with this obsessive mirror-gazing, but in the case of Bombay film, this reflexivity has taken specific forms in the arena of the supernatural. In the age of digital media and media convergence, the planetary paranormal is a specific set of preoccupations and novelties; what we have is a relentlessly reflexive textual domain—not only gazing upon itself, but also compulsively channeling the global in recognizable ways—of the kind that *Zibahkhana* so adroitly demonstrates, in a different context. This is a profoundly global cinema for two primary reasons: for the first time, Bollywood is paying licensing fees for remakes instead of blithely plagiarizing global hits, and also because these films participate quite confidently, and often playfully, in what we might call an international idiom of horror and the supernatural. The planetary paranormal becomes possible in this moment of synergy: a new industrial ecology that includes Hollywood players alongside local entities, a new audience with a larger disposable income, and above all, a public domain that is mediatized and connected to the world's "virtual media culture" in a manner that is unprecedented. Bollywood is imagining the post-national and the planetary in multiple genres, and I contend that the paranormal offers unique gestational spaces for the emergence of a new grammar and idiom. To reiterate, the planetary paranormal, as I conceptualize it here, is a set of innovations and preoccupations that straddle industrial imperatives, cultural shifts, and narrative and generic strategies. In a fundamental sense, this is Bollywood internalizing the gaze of a planetary other; its response is not singular or uniform, but more than a little anxiety seems to propel its unflagging zeal for this constant reinvention of itself.

The planetary paranormal is largely horror, although some aspects of the impetus are visible in fantasy/sci-fi/superhero films as well. In the new millennium, horror finds a digital habitat in at least two different registers. First, much of this cinema is enabled by satellite/cable television and the Internet—made for audiences that are wired into global genres and are thus familiar with the latest global media trends. It is worthwhile to note that the millennium witnessed, among other things, the coining of the term "Millennials" to refer to a whole generation of people born after development of the Internet and steeped in digital cultures and technologies. Among a few others, this urban, affluent, youth demographic has emerged as an important audience segment for Bollywood to address since at least the early 2000s. Moreover, one of the most important lessons that new media scholarship teaches us is that digital media enables new types of social subjectivities to emerge and congeal, because they "*are machines for generating affect* . . . they lie at the very heart of social, circulation and distribution. They generate subjectivity, and they play a crucial role in the valorization of capital."[22] Second, the planetary paranormal tirelessly draws on digital cultures and practices *as content*; computers, cell phones, touchscreen interfaces, and digital images—both high- and low-resolution—saturate these films and often provide the locus where horror gestates or resides.[23] Communication technologies that keep protagonists continuously connected often become conduits for the horrific in this new dispensation. The cybersubject is both the protagonist and the target consumer for this new type of horror cinema: rootless inhabitants of the Worldwide Web who find themselves imperiled by the very same technologies that foundationally constitute them as subjects.

The planetary paranormal is also distinctive in its inscription of temporality. Throughout this book, I have been tracing supernatural entities that are also figures of time—ghosts and monsters of the feudal, the female snake who remains aligned to the mythic, and so on. The past provided the critical coordinates for the supernatural to manifest and make meaning within the genres in question; stories that had been interrupted or left incomplete in the past had to be reckoned with and reconciled in the present. Only then could the present be properly expunged of the supernatural, and the future potentiated. For the first time in the new millennium, we have generic clusters that dovetail almost exclusively with the recent and the present—the genres I discuss here are haunted by figures who are aligned to the contemporary in a manner somewhat distinct from earlier formations. I argue that this obsession with the current, the new, and the concomitant sloughing off of history is an effect of digital media cultures that incessantly redraw and reorganize the map of the novel and the "cutting-edge." Being wired into and participating in a digitally configured "global now"[24] is a foundational aspect of this media imaginary. Not only is media convergence "new" in the sense that its advent is recent, but new media simultaneously claims for itself the role of designating and defining the novum, incessantly—a constant and uninterrupted reinvention of novelty is part and parcel of its ontology. The planetary paranormal profoundly resonates with the temporal aspects of contemporary global media cultures, proclaiming its rightful place in the market of international genres. The sudden appearance of the zombie in Bollywood is a perfect instantiation of this new regime of present-ness.

Information—the content of digital media—is also marked by a new kind of temporality: the instant transmission of data, such that the delay and time lag that so preoccupied scholars of modernity and globalization in other eras is replaced by immediacy.[25] In the digital media ecology with ever-increasing bandwidths, the zombie would have made its way to Indian media sooner or later; however, the swiftness with which the figure in its current avatar migrated to Hindi cinema runs counter to its typical shambling gait. Consider, for example, the circuitous, tangled paths through which the Gothic traveled to Indian cinema—from the Gothic novel to Hollywood cinema to Bombay film, as I elaborated in Chapter 1. In the new media ecology that the planetary paranormal inhabits, that convoluted journey simply becomes unnecessary: the zombie as a global entity is instantly recognizable and readily available for its Bollywood debut. The audience to whom such a figure would signify was similarly in place by 2013, the year in which two zombie films were produced in Bombay: *Rise of the Zombie* (Luke Kenny and Devaki Singh) and *Go Goa Gone* (Krishna D.K. and Raj Nidimoru). Of course two isolated films do not constitute a genre—or even a cycle—proper, but it is noteworthy that they drew on a series of texts and images that were considered "too niche" or risky for Bollywood prior to this particular moment. A third film, tentatively titled *Shaadi of the Dead* (*Wedding of the Dead*) (and later *Rock the Shaadi*) was conceptualized by Balaji Motion Pictures and iRock, but later abandoned. Interestingly, however, Siddharth Jain, the CEO of iRock, produced a graphic novel called *Bloodfest in Bollywood* in order to acquaint young audiences with the genre before the release of the film. In an interview, he elaborated on his efforts:

> *Bloodfest in Bollywood* will be out in October. The idea is to introduce zombies to the young audiences in the most natural way so that when they come and watch our film next summer, they readily recognise the genre. Zombies were first introduced to the world through comics so a graphic novel is, perhaps, the most logical choice. The medium is very youth centric and has a visual appeal that whets the appetite for an Indian zombie film.[26]

Clearly, a novel marketing scheme was necessary to introduce the zombie as a figure to audiences new to it, despite the fact that Jain seemed fairly confident of the genre's youth appeal.

Alongside the reconstituted (glittering, teenage angst-ridden, post-*Twilight*) vampire, the zombie is one of the most iconic pop-culture figures from the new millennium. Intractably undead, zombies lurch through ubiquitous postapocalyptic scenarios, thoughtlessly feeding on the living in multiple media platforms, including graphic novels, film, television, and video games.[27] The Centers for Disease Control in Atlanta, Georgia, recently updated its website to include the following tongue-in-cheek announcement: "If zombies did start roaming the streets, CDC would conduct an investigation much like any other disease outbreak. CDC would provide technical assistance to cities, states, or international partners dealing with a zombie infestation . . . CDC and other federal agencies would send medical teams and first responders to help those in affected areas."[28] Needless to say, zombies have also infiltrated the academy, as the *New York Times* has recently—and rather sensationally—reported.[29] Zombies are us, and we under late capitalism are increasingly more akin to them, as a number of scholars have observed.[30]

The primary reason for the zombie's long and successful career in popular culture, as well as its current visibility, is its ability to allegorize a seemingly endless series of social and political anxieties and upheavals. From slavery, colonialism, and racial tensions, to capitalist consumerism and the monstrosities engendered by market forces,[31] to post 9/11 fears of global warfare, and most recently as the poster child for a liberatory posthumanism,[32] the zombie can embody and incorporate a vast array of sociocultural discourses.[33] Neither completely dead nor wholly alive, the zombie also provokes questions about ontology, consciousness, and subjectivity.[34] In this sense, the zombie is the most burdened metaphor of our times; and perhaps the figure's expressive fecundity also accounts for its motility across global pop cultures.

The prodigious proliferation of the zombie figure in recent years also makes it, unmistakably, a millennial entity, a fact that sits uneasily alongside the speed and pace of the digital moment. Peter Dendle suggests that the zombie's untimely slowness reinforces its status as a "creature of paradox":

> Barely capable of negotiating a set of stairs, the shambling, slow revenant seems an unlikely iconic villain for the cusp of the third millennium. . . . In all its artistic manifestations—film, literature, video games, graphic novels, etc.—the zombie has surfaced in the late twentieth and early twenty-first century as one of the preeminent monsters of the current generation. The zombie holds evident appeal to the technologically savvy, fast-paced generation of young people in the 1990s and 2000s, and through the creature's diverse

iterations and adaptations, the zombie can serve as a mirror to some of this generation's values and notions of identity.[35]

The zombie's ability to function as a tabula rasa of sorts, on which myriad contemporary fantasies and apprehensions can be projected, as well as its status as a specifically millennial monster, makes its recent Bollywood debut especially critical for this inquiry. What does the zombie mean in/to Hindi film? How does it transform the formation's construction of the supernatural in the new millennium? What might the zombie film tell us about Bollywood's industrial compulsions? What might it articulate about troubled times in South Asia? These are some of the questions that inform my analyses below. The zombie is not necessarily a "supernatural" entity in all its avatars; although it is undoubtedly so in its Haitian, voodoo-inspired iterations, more recent zombies in global media have a more rational ontology—often brought about by deadly viruses and contagions that affect and afflict living populations in unpredictable ways.[36] In Bollywood, too, the figure of the zombie is shown to have somewhat scientific, if "unnatural" beginnings, but it is the figure's insistent presentation as a novelty and, indeed, the irrelevance of the question of origins that makes it an exemplar of the planetary paranormal.

Despite obvious differences—for example, a "serious" film versus a comedy—*Rise of the Zombie* (hereafter *ROTZ*) and *Go Goa Gone* (hereafter *GGG*) have more in common than simply zombies. Both films are titled in English, and, given their target audience—the affluent urban youth—this is hardly surprising.[37] But perhaps most tellingly, both films *labor* to situate the zombie in Hindi cinema in significant ways; each film has to clear some generic and formal ground so that the zombie can, in fact, inhabit this unfamiliar terrain.[38] As discussed above, the planetary paranormal is considerably invested in aligning itself formally and stylistically with global genres; the millennial Bollywood zombie film congeals as a particularly telling instantiation of this imperative. Both *ROTZ* and *GGG*, as I show below, are self-consciously more "global" and less *filmi* in their narrative and stylistic idioms. Indeed, it appears that the Hindi film itself has to undergo a process of formal disassembly in order to make room for the zombie—the creature, it appears, cannot simply slouch into Bollywood with any degree of ease.

Both films eschew the song sequence in favor of "sound tracks": songs play over narratively significant images, but characters do not sing or lip-synch to them. The sonic scape of *ROTZ* is heavily influenced by Western rock, punk, and metal, and several of its songs (notably, "Tripwire," "Free Your Soul," and "All Alone") are sung in English; this reliance on recognizably Western musical styles is perhaps also a consequence of Kenny's own career as a musician and television video jockey.[39] Fittingly, *ROTZ* features no music director in its credits; the score is credited to Ray N. Brotherhood, with specific credits to composers and singers who vary by song, including Kenny himself. All of this makes the musical texture of *ROTZ* somewhat different from most Bollywood films.[40] Additionally, the songs are "picturized" in unusual ways as well, often functioning as dissonant counterpoint to images.

However, even more unusual are the film's storytelling techniques, which more accurately simulate the zombie's aimless, lurching gait. A brief plot summary will clarify. *ROTZ* tells the story of Neil Parker (Kenny), a wildlife photographer who travels to a forest to escape an unhappy breakup with his girlfriend, Vinny (Kirti Kulhari). Following a couple of blissful days of communing with nature, he is bitten by a loud, buzzing insect that turns him into a zombie. He begins by eating insects, birds, and small animals, but soon graduates to devouring a series of unsuspecting humans who encounter him. His estranged father, Dr. Dave Parker (Benjamin Gilani), his friend Anish (Ashwin Mushran), and Vinny search for him in vain, while the body count steadily rises. The film closes—somewhat inexplicably—by presenting us with a zombie hoard and the promise of a sequel. This is not an especially abbreviated plot summary, as not much else transpires in the almost ninety-minute screen-duration of *ROTZ*. The traditional Hindi film has often been discussed, and sometimes criticized, for its long-winded, crowded, meandering, and allusive plot lines, or in terms of the figurative, epic energies therein. In *ROTZ*, we can discern a dismantling of the breadth and scale of that entire formal system; it is as though the popular film form has finally lost its tenacious foothold in the present dispensation. *ROTZ*'s formal shrinkage is echoed by the sparseness of characters—we are almost constantly with the solitary Neil in the wilderness; the rest of the characters appear fleetingly to buttress his ordeal. Vinny functions as the perfunctory "love interest" who provides the narrative fulcrum for Neil's initial escape into the wild, but Thapa (Prem Thapa) and the rest of the characters remain shadowy props who appear only so that, as a zombie, Neil can eventually access a range of human bodies to attack and consume. It is also important to note that beyond his self-absorption and his interest in wildlife photography, Neil lacks a biography as much as anyone else; the informational vacuum extends to the protagonist as well. The only aspect of his past that is revealed late in the film is his dysfunctional relationship with his father, a fact that is stated ruefully, but it is of little narrative consequence. In a bid to participate in the multiplex film's discourse of "realism," not only is Neil shorn of the iconic or figurative resonances that the Hindi film traditionally bestows on important characters, he fails to crystallize as a hero—positive or otherwise—altogether.

At this juncture, it is instructive to note that in the most celebrated zombie films, especially George Romero's seminal works, including *Night of the Living Dead* (1968) and *Dawn of the Dead* (1978), a certain incorporation of detail and texture—a certain formulation of realism, particularly in the delineation of space—is of considerable significance. Stephen Harper, for example, draws on Tzvetan Todorov's work to elucidate the kind of realisms that a genre like the zombie film can incorporate:

> The "realism" of *Night of the Living Dead* seems to confound other critical distinctions. In his famous book *The Fantastic: A Structural Approach to a Literary Concept* (1975), Tzvetan Todorov distinguished between two types of verisimilitude: *cultural* verisimilitude and *generic* verisimilitude. The first type refers to texts that aim to be "true to life," like police drama; the second refers to texts in which the narrative details are true to the conventions of the genre. Horror texts tend, of course, to fall into the latter category. *Night of the Living Dead* obviously has a generic verisimilitude—while it observes the conventions of the horror genre, it does not, in a literal sense, correspond to any known reality. Yet the film calls into question Todorov's distinction, since it seems entirely feasible that a world in which zombies *did* exist *would be like the one presented*, giving the film—fantastic as it is—a sense of being "true to life." The plausibility of the zombie outbreak is reinforced by several textual qualities. For example, television news in 1968 appeared in black and white, which would have given *Night of the Living Dead* a documentary-like feel to the film's original audiences, at least. This sense of *verité* is also emphasised in the series of gory still photographs that accompany the film's closing credits and which recall the photojournalism of the Vietnam war. In other words, the film's gritty, "realistic" mode of address confers upon the film a "cultural verisimilitude": the audience is asked to believe that the horrific events depicted *could be happening now.*[41]

I argue that *ROTZ* is unable to mobilize either of these two forms of realism. The notion of "cultural verisimilitude" is unavailable to it because the film makes no effort to situate the zombie within the Indian context in any meaningful way. Although it tries to maintain strict generic verisimilitude, its understanding of genre is so far removed from the formal domain of Hindi cinema that this labor to potentiate and engender a new genre flounders in an unfamiliar terrain. Under any other circumstance, the question of realism—however conceptualized—would be wholly irrelevant vis-à-vis Hindi commercial film; as I have suggested in previous chapters, the ease with which genres of the supernatural have inhabited the *masala* form has everything to do with the latter's constitutive indifference to questions of realism. However, the planetary imperative necessitates a certain embrace of more legible formal characteristics, a heightened sense of the real being the most obvious aspect of that transaction. In other words, by the logic of the multiplex and new Bollywood, realism is—or should be—the payoff in the impetus for making Hindi film more "international." Indeed, packaging generic material in putative mantles of "realism" is a defining characteristic of the larger multiplex phenomenon.

However, for the reasons outlined above, *ROTZ* struggles to make meaning in this sense. The film is, additionally, remarkably spartan in its elaboration of physical spaces. Both interiors and exteriors remain quite imprecise in this film. Neil's apartment and the nightclub he visits before departing for the hills are decidedly generic, and although there is an abundance of low-key, potentially sinister images of nature and wilderness—especially as Neil unsuspectingly soaks in the beauty around him—these, too, remain curiously devoid of character, texture, and density. This is not to suggest, of course, that the popular Hindi film has historically expended much energy in clearly delineating space/place, unless it is of narrative significance. However, even "Bambai" in the old-style Hindi film had to be designated by the insertion of a couple of stock shots of the Gateway of India or of Marine Drive. For a decidedly multiplex film such as *ROTZ*, clear coordinates of space and time ought to be de rigueur in contemporary Bollywood.[42] The film, however, situates Neil in a series of "no-wheres"—the "hills" that he travels to remain nameless, the hamlet that abuts it, which Neil visits on several occasions to make phone calls and procure supplies, is equally blandly called "*shehar*" (city).[43] In other words, although Neil's attempt to escape the strife of his city life by traveling into the natural world is an important causal pivot for the film, neither the space he is escaping nor his solitary campsite quite manifests as a palpable space.[44]

The anonymous sylvan campsite visually dominates the film—much of the action happens in this location, and the bulk of the film's images focus on Neil's campsite and the surrounding forest. And this brings me to yet another curious characteristic of *ROTZ*: its unmistakable slowness and its insistent reliance on repetition, aspects that did not go unnoticed by critics and reviewers, who for the most part, remained unimpressed.[45] As mentioned above, once Neil is bitten by the insect and his transformation into a zombie begins, not much else happens in terms of plot. Images alternate

FIGURE 5.1. *Neil and the wilderness in* Rise of the Zombie.

between shots of wilderness and subjective shots of Neil's faltering memory and confusion about what is happening to him. The last hour of the film includes sequences in which Neil frets about his festering wound as it progressively worsens, growls and lurches around, feeds on creatures, has recurrent flashbacks to his happier days with Vinny (which are signaled through distortions in image and sound), and tries to reach her unsuccessfully on the phone. As his zombie-self strengthens, his pallor and distress are visible, but the film prefers to chart this progressive degeneration through a deliberate system of repetition, with very little variation beyond the use of prosthetic makeup, which becomes increasingly more grotesque. Subjective narration is an important device in this regard, as handheld POVs convey Neil's unsteady, stumbling gait; but beyond his anguish over Vinny and his ghastly appetite for flesh, we come no closer to Neil than we were at the beginning of *ROTZ*.

Recall that earlier templates of the supernatural film were often structured around "performance" sequences—song and dance, monster attacks, or rapes—that functioned as punctuating instances where the supernatural would manifest, unfold, and crystalize, usually along gendered axes. These moments were set pieces, carefully and often spectacularly set aside from the strictly narrative segments. By unmooring itself almost entirely from the old *masala* format, *ROTZ* struggles to meaningfully create such interludes; Neil's monstrous, murderous zombie-self is intercut with increasingly frantic efforts to locate him by his loved ones in Bombay, and this is the closest the film comes in affectively presenting his loss and tragedy. Despite the obligatory shots of Neil gnawing on bloody flesh, dismembered body parts and, on one occasion, ingesting a human eyeball with relish, *ROTZ* remains a remarkably wan and *anemic* film. It is worthwhile to recall that the most compelling zombie films present the destruction and dismemberment of the human body in such a way that it impacts the spectator's body viscerally, in the "heightened tingling of the flesh, with an odd mixture of laughter, anxiety, and disgust."[46] *ROTZ* is unable to conjure up (or mimic) these immediate, violent, sensational affects in any way. The dearth of detail, texture, and variation—informational and stylistic—makes this an unusual Bollywood film indeed, even without zombies. The abrupt conclusion—we do not know what creates the zombie horde that Vinny's panicky voice-over reports, or how Anish and Dr. Parker have become zombie slayers—only increases audience confusion about what the film is *about*, if anything. Re-*locating* the zombie in Bollywood is, evidently, no easy task. Unsurprisingly, the promised sequel was never made.

Go Goa Gone—Bollywood's second zombie film so far—seems decidedly lush and textured in comparison with the skeletal ethos of *ROTZ*, because it is peopled by more characters and features whole hordes of rampaging zombies, instead of a single man's solitary zombification. Before discussing the film in detail, however, it is important to pause and consider the status of a "zom com" in a film culture that is barely familiar with the zombie as a figure. What makes this audacious step—of presenting the zombie in a ludic mode—possible? How can a revisionist formation appear in a context that is only being introduced to a cinematic genre, in this case the zombie film?[47] *GGG* is, in fact, a precise instantiation of the spatial and temporal short circuits that characterize the planetary paranormal, and its novelties do not end here. The generic contortions it attempts are nothing short of astonishing: *GGG* is not content to be simply a zombie film or even a zombie comedy. As an ironic, highly reflexive tribute to globally popular generic cocktails, it is a zombie film married to a "stoner" or "slacker" comedy, reminiscent of *Shaun of the Dead* (Edgar Wright, 2004) and *Zombieland* (Ruben Fleischer, 2009), both of which were made in film cultures (the United Kingdom and the United States, respectively) where the zombie is not only a familiar entity but has reached a point of saturation, and therefore demands reformulation.

FIGURE 5.2. *Zombie-Neil in* ROTZ.

GGG, however, is a confident product that displays no anxiety about skipping these stages of development, consolidation, and restructuring of generic forms. As the segregation of audiences underway since the advent of multiplex theaters continues unabated, a film such as *GGG* can, in effect, conjure up its own niche, elite-youth addressee. The filmmakers and producers of *GGG* insisted at promotional events that knowledge of the zombie as a figure would be unnecessary for appreciating the film.[48] Indeed, the film adopts a pedagogical tone in re-presenting the zombie: it explains the particulars and characteristics of the unfamiliar threat progressively throughout the film, and hence the line "What do we know, what have we learned?" is mouthed by several characters at various points, in signposting new knowledge and forms of awareness. However, I would contend that in its very tone and texture—in the undeniable conceit of its generic conception, to begin with—*GGG* demands (and takes for granted) a kind of audience competence that both exposes its own internal assumptions about current Bollywood viewership and serves to illuminate local contortions of global genres in particularly suggestive ways.

GGG tells the story of three friends, Hardik (Kunal Khemu), Luv (Vir Das), and Bunny (Anand Tiwari), who travel to the "party capital" of Goa and inadvertently find themselves in the middle of a zombie outbreak. Even before the film actually begins, one is struck by its particular brand of hipness and humor. Let me explain. The film is (in part) a stoner comedy, and the two main potheads—Hardik and Luv—spend considerable amounts of time smoking marijuana, seeking it, or talking about it. The song "Babaji Ki Booty" ("Babaji's Weed") is an ode to recreational pot-smoking and is shot in an appropriately "trippy" way. All of that makes the statutory warnings about the dangers of smoking—increasingly more stridently placed in Hindi films under new guidelines from the censor board—apposite for the film in question. As the only star in the film, Saif Ali Khan (who plays Boris) performs in a short "disclaimer" video and condemns smoking as a "terrible thing to do." Immediately following this and the opening credits, the following appears on the black screen:

> Smoking is injurious to Health
> So is Alcohol
> And Drugs
> And Guns
> And a lot of other shit
> So . . . go easy

If the irony of this disclaimer is not immediately apparent to the viewer, the very first sequence of the film features Hardik and Luv smoking pot as they blearily stare at a television screen, surrounded by the paraphernalia of seasoned potheads. These images call into question the sincerity of the anti-smoking disclaimers and the "public service" video that Khan stars in, materials that attempt to frame the film in a certain way. Through humorous counterpoint, this opening sequence exposes the uselessness of statutory warnings, inverting the film's own compliance with a repressive censoring/censuring state mandate.

This is merely one example of a film that is unrelentingly clever and jejune, sophomoric and hip throughout. From the profanity-laced Hinglish dialogue peppered with bon mots and text-message-inspired acronyms such as FYI and BTW ("for your information and "by the way," respectively), to the comic-book-inspired titles and blood that are super-

FIGURE 5.3. *Luv and Hardik smoking pot in* Go Goa Gone.

imposed on images, everything about *GGG* attempts to speak to a specific class-segment of the urban youth audience. Flighty and irreverent, it remains as unmoored and dis-located as *ROTZ*. Mauritius masquerades as Goa in much of the film, as the protagonists head to an island off the coast for a "very underground" rave party.[49] It is also worthwhile to remain attentive to the mainstream perception of Goa as one of the most popular tourist destinations for specifically "foreign" travelers; the meanings that gather around Goa in popular discourse are heavily mobilized by *GGG*. The sound track of the film is rave-music-inspired, especially the song "Slowly, Slowly," which also cheekily refers to the indolent gait of the (imminent) zombies. The lyrics of this song,[50] coupled with the delirium invoked by the combination of young, largely white, beach bodies gyrating to loud music, strobe lights, and the general air of abandon, characterizes best *GGG*'s social referents and political affiliations. The zombie-producing "D2RF drug" in the form of capsules is passed around and consumed with frenzied enthusiasm by the party attendees. Hardik and Luv do not partake, favoring instead the promise of sex on the moonlit beach. Bunny—the serious and innocent one in the group—seems largely oblivious to the sensory excesses that surround him.

Like *ROTZ*, *GGG* gets more repetitive once the zombie hordes arrive, as the trio, accompanied by the gutsy woman Luna (Puja Gupta), struggles to survive successive attacks by feral packs of ravenous monsters. Boris, the macho zombie-killer, with bleached-blond hair and a fake Russian accent, only serves to loosen the film's already tentative grip on anything remotely recognizable;[51] Todorov's "cultural verisimilitude" has slipped away entirely by this point. The group drives, shoots zombies in stylish slow-motion, and continues with comic capers. Here, too, the zombie attacks function in lieu of the song sequence: spectacular interruptions where blood, brains, pierced eyeballs (no doubt an homage to Italian master Lucio Fulci's zombie films, as well as Quentin Tarantino's action sequences) and catastrophically transformed human bodies provide set pieces. As Harper points out, that any zombie film destabilizes questions of verisimilitude goes without saying; the point here is that these young people and the filmic universe they inhabit seem unreal, belabored, and contrived, even without the zombies; the filmic world is potentiated but fails to be anchored to anything, generically and in terms of the social. Indeed, the social—as a referential domain—disappears altogether.

As suggested above, the planetary paranormal in Bollywood operates on the erasure of difference between formations—potentiating a seamless group of winsomely packaged and globally legible products is its basic modality. *GGG* is interesting in that it performs the disassembly of the

FIGURE 5.4. *Zombie attack and the survivors in* Go Goa Gone.

Hindi film not only by rejecting the basics of that form, but also via parody. Beyond the wisecracking dialogue—some of which is reproduced in the epigraph to this chapter—in one particularly comic sequence, Hardik is chased by zombie-Arianna, his former lover, in deliberate, excruciating slow motion, as generic "romantic" music plays in the background. This moment, narratively somewhat redundant, literalizes the traditional Hindi film's most cherished syntax of romantic love: the fabled dancing around trees to music. *GGG*'s own philosophy of love is far removed, consisting of casual breakups, casual sex on the beach, and Hardik and Luv's "moments" with Luna, which do not amount to much. This sequence—and others like it that are strewn throughout *GGG*—brings into sharp focus the fact that if the film is about anything beyond the novelty of zombies, it is about the dismantling and increasing obsolescence of the Hindi film as we know it.

Again, the zombie's continuing popularity is at least partially dependent on its ability to refract deeply felt social and political schisms and anxieties; the figure has been successfully mobilized in given contexts to articulate and amplify larger discourses that remain intrinsic to those contexts. In other words, though undoubtedly global, the zombie requires deep roots in order to convey the political. Its sojourn in Bollywood, on the contrary, has been both brief and abortive—neither *ROTZ* nor *GGG* were commercially successful, despite the massive promotional efforts that accompanied their releases.[52] It is somewhat premature to speculate about the zombie's status in current Bollywood because it can certainly return at a future date in different guises than the ones discussed here. And though it is beyond the purview of this inquiry to fully comment on the reasons for the failure of the zombie experiment in Bollywood, some preliminary observations are in order.

First, the planetary paranormal—a specific conceptualization of the supernatural in the current moment that is completely aligned to the global—has been embraced by the Hindi film industry in an unprecedented way. Following the success of other "off-beat" genres in multiplexes, major studios and production houses are now willing to take chances with such global genres as zombie films, as long as budgets remain relatively modest. Second, the failure of the zombie experiment is not an indication of the fact that Indian audiences are unwilling to watch horror of a certain kind—in fact, the exuberant and enthusiastic response to the trailer of *GGG* online on social media platforms and YouTube belies such an assumption. Shows such as *The Walking Dead* are shown on premier digital television channels, and presumably have garnered a specific audience.[53] Siddharth Jain, whose zombie film did not see the light of day, was quite categorical about this point: "Indian audiences want to see an Indian vampire film or an Indian zombie film and they're not just ready, but demanding it. Look at the huge success of zombie video games and TV shows in the country."[54] The commercial fate of the films above does not quite support this claim. However, I would argue that unlike, for example, the Ramsay brothers' import of the witch or vampire, the zombie got a raw deal in Bollywood.

It is possible to read both *ROTZ* and *GGG* as articulating some kind of disenchantment with the current post-capitalist, commodity-saturated, digital moment. But these would have to be very labored readings indeed. *ROTZ* simply does not provide enough information about Neil's anomie or social vectors for the spectator to have a sense of him as a character; his transformation remains purely a spectacle of prosthetic makeup. In the last few minutes of *GGG*, as the group is finally escaping the infested island, Luna asks for one final time the question that has been repeated as a litany of sorts throughout the film, "What do we know, what have we learned?" The answers are telling: Bunny: "Drugs can f--- you up." Luv: "They can turn you into a zombie, man." Hardik: "Women should always be valued; who knows, one might bite you some day!" Boris: "Karma is bitch, my friends." In other words, *GGG* can finally only congeal as a vacuous cautionary tale about the ill-effects of recreational drugs and youthful promiscuity.

The post-capitalist, posthuman energies that the zombie so effortlessly renders corporeal in other contexts cannot be reproduced here because the films fail—or refuse—to ground the monster in text or history of any kind. The zombie lacks any social coordinates, and shorn of all political energy or intensity, sluggishly shuffles through a hastily generated generic landscape that seems cosmetic at best—as foreign and as moribund as itself. The mythic scaffolding of Hindi popular cinema—that could harness even such an outlandish Dracula figure as Nevla in *Bandh Darwaza*—cannot anchor or situate the zombie in any tangible sense. Along with formal richness and texture, the planetary paranormal, in this instance, eschews the real altogether.

DESIRE AND THE DIGITAL: GHOSTS IN/OF MACHINES

The reader will note that so far, the problematic of gender has all but disappeared from this chapter. Vectors of identity—coordinates of social worlds and belonging—are simply irrelevant to the intractably derivative ontology of the Hindi zombie film. Gender as a particularly potent and affectively charged "scene" for the representation of the supernatural is, however, alive and well in other generic mutations—for example, the globally popular found-footage film, which has also found its way into Bollywood in recent years. In stark contrast to the flightiness of the zombie film, found-footage horror's basic task is to conjure up an immersive world of immediacy and recognition—these are, after all, faux documentaries in a certain sense. The industrial/generic impetus that I have been calling the planetary paranormal embodies a complex series of formal commitments and global aspirations; it does not necessarily imply political vacuity in the manner of the Bollywood zombie film. Neither does it *necessarily* imply a rejection of all forms of realism; after all, the multiplex does exert certain formal pressures in this regard. In fact, one of the most interesting aspects of the planetary paranormal is that it is currently emergent, and therefore unpredictable to a certain degree. Its modalities and guises—both formal and industrial—remain largely fluid and undecided at this point. My intention here is to trace some of its dominant tendencies, even as they mutate and transform. In its determinedly "post-national" found-footage guise, for example, it inscribes an array of social discourses and "real worlds" that attest to the political potentialities inherent in the form.

The observational documentary or verité style that forms the basis for the found-footage aesthetic has a long history in the cinema. In the horror genre, it can be traced back to at least Michael Powell's *Peeping Tom* (1960) and the notorious *Cannibal Holocaust* (1980).[55] Following the sensational success of *The Blair Witch Project* (1999), the found-footage horror film came into its own in Hollywood with the *Paranormal Activity* (2007–2014) films and *Cloverfield* (2008); the Spanish-language *[REC]* (2007) demonstrated that the aesthetics, syntax, and conventions of found footage could be deployed in fairly diverse cultural contexts as well.[56] In Bollywood, Balaji Motion Pictures first explored the found-footage format with Dibakar Banerjee's *LSD: Love, Sex Aur Dhokha* (*Love, Sex and Betrayal*, 2010), and presumably, the success of this small-budget film prompted the studio to experiment with found footage again a year later. Because horror is the generic habitat within which the found-footage idiom has flourished in recent years, Balaji produced *Ragini MMS* in 2011, a film that was marketed on its racy combination of sex and horror. Despite the promotional gimmicks that accompanied the film's release, *Ragini MMS* is not about sex, or more accurately, not *only* about sex. I would argue that the film's efficacy is critically dependent on its canny mobilization of the found-footage aesthetic, as well as its firm grounding in India's digital dispensation.

Ragini MMS is about a young couple, Ragini (Kainaz Motiwala) and Uday (Rajkumar Rao), who travel to a desolate bungalow outside Bombay for an intimate weekend. Unbeknownst to Ragini, the entire house is booby-trapped with hidden cameras so that irrespective of room or location, their sexual encounters will be digitally recorded to create an MMS video.[57] Uday has promised this video to a shadowy character named Guruji in exchange for a break in the movies. Once they arrive at the bungalow, however, their steamy tryst is interrupted by a malefic female spirit who kills Uday, and though Ragini escapes with her life, the traumatic experience propels her into a mental asylum. The police abruptly stop investigating the case. The MMS, we are told, via a series of somber concluding title cards, began circulating months after this incident.

Opening and closing titles are not the film's only claim to presenting "real" events, of course. In mobilizing the found-footage aesthetic, *Ragini MMS* uses primarily two different sources for the image: Uday's digital, handheld video camera, and the multiple "camera feeds" that remain stationary in the manner of CCTV cameras while surveilling the entire haunted dwelling; there is also a third "neutral" camera source, but the film uses it sparingly, as this "view" interrupts its status as a "meta-MMS." Like *The Blair Witch Project*, which, "emblematically released just as the new millennium was approaching, pointed the way for the new-media marketing of films today,"[58] Balaji promoted *Ragini MMS* via strategies unusual for the time. The film's alleged status as an extended MMS clip was its first and most audacious claim. The MMS is the most single-mindedly sexual form of digital media that circulates via cellular phones in India. Since 2004, dozens of "MMS scandals" have come to achieve a specific kind of prurient popularity in the public imagination. Shaunak Sen recounts the stories of the most infamous MMS scandals:

> The first "MMS scandal" (now almost a codified generic description for pornographic videos involving heterosexual couples in sexual positions shot on cellphones) to get widely discussed in popular media was the infamous "DPS MMS scandal" in 2004. The video involving two 17-year-old students from the posh Delhi Public School R. K. Puram became something of a media sensation, when someone uploaded it for public auction on the online auction/shopping siteBaazee.com. This spiraled into a full blown media event as the then CEO of the online auction company was booked under the obscenities section of the IT Act (2000), and the Delhi court stipulated that anyone found possessing the clip could be imprisoned for six months and/or charged a fine up to 10,000 rupees. The clip spread like a contagion across cities, spawning a number of similar MMS related "scandals" soon after. Following these were other prominent "cases" that caught the media eye, like the Mona Chopra MMS in 2006, the "Sahranpur MMS" in 2009, the JNU "sex scandal" in 2011 and a string of celebrity MMS's—the Shahid Kapoor–Kareena Kapoor "kiss" clip in 2004, the Riya Sen–Ashmit Patel sex video in 2005, the Soha Ali Khan "beauty saloon" [*sic*] clip, the '*baba-MMS*' involving Godman Nithyananda with Tamil actresses Ranjitha and Yuvarani, the Sania Mirza "shower footage'" MMS and so on. These MMS clips create their own circulation economies, proliferating across cellphones via Bluetooth in school canteens, tuition centers, playgrounds, and boy's hostels; or a plurality of video portals, social media pages, porn websites, dedicated chat rooms and forums (to the point that most Indian porn sites now have a separate page banner heading called "MMS").[59]

As Sen points out in his analysis of *Ragini MMS*, the film rather shrewdly inserted itself into a public domain already enmeshed with the voyeurism and prurience that surrounds the very idea of a new, illicit MMS. By placing signs proclaiming "Have you seen Ragini's MMS?" and "Ragini sat here once," on suburban auto-rickshaws in Bombay, the marketing team clearly sought to capitalize on the real bodies that become the subjects of digital media in the viral and spectral pathways of the digital. In other words, an important component of Balaji's marketing strategy was—however nebulously—to tether the fictional story of the film to "real" women whose often-unauthorized images circulate in this manner.[60]

But the intrigues that gathered around the film even before its release do not end here. A week or two before the release of the film, Ekta Kapoor announced that *Ragini MMS* was largely based on the real-life experiences of a young woman from Delhi. Deepika, who was soon "unveiled," in a manner of speaking, had gone out with her boyfriend and experienced a series of paranormal events; *Ragini MMS* was, at least to an extent, her story.[61] In an interview before the release of the film, Kapoor confidently declared,

> It was completely done by the producers and they had met this girl and given us the story. We definitely had to make sure the movie is done like American movies are done. There was no footage that we could get but we worked on other things. I can't reveal where the real story happened though I have taken the permission from the girl but how much of her life I can reveal in public, or talk about in an interview is not yet decided.[62]

What exactly transpired following this collaborative moment is somewhat unclear, but thereafter, Deepika approached the media herself, claiming that Kapoor has misled her and was unwilling to show her the finished film. She also claimed that she was considering legal action against Balaji.[63] Although some journalists sympathized with the young woman's plight, others dismissed it as a publicity stunt contrived by the marketing department at Balaji in order to heighten the already considerable "buzz" that surrounded *Ragini MMS*. The controversy apparently lost steam after the film's release, and I have not been able to find evidence of any lawsuit against the production house, either. In any event, the veracity of the allegations and counter-allegations that provided considerable fodder to the tabloids is less important than the effect it produces. In the case of *Ragini MMS*, the Deepika episode added yet another layer of "realism" to the fictional film. Although the producers did not claim that the film was nonfiction, these other stories—of recent MMS scandals, of Deepika's largely unspecified "experience"—overlaid and provided a certain "thickness" to the film in question.

Beyond these extra-diegetic resonances, the sharply etched characters and the naturalism of performances bolster the documentary feel of *Ragini MMS*. Rajkumar Rao's Uday is particularly effective as a "violently misogynistic and penetrative figure,"[64] the gaping chasms of class, social capital, and desire for upward mobility writ large on his body and disposition. Uday's vernacularized, profanity-laced speech and aggression toward Ragini and her snobbish, English-speaking friends is as much a product of his social un-belonging and desperation, as of an excessive, malignantly configured masculinity. Motiwala as the typical "South Bombay" girl—the film's titular imperiled ingenue—for her part demonstrates remarkable grit and strength as the horror of the situation dawns on her. Ragini's horror is of course doubled: not only does she have to reckon with her attempted prostitution by a trusted partner, she simultaneously has to battle the enraged supernatural entity that eventually murders him. The fact that she is handcuffed to a bed through most of her protracted ordeal only increases the spectator's empathic terror. But beyond these credible and textured performances by the young actors, what cements *Ragini MMS*'s status as an exemplary found-footage horror film is the aesthetic quality of its images and the domain of visuality that it elaborates.

Despite the immateriality implied by the dots and pixels of the digital image, I would contend that *Ragini MMS* paradoxically renders the abortive erotic encounter between Ragini and Uday in noticeably corporeal ways. The cornerstone of the found-footage genre is, of course, the ontology of the digital image itself, the "fly on the wall" eye of the camera. The "verité" credentials of observational documentaries that the found-footage horror film seeks to reclaim is dependent on a certain performance of digital technology, critical to which is a display of amateurishness. This is precisely the kind of technique that Steven Shaviro has described as cinema's "performative and instrumental self-reflexivity: the equipment with which the film was shot . . . is itself present within the diegesis, and plays a major role in the events of the film."[65] As noted above, in *Ragini MMS*, there are primarily two different kinds of digital images—the static cameras that surveil the home, and Uday's digital camera that he constantly uses to record Ragini and also to shield himself. The portable video camera, writes Jane Roscoe, "can penetrate the most personal and intimate spaces." And it is this shaky, occasionally out-of-focus, handheld image that captures the intimacy between Uday and Ragini with immediacy and a certain kind of "authenticity," which is its raison d'être in this context; as Cecelia Sayad notes, "[a]bsorbing the camera into the narrative world, the found footage horror movie merges the film and the extrafilmic" in especially palpable ways.[66] This replication of amateur video recording, so beloved of reality television, for example, is "also central to creating this feeling for viewers that we are watching the story unfold in an unmediated way," despite the fact that we know that our voyeurism is dependent on the couple being within a hyper-mediated environment.[67] Prior to the scenes of intimacy, we have already been shown just how rigged with cameras the entire mansion is, and we are aware that not even the bathroom is a "safe space" in terms of surveillance and recording. However, the power of the "documentary look" is precisely that it is able to short circuit, or at least temporarily disable, the fictional scaffolding of the film. In other words, Uday's digital video camera—which performs multiple functions in the film—*appears* to render the film as a "real MMS" of two people having sex. This "authenticity" is bolstered by the editing—the film cuts back and forth between the static long-shots of the implied hidden cameras and extreme close-ups of bodies, skin, and frenzied caresses being filmed on Uday's camera that is awkwardly perched next to the couple on the bed. And this shifting between two different kinds of images actually serves to disrupt the voyeurism inherent in an MMS video, while paradoxically rendering it more real. The lighting remains steady and flat; the static camera angles down from top shots, while the portable video camera clumsily offers close-ups.

In *Ragini MMS*, the spectrality of the digital idiom is counterbalanced by the robust physicality of the couple's intimate exchange;[68] the solid corporeality of their erotic encounter—paradoxically—belies the mediated nature of the visual terrain engendered here. As Sen notes, the MMS cannot really materialize, because Uday and Ragini's lovemaking is constantly interrupted by sinister noises, untimely visits from friends, and finally the malevolent specter who remains (largely) invisible as she summarily dispatches with Uday. Despite the prurience of publicity gimmicks and promotional strategies, *Ragini MMS* is remarkable in its repeated rejection of the prurient, voyeuristic gaze of the camera. Even as the sexual escapades unfold before our eyes and the eyes of dozens of cameras qua split screens, the film remains an exercise in the frustration of the libidinal gaze—unlike Ragini herself, the film is a tease, a titillating promise of pornographic material that endlessly defers but never delivers the climactic money shot. On the contrary, the only sex act that we witness in its entirety—Pia (Janice) and Jigar's (Rajat Kaul) sex in the bedroom—abruptly ends in premature ejaculation, yet another instance of a failed promise. Visceral, recognizable, and immediate, the found-footage aesthetic in *Ragini MMS* simultaneously harnesses a certain kind of robust "realism" of context, while gesturing to

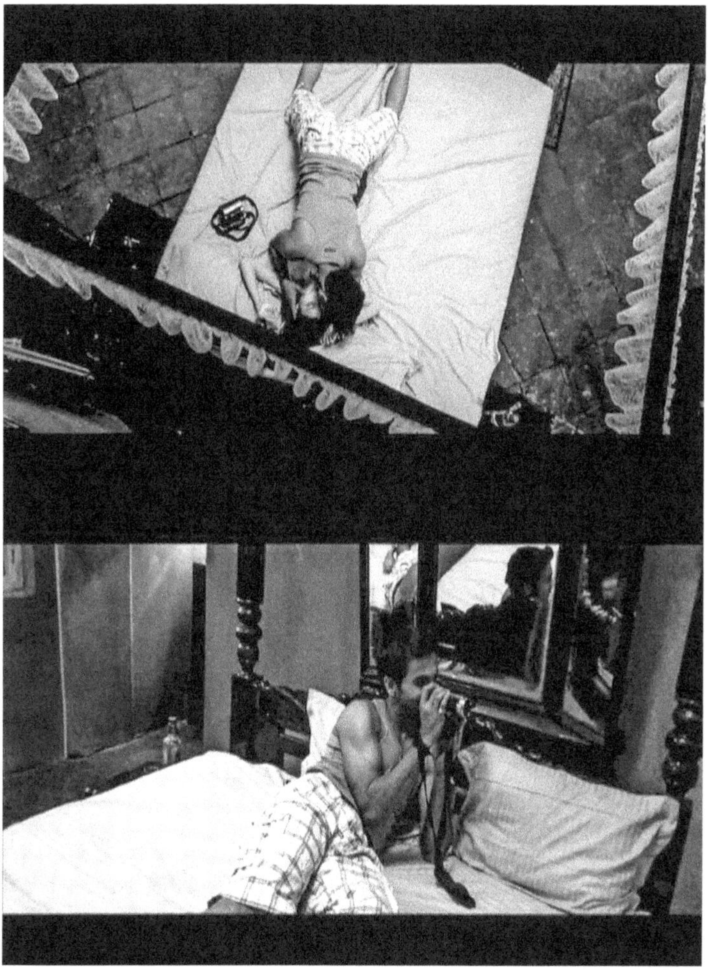

FIGURE 5.5. *Sex and voyeurism in* Ragini MMS.

an endlessly proliferating digital economy of images that operates through spectral conduits.[69] *Ragini MMS* is a compelling instantiation of India's digital zeitgeist—the imbrication of the social and the digital has altered the perceptual domain to a degree where the "real" and the "fictional" can easily masquerade as each other.

The politics of *Ragini MMS*, as I note above, are clearly aligned along class and gender lines. Perhaps Uday is punished for his masculine arrogance, his easy sense of entitlement over Ragini's body, and for his real and attempted violence against her.[70] However, the fact that Ragini herself just barely survives the trauma puts a certain fillip on the terrifying proceedings. The specter—who insists she is not a witch throughout, in a guttural Marathi—will not let Ragini escape unpunished either, even though she is "innocent" and repeatedly declares as much. Why, then, must Ragini suffer?[71] The fact that the film makes no attempt to explain the specter's backstory only adds to its power as a *horror* film, the genre that must clear up spaces so that past crimes and misdemeanors can be laid to rest in the present. The spectator—liberated from the female ghost's specific biography—is free to imagine a series of structural inequities and violence that feeds its irrational wrath; the trope of a village woman brutally murdered, even as she protests her innocence, easily concatenates with a whole array of oppressive if imprecise narratives that continue to circulate with alarming regularity in India.[72] Unlike the zombie film, where the past is absent, if not wholly irrelevant, the digital ghost film stages a return of the revenant within its newly mediated formal universe. The ghost—and the narratives of injustice that she embodies—does not have to return as a seductive wraith via the archetypal plaintive song; in *Ragini MMS*, she is allowed to come back for vengeance, even as she remains a pixilated and barely visible smudge on the wall.

Modern, metropolitan life-worlds are inextricably enmeshed with the digital in India today. The planetary paranormal that I have been tracking throughout this chapter remains especially attentive to this new kind of rapaciously aspirational social domain. If there is any critique of India's post-industrial, media-saturated, modernity in Bollywood horror, it is to be found in the disturbances that manifest themselves in the digital media that form the narrative content of these films. Aspects of social worlds that are insufficiently expunged, affective histories that are only partially erased, return as dots, traces, and smudges on digital screens and interfaces. The neatly ordered, commodity-glutted images that form the visual bulwark of these films come to be increasingly *distorted*—bent out of shape, fuzzily out of focus, pixilated and stretched—as recalcitrant revenants return to seek justice and redemption. Other films of the genre in which ghosts—almost always wronged women, perhaps echoing the success of female specters in Japanese and Korean horror—return via the digital include *Click* (Sangeeth Sivan, 2010) and *3G: A Killer Connection* (Sheershak Anand and Shantanu Ray Chibber, 2013), among several others.[73]

3G: A Killer Connection's inscription of digital domains and its effects on contemporary coupledom is considerably complex. In this film, a similar modern couple, Sam (Neil Nitin Mukesh) and Sheena (Sonal Chauhan), encounter the paranormal via a distressing series of ghostly calls that Sam receives on his 3G-enabled, secondhand cellular smartphone. Even before Sam purchases his new phone in Fiji,[74] we see him working with enormous touchscreens that magically extend his body into the realm of the virtual, a diegetic representation of the "augmented reality" that forms the core narrative preoccupation in this film. From ghostly calls to violent video clips that inexplicably seem to show a woman's brutal murder, in *3G* terror is entirely transmitted via digital cellular technology. As the owner of this "haunted phone," Sam becomes possessed by its dead former user, undergoing a complete personality transformation; indeed, Sam's body becomes an extension of the haunted phone and vice versa—mutually constituting digital affects of the terrifying kind. We eventually learn that the murdered woman was Chaima/Jasmine (Mrinalini Sharma), whose fiancé, Mong (Asheesh Kapur), killed her in a fit of jealous rage when he discovered that unbeknownst to him, she had had a double life: she had been working as a prostitute/porn star. In this film's universe, the differences between these careers do not amount to much. Chaima's pornographic videos had been downloaded and enjoyed thousands of times from a website also titled "3G," and Mong, as the rightful claimant to Chaima's body/sexuality, had killed her before committing suicide. The climax comes full circle when Sam—now completely possessed by Mong—tries to kill Sheena instead, in the same spot where Mong had proposed marriage to Chaima before murdering her. Seamlessly moving between past and present episodes of violence via a vertiginous series of doublings, the climax sequence is a telling elaboration of what the digital domain signifies as content in Hindi film.

One of the most perplexing aspects of *3G* is the very notion of haunting. Sam becomes haunted by both Chaima's spirit—now trapped inside video clips that show her either having sex or dying—and Mong's rage, which, *Ju-on*-like (*The Grudge*, Takashi Shimizu, 2002), gathers momentum after his death.[75] The very notion of the spectral gets garbled in these multiple relays and displacements. In other words, haunting in 3G does not simply happen *via the digital*; the terrain of digital technology and its many screens and interfaces *become* the evil that exacts a price on social and sexual contracts. Exactly like the films in the earlier *Paranormal Activity* series, *3G* "modulate(s) the affect of fear through, and with direct attention to . . . digital technologies, and the larger social and economic relations within which such technologies are embedded."[76]

In *3G*, what is revealed at the end is, in some ways, far more horrific than the fate that befalls Ragini, because Ragini's MMS never gets created, at least not in the way that Uday would have wanted. But Ragini's worst nightmare comes true in Chaima's story. Chaima prostitutes herself—willingly, we are meant to infer—and is therefore not only killed but also condemned to an endlessly downloadable, horrific afterlife. Before killing Chaima, Mong asks, "Was I just another customer for you? I will

FIGURE 5.6. *Sam and his haunted phone in* 3G.

call all my friends, they will all f—k you and pay you—and then I'll make a video of you. Will that be fun? Won't you enjoy that?" The online traffic in women's bodies reduces them to interchangeable bytes of accessible data; that is why Sam sees Chaima during the climax, and not Sheena. In the double logic of the film, this substitution makes perfect sense. As Mong continues to live on in Sam's phone, *3G* ends with a somber end title proclaiming that "13,000 adult clips are downloaded every minute on mobile networks worldwide . . . Resulting in 27 percent of personal relationships breaking up." What is remarkable is that *3G* began with an opening title-card that read: "4.3 billion mobile users in the world . . . Every minute 60 thousand calls from unknown sources are received worldwide . . . People believe these are spirits trying to connect to our world." The film, however, concludes with its primary preoccupation—which is not, after all, dead people communicating through cellular technology, but the digital terrain opening up spaces where women's bodies and sexualities can no longer be adequately policed or disciplined. The specter of unruly female behavior on online portals—with unthinkable consequences for men, women, and social relations—haunts *3G* more powerfully than anything else. *3G* can be productively read as a sequel to *Ragini MMS* in a certain sense—Chaima's video ends up being consumed in a way that Ragini's presumably does not; both their stories demonstrate that Hindi cinema's most enduring anxieties about gender and sexuality are today being projected onto the realm of digital media and technology.

The domain of digital technologies congeals in Hindi horror as always already imbued with dreadful potentialities. In this film and others—such as the much-discussed *13 B*, which deploys television instead—new technologies in general and communications technologies in particular become the exclusive gestational spaces and conduits for the eruption and elaboration of the paranormal. Alongside everything else, the digital in this instance becomes the interface where the past can "screen" itself—render itself present and palpable. But in presenting the universe of digital and new media as always already haunted, the Bollywood horror film also proffers a commentary on the present, an immanent critique of the contemporary. In this sense the planetary paranormal continues the modality of the supernatural that has come before.

The Hindi digital ghost-film genre remains clearly indebted to J-horror films like *Ringu* (*The Ring*) and *Kairo* (*Pulse*), and the "techno-terror" wave more generally in East Asian horror cinema, although it lacks the former's philosophical bleakness. But in remaking the originals within the Bollywood format—*Click*, for example, features several song-and-dance sequences—the genre also indexes an attempt to harness and vernacularize/hybridize the planetary popularity of the formation. The planetary paranormal—the larger impetus within which Hindi horror film embeds itself—additionally gestures to a new industrial ecology via altered notions of licensing and copyright regulations. Although earlier "remakes"—such as *Click* and *Naina* (Shripal Morakhia, 2005, remake of the Hong Kong–Singapore co-production, *The Eye*, Pang Brothers, 2002)—remained unauthorized and mired in controversies and allegations of plagiarism, New Bollywood is for the first time buying rights to legally remake international horror hits in the new millennium. The recent *Alone* (Bhushan Patel, 2015), for example, is an authorized remake of the Thai film of the same title, advertised and publicized as such.[77] Like *Click*, *Alone* includes a series of song sequences, shot in the lush backwaters of Kerala. Although the adaptative process in these remakes does not end at the inclusion of song sequences, that tried and tested staple appears to be the very first gesture toward indigenizing international genre films in New Bollywood. Similarly, Hindi cinema's "first" creature-feature, predictably titled *Creature* (Vikram Bhatt, 2014), not only includes songs but also taps into mythic temporalities, much like the snake film I discussed in Chapter 3. The creature is a "Brahmrakhshas"—a specially cursed being who can be found in both the Vedas and local folklore. Despite its entrepreneurial heroine and the 3D technology and the VFX work that brings the lizard-like creature to life, the film remains strongly tethered to multiple pasts of Hindi cinema. In other words, the planetary paranormal is not aligned to a single impulse in the present Bollywood industry. Although it sometimes dictates that the "eccentricities" of Hindi film be wholly expunged—as in the zombie film—at other times, it is the global genre formats that are reworked and repurposed to make room for Bombay cinema's typical pleasures. And as always, the presentation of the supernatural becomes a site of struggle: over formal aspects and political imperatives.

Epilogue

Can we speak of "ghosts" without transforming the whole word and ourselves, too, into phantoms? Such a question and the worry within it . . . lies at the very heart of modernity.

—JEAN-MICHEL RABATÉ, *THE GHOSTS OF MODERNITY*

IT IS DIFFICULT NOT TO BE REMINDED OF STANLEY KWAN'S *Rouge* (1987) while watching Reema Kagti's recent thriller, *Talaash* (*Search*, 2012). Both films feature melancholic female ghosts who used to be prostitutes in life. Both women return after death to redress the injustices that befell them in life. Both visit the living for a reckoning of sorts: Fleur (Anita Mui), to meet her estranged lover, and Rosie (Kareena Kapoor), to bring her murderers to justice.[1] However, the differences, too, are unmistakable: whereas Fleur travels to the present (the crucial year 1987) from 1930s Hong Kong, Rosie's transition to a ghostly afterlife is more immediate—she returns less than two years after her death. Fleur is an anachronism; her un-belonging in an unrecognizable contemporary urban milieu lies at the heartbreaking core of Kwan's film.[2] Rosie, on the other hand, is street smart in the literal sense—completely at home in the cityscape and conversant with the alleys and highways she cruises for potential clients; indeed, she blends in so well as to be virtually indistinguishable from the living prostitutes at the brothel. Fleur's existence as a ghost is apparent from early on in *Rouge*; Rosie's status as a restless, vengeful spirit is the big reveal that constitutes the climax of *Talaash*. But the most staggering difference is in terms of the relationships these ghosts form with the humans in each film. Fleur's interactions with the young couple (Alex Man and Emily Chu) enable them to realize the transformative potential of love and loss, but Rosie's human friend, Surjan Singh Sekhawat (Aamir Khan), is humanized and healed by the specter.

Talaash is a compelling illustration of Hindi cinema's continuing negotiation of the supernatural, even as it updates these formal and narrative maneuvers for the new millennium. Surjan is the haunted hero par excellence: an insomniac unmanned by grief and guilt over his young son's accidental death, he prowls the dark streets searching for answers while his marriage disintegrates, and his wife, Roshni (Rani Mukerji), suffers in solitude. Surjan is fascinated by Rosie when he meets her during the course of a murder investigation, and she seems to have important information about the case. In keeping with Hindi cinema's more recent formal tendencies, Rosie does not actually sing as she lures the male protagonist into specific spaces, but the song "Jiya Lage Na" ("My Heart Is Restless") plays over a key sequence as he follows her around crowded streets, garishly lit bars, and seedy hotels. In other words, the enchanting spell Rosie casts on Surjan, and his capitulation to her charms, is very similar to the modality of romance elaborated in the Gothic film of the 1950s and 1960s that I explored in the first chapter of this book. Of course, considering the vastly altered media landscape that Bollywood now straddles, there are notable differences as well: for example, when Rosie takes Surjan to the socially unsanctioned space of the hotel for a night, instead of seducing him into a sexual encounter, she lulls the exhausted cop into a deep, dreamless sleep. Surjan, the taciturn police investigator, is rendered strangely vulnerable by his inner anguish and inability to share it with anyone, except the ghostly woman whom he is drawn to against his will. Rosie herself is an odd sort of succubus: part femme fatale who toys with the hero's unraveling composure, part ghostly apparition whose melancholy over her own murder is palpable in *Talaash*. If Fleur suffered from a surfeit of memory—unable to disentangle herself from the past—Rosie's tragedy hinges on the near complete absence of memory that seems to characterize the heartless contemporary: "Imagine, sir, a girl disappears and no one even notices that she's gone," she laments. Rosie is both an erotic conundrum and an emotional refuge for Surjan, but also, crucially, a ghost in the real sense. She haunts the spaces of the living until Surjan uncovers the truth of her murder and revenge. Unlike the faux ghosts of earlier eras who were circumscribed within crumbling feudal *havelis*, Rosie can come and go as she pleases, generally rendering the entire urban environment as an uncanny, haunted topos.[3] Interestingly, the film does not end until Surjan disinters her carelessly buried corpse on the beach; Rosie's pitifully desiccated, bejeweled, skeletal hands echo the remains of another luckless woman in Hindi cinema: Chhoti Bahu (Meena Kumari) from *Saheb Biwi Aur Ghulam* (*King, Queen, and Knave*, Abrar Alvi,

1962). *Talaash* is, thus, both sumptuously Gothic—replete with twisted secrets, occluded histories, and decaying bodies—and competently and confidently global in pace, tone, and texture.[4]

Indeed, one of the film's strengths is its cinematography and editing. Diffuse lighting, saturated neon colors, and digital photography render the night shots both luminous and dreamlike. Liberal uses of slow motion and syncopated editing during the song sequences are especially efficacious in conveying the haunted, restless tenor of Surjan's existence. However, it is the images of water and the sensation of drowning that the film most deftly mobilizes to generate affect. Hindi commercial cinema conventionally uses water to eroticize star-bodies in song sequences, but *Talaash* is a sodden film throughout. Almost every single character in the film is drowning or has drowned, in a way that is both literal and symbolic: Karan (Jineet Rath), Surjan's dead son, falls into a lake while playing and drowns; Roshni is sinking in loneliness and isolation; Rosie's pitiful, shallow grave is on the beach and she remains strongly associated with the sea; Armaan Kapoor (Vivan Bhatena), the movie star, is pursued by Rosie's ghost until he drives his car into the heaving ocean; and finally, Surjan himself discovers the truth as a spectral Rosie saves him from drowning in an extended underwater sequence. If affect is cinematically generated through an "inventory of shimmers" and the way in which images generate bodily sensations, *Talaash* is an invitation to surrender to water and memories.[5] The film is difficult to summarize via a simple plot description precisely because much of its power derives from the ineffable: the dexterous dovetailing of style, mood, and emotion.

But *Talaash* is *also* about bodies, particularly the bodies of prostitutes—encased in lycra, cheap baubles, and garish makeup that camouflage scars and bruises. Labor embodied, these women are used and abused, pursued, haggled over, purchased, killed, and often abandoned and forgotten. Their bodies are simultaneously abjectly productive and imminently disposable. This is why it is so important that Rosie's corpse be exhumed. It is not enough to punish her murderers; in the ethical schema of the film, the violence on and violation of female bodies can only be redressed when they are restored to a state of dignity and grace. Derrida's impassioned call to be with and speak to the ghost is made palpable here, as the revelation of the truth in this film is also a matter of a general accountability, of accepting responsibility for the crimes that have been perpetuated against Rosie (and many others like her) in the past.[6] It is only when Surjan *learns* to listen to Rosie's cryptic pronouncements that he is able to see the light—he must become a credulous believer and a bit of a phantom himself in order to access and literally uncover the truth.

In Surjan's recovery and rehabilitation—in the last scenes, he finally seeks solace in his wife's embrace and weeps uncontrollably, thereby purging himself of guilt and despair—we have the precise obverse of the operations that enabled the remasculinization of the Gothic hero in the 1950s and 1960s. Instead of the expulsion of the feminine and the supernatural, it is, in fact, the ethical acceptance of the irrational that enables the reconstitution of the heterosexual couple. *Talaash* does not feel the need to debunk or exorcize phantoms; instead, it is the recognition of the other that finally constitutes characters as subjects. By the same token, the investigative thriller comes to be more capacious: it is now a form that is able to make room for these other energies—spectral, feminine, childlike, and queer. Millennial Bollywood, then, does not suffer the same anxieties that earlier iterations of the supernatural film did. Having traversed a swath of historical moments, industrial imperatives, and formal contortions, the supernatural no longer needs to defend or belabor its existence in Hindi cinema. *Talaash* both invokes and adroitly reconfigures the Gothic ghost film of earlier eras, illustrating precisely the (re)iteration-innovation axes that I have been tracing throughout this book.

In *Haunting Bollywood*, I have been mapping the story of the Hindi supernatural film from the late 1940s to the present. At the core of this narrative has been the generic and formal restructuring that the supernatural has subjected the formation to. For example, the Gothic film in the 1950s and 1960s tantalizingly broached the subject of ghosts through songs and hauntings, only to disable these impulses in conclusion. The figuration of a rational discourse and a modern citizen-subject was a matter of singular importance, and therefore, the supernatural remained a nascent impulse at best in the genre in question. Gender and sexuality remain equally critical axes of making meaning in terms of supernatural elaboration; and as *Talaash* so deftly demonstrates, this still remains the case. Formal and generic habitats of the supernatural, I have argued, often hinge on the "performance sequence" in Hindi cinema; thus, the female ghost haunts via song, the magical shape-shifting serpent seduces via the allure of dance. In the Ramsay horror film, disco songs, rapes, and monster attacks constitute the delirious *masala* assemblages that typified the 1970s and 1980s.

Song-and-dance sequences—their abundant inclusion or complete excision—also depends on the specific historical moment that the supernatural finds itself tethered to. Therefore, in Bollywood's recent bid for global legibility, some horror films streamline the form and purge it of the *masala* altogether. However, for every *Bhoot* that is taut, sleek, and songless, the excesses of the Vikram Bhatt musical-melodrama-horror film return us to Hindi cinema's most enduring pleasures. In other words, although generic and formal novelties—like recent zombie films or found-footage films—appear on the filmic horizon, Hindi cinema's traditional formal assemblage continues to host the supernatural in multiple ways.

The cinema of the supernatural has rarely been A-list fare, and this, for the most part, remains true in contemporary Bollywood. These films are often made on fairly tight budgets, a factor that enables them to make profits among certain segments of the audience. Who this intended audience is has shifted quite dramatically over the course of the decades that I trace in *Haunting Bollywood*. Although the 1950s and 1960s Social film aimed for a "modern" and national audience, the *masala* horror and snake films of the 1970s and 1980s unabashedly wooed working-class audiences in cities and small towns, and mobilized thrills and sensations accordingly. Likewise, post-liberalization Bollywood has given the supernatural a facelift in order to make its genres more suitable for the plush multiplex theater and putative elite audiences. But the social circulation of texts reveals only a part of the story. For example, if the formal or narrative peculiarities of the snake film or the Ramsay horror extravaganza are best illuminated by the historical and political exigencies of Emergency India, what explains their continued popularity in the era of new media? These genres have managed to gain something of a reputation in cult film circles globally, thanks to their circulation via the Internet and the many online platforms it has spawned. Serials based on ghosts, monsters, and magical snakes have found space on television as well, confounding our assumptions about the "middle-class" nature of the medium in addition to the class-based appeal of these sensationalist forms.[7]

In *Haunting Bollywood*, I explore the genres of the supernatural within their immediate historical and ideological contexts, but I also track their dispersal along other and more untimely media ecologies. In the case of the supernatural, historical tethers rarely furnish all the answers. For example, consider the paradox of the snake film: although older films such as *Nagin* and *Nagina* have garnered newer audiences and fan communities through electronic conduits of dispersal, the formation has not been easily upgraded to a CGI avatar, as evidenced by the colossal critical and commercial failure of *Hisss*. Conversely, not all generic formations can easily be domesticated within the textual enclosure of Hindi cinema, either; the failure of the recent zombie films attests to the fact that the supernatural genres have to maintain the delicate balancing act between local codes and global impulses.

But the supernatural—perhaps even more pointedly than other genres—also demonstrates that Bombay cinema has always been in dialogue with global forms. Whether in terms of adapting proto-Western Gothic tropes qua the feudal in earlier periods, or the more recent obsession with such generic novelties as creature-features, the supernatural has always pushed Hindi cinema into new and unfamiliar territories. The productive tension between global and local, old and new has been at the heart of the story I have explored in this book. For instance, the recent horror/fantasy film *Ek Thi Daayan* (*There Was Once a Witch*, Kannan Iyer, 2013) simultaneously draws on local archives of folklore and myths about witches but presents this material in a hyper-digitized visual universe that is remarkably novel; the film fuses the mythic material to a performance of digital technology in a manner that proclaims its confident cosmopolitanism and globality. The recent *Khamoshiyan* (*Silences*, Karan Darra, 2015) from the Bhatt assembly-line liberally "borrows" from *Psycho* (Hitchcock, 1960), even as it transplants the tropes of a preserved corpse in a lonely hotel into an erotic triangular fantasy, involving black magic, beautiful protagonists, and soulful love songs. Thus, contrary to popular belief, the supernatural in Hindi cinema is rarely an inward-looking impetus; if anything, it continues to innovate and update in tandem with planetary developments. The supernatural has also found other habitats in the new millennium—including new types of comic books, graphic novels, and video games.

This is an exciting time for Indian horror studies, both because Bollywood continues to make films with supernatural themes in increasing numbers, and because scholarly work on these films has begun in earnest in recent years. For a long time, these films were not considered worthy of scholarly exploration, not only because they were considered too marginal to be taken seriously but also because their profligate energies could not be easily corralled into recognizable theoretical enclosures. But an increasing number of studies have shown that there are multiple histories of the commercial cinema in India, and all of these strands are generative of the contemporary formation that is global Bollywood. *Haunting Bollywood*, too, has tracked a history that is not necessarily linear, and one in which straightforward causal connections among genres, cycles, ideologies, and the supernatural remain fractious at best. Many of the filmic formations I have explored in this book remain intractably resistant to neat theoretical grids, and likewise, my analytical lenses have sometimes been eclectic as well.

I have also refused to relinquish my cinephiliac pleasure in writing this book. Although many of the films I discuss here remain disturbing, terrifying, or downright objectionable, I have surrendered to their complex seductions willingly. It is impossible to write a book about enchanted traditions without allowing oneself to be somewhat captivated in the process.

Finally, *Haunting Bollywood* demonstrates that the irrational and the fantastic continue to nurture Hindi cinema, as they have from the earliest years; this cinema, in turn, continues to allow itself to be imbued by these energies. Indeed, alongside music and melodrama, the supernatural may be this formation's most enduring tendency.

Notes

INTRODUCTION

1. See, for example, Shubhajit Chatterjee, "On Disreputable Genres: B Movies and Revisionary Histories of Bombay Cinema," *Marg* 64 (4) (2013): 32–41.

2. That mythologicals and devotionals have received more scholarly attention can be explained by their deep history and provenance. India's earliest surviving films, at least those credited to Phalke, are mythologicals. The reputation of devotionals such as *Sant Tukaram* (1936) is similarly buttressed by the fact that Prabhat Studios produced it. In other words, these particular formations have crystalized as cherished objects of historical inquiry for a variety of different reasons.

3. For an excellent reassessment of the history of early Indian cinema and the importance of visceral, "sensationalist" genres like oriental fantasy and action-adventure-stunt films in the silent era, see Kaushik Bhaumik, "Querying the 'Traditional' Roots of Silent Cinema in Asia," *Journal of the Moving Image* 7 (2008), at www.jmionline.org/articles/2008/querying_the_traditional_roots_of_silent_cinema_in_asia.pdf (accessed December 12, 2015). See also V. Dharamsey, "The Advent of Sound in Indian Cinema: Theater, Orientalism, Action, Magic," *Journal of the Moving Image* 9 (2010), at www.jmionline.org/articles/2010/the_advent_of_sound_in_indian_cinema_theatre_orientalism_action_magic.pdf (accessed December 12, 2015). For the continuing impact of these early genres on more recent Hindi cinema, see Rosie Thomas, *Bombay Before Bollywood: Film City Fantasies* (Albany: SUNY Press, 2013).

4. See Pete Tombs, "The Beast from Bollywood: A History of the Indian Horror Film," in *Fear Without Frontiers: Horror Cinema Across the Globe*, ed. Steven Jay Schneider, 243–253 (Godalming, England: FAB Press, 2003); Sangita Gopal, *Conjugations: Marriage and Form in New Bollywood Cinema* (Chicago: University of Chicago Press, 2011); Kartik Nair, "Fear on Film: The Ramsay Brothers and Bombay's Horror Cinema," *Sarai Reader* 8 (2008): 254–261; Kartik Nair, "Taste, Taboo, Trash: The Story of the Ramsay Brothers," *Bioscope: South Asian Screen Studies* 3 (2) (2012): 123–

145; Kartik Nair, "Temple of Womb," *New Inquiry*, last modified July 23, 2013, accessed January 2015, at http://thenewinquiry.com/essays/temple-of-womb/; and Valentina Vitali, "The Evil I: Realism and Scopophilia in the Horror Films of the Ramsay Brothers," in *Beyond the Boundaries of Bollywood*, ed. Rachel Dwyer and Jerry Pinto, 77–101 (New Delhi: Oxford University Press, 2011).

5. Ashis Nandy, "Slum's Eye View of Politics," introduction to Ashis Nandy, ed., *The Secret Politics of Our Desires: Innocence, Culpability, and Indian Popular Cinema* (London: Zed Books, 1999).

6. Colin Davis, "*État Présent*: Hauntology, Specters and Phantoms," in *The Spectralities Reader*, ed. María del Pilar Blanco and Esther Peeren (New York: Bloomsbury, 2013), 54.

7. Ibid., 53.

8. Jeffrey Andrew Weinstock, "Introduction: The Spectral Turn," in *The Spectralities Reader*, ed. Pilar Blanco and Peeren, 63.

9. Key works that remain indebted to Derrida's notion of ghosts, specters, and hauntologies include but are not limited to Avery F. Gordon, *Ghostly Matters: Haunting the Sociological Imagination* (Minneapolis: University of Minnesota Press, 1997); Jeffrey Sconce, *Haunted Media: Electronic Presence from Telegraphy to Television* (Durham, NC: Duke University Press, 2000); Julian Wolfreys, *Victorian Hauntings: Spectrality, Gothic, the Uncanny and Literature* (New York: Palgrave Macmillan, 2001); Bliss Cua Lim, *Translating Time* (Durham, NC: Duke University Press, 2009); María del Pilar Blanco and Esther Peeren, eds., *Popular Ghosts: The Haunted Spaces of Everyday Culture* (New York: Continuum, 2010); and María del Pilar Blanco, *Ghost-Watching American Modernity* (New York: Fordham Press, 2012).

10. Weinstock, "Introduction," 63.

11. María del Pilar Blanco and Esther Peeren, "Introduction: Conceptualizing Spectralities," in *The Spectralities Reader*, ed. Pilar Blanco and Peeren, 9. Indeed, for Derrida, as these scholars observe, the ethical potentialities of haunting remain primary: "[T]o believe or not believe in ghosts no longer involves a determination about the empirical (im)possibility of the supernatural, but indicates contracting validated attitudes—a welcoming seen as ethical and enabling, and a rejection considered unethical and dispossessing—towards the uncertainty, heterogeneity, multiplicity, and indeterminacy that characterize language and Being because of their inevitable entanglement with alterity and difference. Derrida, then, far from being a ghostbuster . . . uses the figure of the ghost to pursue (without ever fully apprehending) that which haunts *like a ghost* and, by way of this haunting, demands justice, or at least a response."

12. Sconce, *Haunted Media*, 4.

13. Jacques Derrida, *Specters of Marx*, trans. Peggy Kamuf (London: Routledge, 2006), 4.

14. See for example, Tom Gunning, "An Aesthetic of Astonishment: Early Film and the [In]Credulous Spectator," *Art and Text* (Fall 1989).

15. Tom Gunning, "To Scan a Ghost: The Ontology of Mediated Vision," in *The Spectralities Reader*, ed. Pilar Blanco and Peeren, 226.

16. Even in instances when the supernatural entity remains spectral—such as in some of the more contemporary horror films like *Bhoot* or *1920*—it asserts its presence by possessing other bodies; the fact of haunting remains arguably embodied in much of Hindi cinema.

17. Linda Williams, "Film Bodies: Gender, Genre, and Excess," *Film Quarterly* 44 (4) (1991), 4.

18. For Clover's theorization of gender and spectatorship, see Carol J. Clover, *Men, Women, and Chainsaws: Gender in the Modern Horror Film* (Princeton: Princeton University Press, 1993). Barbara Creed's *The Monstrous Feminine* is another key work that brought together questions of gender, the (female) body, and the horror film. Drawing particularly on Julia Kristeva's conceptualization of abjection, Creed argues that the horror film "would appear to be, in at least three ways, an illustration of the work of abjection. First, the horror film abounds in images of abjection, for most of which is the corpse, whole and mutilated, followed by an array of bodily wastes such as blood, vomit, saliva, sweat, tears, and putrefying flesh. In terms of Kristeva's notion of the border, when we say such-and-such a horror film 'made me sick' or 'scared the shit out of me,' we are actually foregrounding that specific horror film as a 'work of abjection' or 'abjection at work'—almost in a literal sense. Viewing the horror film signifies a desire not only for perverse pleasure (confronting sickening, horrific images/being filled with terror/desire for the undifferentiated) but also a desire, once having been filled with perversity, taken pleasure in perversity, to throw up, throw out, eject the abject (from the safety of the spectator's seat)." Barbara Creed, *The Monstrous-Feminine: Film, Feminism, Psychoanalysis* (New York: Routledge, 1993), 10. This large body of feminist scholarship has critically informed my readings of gendered bodies in Hindi film.

19. Judith Halberstam, *Skin Shows* (Durham, NC: Duke University Press, 1995), 21.

20. Ibid., 24. At another point in the introduction, Halberstam clarifies the point, writing, "The body that scares and appalls changes over time, as do the individual characteristics that add up to monstrosity." Although race, class, and nationality remain important optics for Halberstam's analysis, he argues that the focus of monstrosity has shifted primarily to gender and sexuality within fictional modes in the twentieth century, especially in film.

21. Steven Shaviro, *The Cinematic Body* (Minneapolis: University of Minnesota Press, 1993), 10, 1.

22. Ibid., 26, 7. In this conceptualization of affect as a pre-cognitive, sensory force, he is echoed by Brian Massumi, who argues for the autonomy of affect: "(A)ffects are *virtual synesthetic perspectives* anchored in (functionally limited by) the actually existing, particular things that embody them. The autonomy of affect is its participation in the virtual. *Its autonomy is its openness.* Affect is autonomous to the degree to which it escapes confinement in the particular body whose vitality, potential for interaction it is. Formed, qualified, situated perceptions and cognitions fulfilling functions of actual connection or blockage are the capture enclosure of affect. Emotion is the most intense (most contracted) expression of that *cap-*

ture—and of the fact that something has always and again escaped." Brian Massumi, *Parables for the Virtual: Movement, Affect, Sensation* (Durham, NC: Duke University Press, 2002), 35.

23. Shaviro, *Cinematic Body*, 85.

24. Ibid., 129.

25. Emphasis in original. Dudenhoeffer's work takes the research on body and affect a step further. Using four major animal tissue types—muscle tissue, connective tissue, nervous tissue, and epithelial tissue—he argues that "horror cinema turns on revealing what we cannot comfortably reveal, on transposing outside us what must remain on the inside, on disclosing what seems impossible to ever visualize or claim as our own—the flesh in its fullest microcellular, multifunctional, and inter-systemic complexity, an anatomic complexity irreducible to the sex organs or erotogenic zones, to the skin or the sense mechanisms, or to the central nervous networks." Larrie Dudenhoeffer, *Embodiment and Horror Cinema* (New York: Palgrave Macmillan, 2014), 5–6.

26. Some of the most important and interesting theorizations of monsters in cinema have come from queer theorists such as Harry Benshoff and others.

27. Arjun Appadurai describes the concept of rasa thusly: "Indian aestheticians have singled out eight feelings (bhava) that all persons experience in their lives: love, mirth, grief, energy, terror, disgust, anger and wonder . . . In the poetic context, each of these is transformed into a corresponding mood (rasa), a generalized, impersonal feeling capable of being understood by other persons in similar states. In drama, these moods are expressed in a publicly understood set of gestures, and both the dramatic performance and its critical analysis involve the appraisal of these gestures . . . The object is to create a chain of communications in feeling, not by unmediated empathy between the emotional 'interiors' of specific individuals but by recourse to a shared, and relatively fixed set, of public gestures." Appadurai, "Topographies of the Self: Praise and Emotion in Hindu India," *Language and the Politics of Emotion*, ed. Catherine A. Lutz and Lila Abu-Lughod (Cambridge, UK: Cambridge University Press, 1990), 106–107. For the applicability and use of affect theory vis-à-vis non-Western texts and its resonances with *rasa*, see also Sneja Gunew, "Subaltern Empathy: Beyond European Categories in Affect Theory," *Concentric: Literary and Cultural Studies* 35 (1) (2009), 11–30.

28. Tom Gunning, "The Cinema of Attractions: Early Film, Its Spectator and the Avant-Garde," *Wide Angle* 8 (3 and 4) (1986), 63–70.

29. Lalitha Gopalan, *Cinema of Interruptions: Action Genres in Contemporary Indian Films* (London: British Film Institute, 2002); and M. Madhava Prasad, *Ideology of the Hindi Film: A Historical Construction* (New Delhi: Oxford University Press, 2001).

30. Even the Social, with its strong narrative preoccupations, was a generic amalgam:

> The social film drew on multiple genres—musicals, romantic comedy, action-adventure, and drama—in order [to] satisfy the demands placed upon the medium. Thus the typical film focused on one or more "relevant"

> issues; including add-ons, like rural vignettes, comedy routines, and thrills that helped to draw in the masses; and utilized devices like song and dance in order to promote contemporary fashions and lifestyles. So perfect was this formula that the social film survived almost intact for two decades. (Gopal, *Conjugations*, 5–6)

31. Rick Altman, *Film/Genre* (London: British Film Institute, 2006), 14.

32. Madhava Prasad, for example, has argued that the subgenre of the women's film, popular in the 1960s, was eventually absorbed into the "supra-generic social." Prasad, *Ideology of the Hindi Film*.

33. Sangita Gopal and Sujata Moorti, "Introduction: Travels of Hindi Song and Dance," in *Global Bollywood: Travels of Hindi Song and Dance*, ed. Gopal and Moorti (Minneapolis: University of Minnesota Press, 2008), 28.

34. For more on the reincarnation genre, see Neelam Sidhar Wright, "The Soul Gets Typecast: The Reincarnation Film in Hindi Popular Cinema," *New Cinemas: Journal of Contemporary Film* 12 (1 and 2): 113–132.

35. Gopal and Moorti, "Introduction," 2.

36. Prasad, *Ideology of the Hindi Film*; Gopal and Moorti, "Introduction"; and Anna Morcom, *Hindi Film Songs and the Cinema* (Farnham, UK: Ashgate, 2007).

37. Gopal and Moorti, "Introduction."

38. See, for example, Gopal, *Conjugations*.

39. Gopal and Moorti, "Introduction," 5.

40. Jo Collins and John Jervis, eds., *Uncanny Modernity: Cultural Theories, Modern Anxieties* (New York: Palgrave Macmillan, 2008), 2.

41. Ibid.

42. Jean-Michel Rabaté, *The Ghosts of Modernity* (Gainesville: University Press of Florida, 1996), 3.

43. Timothy Mitchell, ed., *Questions of Modernity* (Minneapolis: University of Minnesota Press, 2000), xiv.

44. Dipesh Chakrabarty, *Provincializing Europe: Postcolonial Thought and Historical Difference* (Princeton: Princeton University Press, 2000), 8.

45. Mitchell, *Questions of Modernity*, xiv.

46. See, for example, Chakrabarty, *Provincializing Europe*; and Saurabh Dube, *Enchantments of Modernity: Empire, Nation, Globalization* (Delhi: Routledge India, 2009).

47. Prasad, *Ideology of the Hindi Film*, 2.

48. Ibid., 7.

49. Lim, *Translating Time*, 149.

50. Ibid., 2.

51. Ibid., 12.

52. See, for example, Aswin Punathambekar, *From Bombay to Bollywood: The Making of a Global Media Industry* (New York: New York University Press, 2013); and Tejaswini Ganti, *Producing Bollywood: Inside the Contemporary Hindi Film Industry* (Durham, NC: Duke University Press, 2012).

53. See Gopal, *Conjugations*; and Ganti, *Producing Bollywood*.

54. See, for example, Gopal, *Conjugations*, Chap. 3, "Fearful Habitations: Upward Mobility and the Horror Genre," 91–123; Bishnupriya Ghosh, "The Security Aesthetic in Bollywood's High-Rise Horror," *Representations* 126 (1) (2014), special issue, *Financialization and the Culture Industry*: 58–84.

CHAPTER ONE: HAUNTED *HAVELIS* AND HAPLESS HEROES

1. A slightly different version of this essay was published in Meheli Sen and Anustup Basu, eds., *Figurations in Indian Film* (Hampshire, UK: Palgrave Macmillan, 2013).

2. Earlier in the essay, David Punter and Glennis Byron write, "We might refer to this, then, as history written according to a certain logic: a logic of the phantom, the revenant, a logic of haunting, and it is here that we might see the connection with the postcolonial coming most clearly into view. The very structure of the term 'postcolonial' itself, its apparent insistence on a time 'after,' on an 'aftermath,' exposes itself precisely to the threat of return, falls under the sign of an unavoidable repetition. . . ." David Punter and Glennis Byron, *The Gothic* (Malden, MA: Blackwell, 2004), 55. Fittingly, scholars of postcolonial literature have been especially attentive to the uncanny and the spectral in the works of, for example, Amitav Ghosh and Arundhati Roy. See Bishnupriya Ghosh, "On Grafting the Vernacular: The Consequences of Postcolonial Spectrology," *boundary 2, an international journal of literature and culture* 31 (2) (2004): 197–218.

3. William Hughes and Andrew Smith, "Introduction: Defining the Relationships Between Gothic and the Postcolonial," *Gothic Studies* 5 (2) (2003): 1–6. Emphasis in original.

4. Michelle Giles, "Postcolonial Gothic and *The God of Small Things*: The Haunting of India's Past," *Postcolonial Text* 6 (1) (2011): 1–15.

5. Philip Holden, "The 'Postcolonial Gothic': Absent Histories, Present Contexts," *Textual Practice* 23 (3) (2009), 356.

6. Ibid.

7. See Vijay Mishra, *Bollywood Cinema: Temples of Desire* (New York: Routledge, 2001). See also the author's analysis of Madhumati in Chap. 4, "New Uses of the Romantic-Mythic Tradition," in Sumita Chakravarty, *National Identity in Indian Popular Cinema, 1947-1987* (Austin: University of Texas Press, 1993).

8. Rachel Dwyer, "Bombay Gothic: On the 60th Anniversary of Kamal Amrohi's *Mahal*," in *Beyond the Boundaries of Bollywood*, ed. Rachel Dwyer and Jerry Pinto (New Delhi: Oxford University Press, 2011), 136.

9. South Asian literature has a robust body of work that invokes the supernatural, of course, but rarely do the films I discuss here tap into that archive. Rabindranath Tagore's famous short story "The Hungry Stones" is only one example of a text that is replete with Gothic energies. For a provocative reading of spectrality, historicality, and literary form in Tagore's work, see Suvadip Sinha, "Ghostly Predicament: Narrative, Spectrality and Historicality in Rabindranath Tagore's 'The

Hungry Stones,'" *Interventions: International Journal of Postcolonial Studies* 15 (7) (2015): 728–743.

10. "*Kohraa*: The Beaten Track," *Filmfare*, May 1, 1964.

11. Indeed, *Kohraa* includes a shot of a sluggishly drowning car—in lieu of the novel's boat—which is an exact replica of the justly famous shot in *Psycho* (1960), cementing its reputation as an adaptation of Hitchcock rather than du Maurier's original text.

12. "*Woh Kaun Thi?*: Sensitively Directed," *Filmfare*, March 6, 1964.

13. Vijay Mishra, for example, has argued that tropes of reincarnation are foundational to Bombay cinema's recasting of the Gothic as a postcolonial form, noting that "reincarnation was a very real contribution to the general theory of the gothic. In other words, India presented the gothic with a narrative which its European form never had. . . . Indian reincarnation now invests the supernatural with another history and a memory of it in the new life. Recalling one's past life—and one that reworked the principle of the double—is thus an instance of an uncanny duplication, a mirroring of real, present history with an unreal past history whose authenticity is available only to the person who remembers. The colonized thus expand a genre of the colonizer and then internalize it into their own artistic domains." Mishra, *Bollywood Cinema*, 51.

14. The cluster of films I am engaging here is not meant to suggest that the Gothic remains limited to Hindi-language cinema or dies a sudden death in the mid-1960s. On the contrary, generic conventions remain strong in later color films such as *Mera Saaya* (*My Shadow*, 1966) and *Neel Kamal* (1968), through at least *Naqaab* (*The Veil*, 1989). *Lekin* (*But*, Gulzar, 1990), which adapts Tagore's short story "The Hungry Stones," is a more recent iteration of the Gothic film, which also recalls Tapan Sinha's earlier Bengali adaptation *Khudito Pashan* (1960). Bengali films such as *Kuheli* (*Mystery*, Tarun Majumdar, 1971) channel Gothic tropes in very similar ways. Other generic clusters, for instance, horror films in the 1970s and reincarnation films of all periods, appropriate Gothic modalities in significant ways. However, I would argue that the introduction of color and the attendant infusion of a certain kind of naturalism do transform the tone and texture of these later films to a considerable degree. The dismantling of the Nehruvian consensus in the mid-1960s additionally impacts the stakes involved in gendering the genre in a specific way.

15. Bombay Talkies' German cinematographer, Josef Wirsching, infused *Mahal* with an eerie expressionism that later films clearly drew on.

16. John Jervis, "Uncanny Presences" in *Uncanny Modernity: Cultural Theories, Modern Anxieties*, ed. Jo Collins and John Jervis (New York: Palgrave Macmillan, 2008), 18.

17. Sound effects or noises are also critical conduits for the creation of "Gothic atmosphere" in the genre. Especially important are sounds of storms and wind, the chiming of clocks, the tinkle of jewelry worn by ghosts, and so on.

18. Mishra, *Bollywood Cinema*, 52.

19. Dwyer, Hsu, and Mishra all comment on the absence of real ghosts and the supernatural in their respective discussions of *Mahal*.

20. Brian Baker, "Gothic Masculinities," in *Routledge Companion to the Gothic*, ed. Catherine Spooner and Emma McEvoy (New York: Routledge, 2007), 166.

21. The female ghost, the central trope I explore here, would also become a generic motif—almost a typological figure—in later horror films. The figure becomes so clichéd that it reappears in other media as well, for example, in the music video for Bally Sagoo's remix of the song "Noorie," produced in the 1990s. An entirely different film titled *Bees Saal Baad*, unambiguously a horror film, was made by Rajkumar Kohli years later in 1988, alerting us to the connections between the two genres.

22. Jacques Derrida, *Specters of Marx*, trans. Peggy Kamuf (London: Routledge, 2006), 5.

23. See, for example, Ravi Vasudevan's discussion of the social in Ravi Vasudevan, "Shifting Codes, Dissolving Identities: The Hindi Social Film of the 1950s as Popular Culture," in *Making Meaning in Indian Cinema*, ed. Ravi Vasudevan, 99–121 (New Delhi: Oxford University Press, 2000).

24. For a rich theorization of the relationship between the nationalist *bildung*, literature, and the spectral, see Pheng Cheah, *Spectral Nationality: Passages of Freedom from Kant to Postcolonial Literatures of Liberation* (New York: Columbia University Press, 2003).

25. Some films of a slightly later period do feature male protagonists who venture from cities to villages, but they do so in order to bring the developmentalist imperative to rural areas, attempting to induct the village under its aegis, as it were. Examples would include *Shikar* (*The Hunt*, 1968), *Izzat* (*Honor*, 1968), *Tere Mere Sapne* (*Your Dreams and Mine*, 1971), and *Zindagi Zindagi* (*Life Life*, 1972).

26. The double operates as more than a narrative convention in the Gothic. Doppelgängers do not simply befuddle and confuse, they function as metaphors for the general instabilities that afflict subjects and characters in these films. The ghostly double ruptures presence, wholeness, nationalist histories, and ontology in a fundamental way in all the films under discussion here.

27. Mary Ann Doane, "Paranoia and the Specular," in *The Desire to Desire: The Woman's Film of the 1940s* (Bloomington: Indiana University Press, 1987), 39.

28. During one of their early encounters, Kamini clearly tells Hari Shankar that he can never touch her, and that they can be unified in spirit only in death.

29. This is not to suggest that Madhubala's youthful radiance is inconsequential in the film's generation of meanings. However, the song signposts most emphatically the strength of her spell.

30. Emphasis in original. See Michel Chion, *The Voice in Cinema* (New York: Columbia University Press, 1999), 24.

31. Rick Altman has also argued that sound in the cinema is a powerful tool for generating enigmatic and uncanny effects: "The ramifications of sound's relative freedom as compared to the image are many; two in particular concern us here: 1) sound's ability to be heard around a corner makes it the ideal method of introducing the invisible, the mysterious, the supernatural (given that image = visible = real); 2) this very power of sound carries with it a concomitant danger—sound will

always carry with it the tension of the unknown until it is anchored by sight." Rick Altman, "Moving Lips: Cinema as Ventriloquism," *Yale French Studies* (60), Cinema/Sound (1980), 74.

32. Chion has also complicated his notion of the acousmetre by suggesting that the acousmatic voice is like the voice of God: "What are his powers? The powers are four: the ability to be everywhere, to see all, to know all, and to have complete power. In other words: ubiquity, panopticism, omniscience, and omnipotence." Chion, *The Voice in Cinema*, 24. Although the female ghost in the Hindi Gothic rarely harnesses this many powers, insofar as the spectral song demands complete submission, this layering works well for the Gothic.

33. Neepa Majumdar, "The Embodied Voice: Song Sequences and Stardom in Bombay Cinema," in *Wanted Cultured Ladies Only! Female Stardom and Cinema in India, 1930s–1950s* (Chicago: University of Illinois Press, 2009), 187–188.

34. In fact, achieving the aural quality of haunting was a key goal for Kamal Amrohi and Khemchand Prakash in the sound-recording process:

> In an interview, Lata Mangeshkar once told me how much inventiveness Amrohi, composer Prakash and she brought to the recording to give the song a ghostly feel: she stood in a corner of the studio, with the microphone at its centre and walked towards the microphone singing the opening verse, from *Khamosh hai zamana . . . to is aas key sahare*, and when she got close to the mike, she sang the refrain, *Aayega, aayega. . . .* After much trial and error with this procedure, the song was finally recorded to everyone's satisfaction. (Nasreen Munni Kabir, "Palace of Delusion: Kamal Amrohi's *Mahal* Is Our First Reincarnation Thriller," *Outlook India*, last modified June 4, 2012, accessed May 11, 2013, at www.outlookindia.com/magazine/story/palace-of-delusion/281005)

35. Sanjay Srivastava, "Voice, Gender and Space in Time of Five-Year Plans: The Idea of Lata Mangeshkar," *Economic and Political Weekly* 39 (20) (2004): 2019–2028.

36. Ibid., 2025.

37. Ibid., 2026.

38. See Majumdar for a detailed analysis of Lata's on-screen and off-screen personas.

39. Mani Kaul's *Duvidha* (*Dilemma*, 1973) and its Bollywood remake *Paheli* (*Puzzle*, Amol Palekar, 2005) are based on a folktale featuring ghostly beings who impersonate as spouses as well.

40. Chion, *The Voice in Cinema*, 23.

41. In one particularly important instance, he hears the song wafting to him as he sits in a park or garden beside a body of water. Greatly agitated, he rushes home, only to hear it being sung from within his locked, empty house.

42. Tithi Bhattacharya describes the ghostly protagonist of Tagore's story *Manihara* in similar terms, in terms of the intrusion of an uncanny female presence into the modern home: "It is not merely the house, but the *home*, the bastion of modern safety, the heart of bourgeois selfhood that is rendered unstable here

. . . The domestic space is not offered any respite from this deep unsettling fear." Tithi Bhattacharya, "Deadly Spaces: Ghosts, Histories and Colonial Anxieties in Nineteenth-Century Bengal," in *Postcolonial Ghosts, ed.* Mélanie Joseph-Vilain and Judith Misrahi-Barak (Montpellier: Presses Universitaires de la Méditerranée, Collection Les Carnets du Cerpac, no. 8, 2009), 148.

43. Dwyer, "Bombay Gothic," 144.

44. Sandhya tries to become intimate with Anand in the remarkably erotic song sequence, *Lag Ja Gale* ("Come into My Arms"), also sung by Lata. However, Anand is not able to overcome his fears and this attempt at seduction, too, remains incomplete.

45. Although Hari Shankar never sings in *Mahal*, he does play the piano, and Anand participates in a rock-and-roll song-and-dance number and also sings a love duet. But all these musical interludes take place before Seema is murdered and Sandhya's ghostly sightings become frequent.

46. Radha, as it turns out, was indeed masquerading as the ghost, but it is her human, corporeal, playful avatar that bewitches Kumar.

47. Contemporary reviews of the film lauded its style, even as they remained somewhat skeptical of screenplay and narrative. For example, the (habitually acerbic) critic at *Mother India* lamented:

> Quite an amount of suspense is maintained in the story but there are many loose bits which give away the secret. The production values are quite suitable, the sound and photography being particularly successful in creating an eerie atmosphere. The music is attractive. The song that is supposed to have a haunt has it. Usually the Indian pictures promise one thing and give another. The lyrics are well-worded. The direction is quite competent. The director would have done better had he had a better screenplay. ("*Bees Saal Bad*, a Murder Mystery: Good Time-Killer for the Masses," *Mother India*, July 1, 1962)

In the same vein, the *Filmfare* critic also compliments the film's stylistic aspects, especially its music, cinematography, and editing:

> Appropriate background music and hauntingly melodious songs, particularly the "kahin deep jale kahin deep" number, further enhance the appeal of "Bees Saal Baad," which marks the debut of maestro Hemant Kumar as a Hindi film producer and of art director Biren Naug as a sensitive director. Marshal Braganza, who has photographed several hit films, successfully creates the eerie atmosphere which is absolutely necessary to the film. In technical values, setting, décor and especially, editing it is a first class production. ("'Bees Saal Baad' Grips, Despite Several Failings," *Filmfare*, June 1, 1962)

48. The swamp of reeds is a particularly rich space for the creation of the acousmatic song and for building suspense in *Bees Saal Baad*.

49. Derrida, *Specters of Marx*, 6.

50. Walter Benjamin, "Theses on the Philosophy of History," in *Illuminations*, ed. Hannah Arendt, trans. Harry Zohn, 253–264 (New York: Schocken Books, 1969).

51. Bliss Cua Lim, "Spectral Time, Heterogeneous Space: The Ghost Film as Historical Allegory," in *Translating Time: Cinema, the Fantastic, and Temporal Critique* (Durham, NC: Duke University Press, 2009), 149.

52. Dwyer, "Bombay Gothic," 139.

53. Lim, "Spectral Time, Heterogeneous Space," 152.

54. A notable exception is *Bees Saal Baad*, where Lata's song is not only heard by the hero Kumar, but the entire village community responds with alarm to its eerie quality.

55. Hari Shankar travels for three years constantly in the company of his beleaguered wife, Ranjana, in an unsuccessful attempt to find peace. Anand is also taken to Simla to "recuperate," but, of course, Sandhya's song follows him there as well and the convalescent vacation is soon aborted.

56. In many of Ann Radcliff's novels, ghosts turn out to be figments of characters' imaginations:

> Radcliffe's ghosts illustrate how an overwrought (and therefore Gothic) imagination can become overly stimulated by fantastical ideas. In *The Mysteries of Udolpho* (1794) and *The Italian* (1797) Radcliffe's ghosts expose the provenance of imaginative and emotional excess. Her ghosts are bogus, employed by villains to dupe superstitious 'heroes' and thus doubly spectral—the ghost of a ghost as it were. Such ghosts participate in the female Gothic's language of subtle and implied terrors. (Andrew Smith, "Hauntings," in *Routledge Companion to the Gothic*, ed. Spooner and McEvoy [New York: Routledge, 2007], 147)

57. Wendy F. Hsu, "Between Narrative and Expressive, Fantasy and Melodrama in Bombay (Bollywood) Film," *Virginia Review of Asian Studies* 5 (2003), 6.

58. In *Mahal*, for example, the last half hour is thick with policemen, lawyers, judges, the general public at the hearing, and so forth.

59. Michel Chion, *Audio-Vision: Sound on Screen*, trans. Claudia Gorbman (New York: Columbia University Press, 1994), 130.

60. Reviewers of the time noted this contrived climax and closure as well; one of them scornfully noted: "A dozen or more villains appear at the end as if by magic; they are delivered to the audience in package form—under arrest. Then a policeman gives a summary of the news before the camera. Don't ask us how villains, policeman, heroine, 'ghost' and hero come together in the haunted house . . . The film falls flat on its face at the end, but it was good going most of the way." See "*Woh Kaun Thi?*: Sensitively Directed," 33.

61. In *Mahal*, there are multiple dissolves between Asha's testimony in the courtroom and scenes from the past, where she sings to Hari Shankar and convinces him of her ghostly desire. *Woh Kaun Thi?* uses a plethora of visual effects—split screens, irises, and so on—to help spectators revisit and recalibrate the earlier sequences of haunting.

1. This type of rehabilitation of a previously "debased" and marginalized formation is similar to what Sconce had described as the paracinematic drive:

> paracinema is . . . less a distinct group of films than a particular reading protocol, a counter-aesthetic turned subcultural sensibility devoted to all manner of cultural detritus. In short, the explicit manifesto of paracinematic culture is to valorize all forms of cinematic "trash," whether such films have been either explicitly rejected or simply ignored by legitimate film culture. In doing so, paracinema represents the most developed and dedicated of cinephilic subcultures ever to worship at the "temple of schlock."

It is precisely a paracinematic moment that enables the Ramsay films—and other forms of its kind like the copycat films of Mohan Bhakri and Vinod Talwar—to have a global fan-base on the Internet in the current moment. See Jeffrey Sconce, "'Trashing' the Academy: Taste, Excess, and an Emerging Politics of Cinematic Style," *Screen* 36 (4) (1995): 371–393.

2. Grady Hendrix, "Kaiju Shakedown: The Ramsays of Bollywood," March 20, 2015, available at www.filmcomment.com/blog/kaiju-shakedown-the-ramsays-of-bollywood/.

3. Sleaze, as Sconce reminds us,

> is less a definable historical genre than an ineffable quality—a tone that is a function of attitude as much as content—it by necessity evokes a whole range of textual issues, from the industrial mechanics of low-budget exploitation to the ever shifting terrains of reception and taste. Sleaziness is a presence that must be inscribed into a text by some manner of evaluation and critical labor; that is, sleaze is a feeling one has about a film . . . that requires judging, if only in one's imagination, that there is something "improper" or "untoward" about a given text. Often sleaziness implies a circuit of inappropriate exchange involving suspect authorial intentions and/or displaced perversities in the audience. (Jeffrey Sconce, ed., *Sleaze Artists: Cinema at the Margins of Taste, Style, and Politics* [Durham, NC: Duke University Press, 2007], 4)

4. The term "integrated" may be something of a misnomer, however, because many of the Western influences in the Ramsay film remain "attractions"—stand-alone tropes, motifs, or set pieces that are randomly inserted into plots that share extremely tenuous links with the originals.

5. "The Ramsay movies mirrored beliefs prevalent in rural India, such as a chudail (witch) whose feet do a 180 degree turn before she reveals herself or a medieval curse that holds true in present day. The Censor Board would order a disclaimer preceding some films to rubbish any superstition they might encourage. . . . The Ramsays mixed and matched from horror movies from around the world.

Their movies are full of influences for a horror aficionado to spot. Gothic horror sequences with an overdose of smoke and diffused blue light. Stuffed animals from Alfred Hitchcock and Hammer movies. The use of primary colour filters from Italian horror maker Mario Bava's *Black Sabbath* and *Blood and Black Lace*. Chase sequences from American slasher films like *Black Christmas* (Bob Clark) and *Friday the 13th* (Sean S. Cunningham). And an obsession with Bram Stoker so that coffins house creatures of every faith, even those vanquished by an Om sign or Shiva's trident. The brothers' films rarely matched these movies in their execution, but the lodestone of Ramsay horror, the gore—rolling heads, blood baths and ghastly faces—often helped mask the lack of technical expertise or inability to sustain a mood." Rishi Majumder, "Ramsay International," *Motherland* 7 (2012), last modified May 2012, accessed December 2004, at www.motherlandmagazine.com/ghost-issue/ramsay-international.

6. Pete Tombs, Valentina Vitali, and Sangita Gopal all read the Ramsay film as an unprecedented novelty in the media landscape of this period.

7. The Ramsays insist that they do not "copy," but instead "Indianize" foreign films, whose storylines seem to be "small." This restructuring is essential for ensuring that plots and elements "can be digestible to local audiences." Tulsi Ramsay, interview by Meheli Sen, Bombay, July 8, 2009.

8. Notably, some Ramsay films are "thrillers"—*Do Gaz Zameen Ke Neeche*, *Aur Kaun*, *Telephone*, and so on—but did not have supernatural agents after all, in yet another resonance with the old Gothic film.

9. A contemporary review of *3D Saamri*, for example, contains the following paragraph:

> But Tulsi and Shyam Ramsay's little baby, for all the mystery of its hero being a great practitioner of the black arts, is that unusual horror film that is more a laugh raiser than a hair-raiser, and the mirth it engenders is entirely due to the characters in their story projecting abject fear in situations that are positively funny rather than fearsome. So instead of *Saamri* scaring the people out of their wits, it nearly gives them a stich in their side from laughing at its easily scared characters and their follies. ("*Saamri*: Horror's New Dimension," *Screen*, November 22, 1985, 4)

Even more disdainful was Sudhir Gaikwad's review of *Bandh Darwaza*:

> [Y]es people, it's happened—the Ramsay clan's (India's answer to Hitchcock, Hammer films, Spielberg and all the rest) latest horror comes a-splashing goo and gore, spewing forth hocus pocus and gobbledy-gook across the city's movie screens—unimaginatively and irreverently titled (like all the rest of the film is unimaginative and ludicrous) *Bandh Darwaza*. The central figure of the film, undead monstrous vampire Nevla (Anirudh Agarwal) is a cross between Count Dracula, Frankenstein, a senile Michael Jackson, gone-to-seed Mick Jagger and a laboratory variety skeleton.
>
> Plastence [*sic*] veins popping across his forehead, jackboots, waistcoat,

> tails, satin cloak and bloodshot eyes, the kind one has after an all-night binge with a caseful of Bullfighter rum (no water), Nevla the Don of darkness flits about, choking a maiden here, piercing another's slender neck there, thereby causing much distress to citizens around Kali Pahadi. ("*Bandh Darwaza*: Howls, Cowls and Scowls," *Maharashtra Herald*, June 18, 1990)

The regional language presses were equally scathing toward the Ramsay film and its intended audiences; for example, the Marathi-language review of *Veerana* ran thusly:

> Ghost/horror stories and such melodramatic forms have their own viewership. These viewers expect to be entertained through extreme or shocking elements in the film. They do not bother about the story or the philosophy behind it. The Ramsay brothers have made a mark in this type of filmmaking. They do not even pretend to have any other stake in their filmmaking, that is the refreshing part.
>
> *Veerana* is that kind of a film by them. But despite having thoroughly combed through this narrow style of storytelling, the director brothers, Tulsi and Shyam Ramsay, seem not to have been moved to look for anything new in this small area that they inhabit. They keep using the same formulae of haunted stories, the same tricks for creating fear (a black cat, a beautiful girl on the road asking for a lift, the car losing control). They are not successful with creating fear through these fantastic means, so then they end up using crude masks as well and end up failing in their attempt. (Ashok Rane, "The Shortage of Newness in Ramsay Brothers' Story!" *Mumbai Sakal*, May 13, 1988)

The earlier *Dahshat*, similarly, provoked scorn from the film critic of *Kesari*, a major Marathi publication:

> Sorry, it is impossible of all the Ramsay brothers here for lack of space. The newest familial effort emerging out of the fear-foundry is "Dahshat." Leave aside experiencing the terror in the title, one fails to feel an iota of fear in this movie. One cannot doubt the sincerity of devotion of the Ramsay brothers to the genre of haunted film. But the audience collapses in laughter instead of fear at this relentless attempt to induce fear. Because of the familiarity [with this kind of approach], they mock the horror in the movies of the Ramsay brothers. In this movie, "Dahshat" by the Ramsay brothers, the dish made by 7 cooks becomes a film to mock rather than a horror film. (Aruna Antarkar, "Seven Cooks [De]Construct a Dish," trans. Anjali Nerlekar, *Kesari*, July 14, 1981)

10. Pete Tombs, whose essay was one of the first overviews of horror in Indian cinema, could only manage a tone of embarrassed affection for the genre: "The films must have a monster and the monster must look gruesome. Filmmakers talk about the concept of a 'horror face,' meaning that the evil within the creature must

be outwardly visible. Due to the lack of special effects available until quite recently, this generally meant that the monster looked like it had a three-day-old pizza stuck to its face. Fangs would have to be real whoppers, at least four or five inches in length, and the monster must always be a lumbering giant." Pete Tombs, "The Beast from Bollywood: A History of the Indian Horror Film," in *Fear Without Frontiers: Horror Cinema Across the Globe*, ed. Steven Jay Schneider (Godalming, UK: FAB Press, 2003), 245–246. Similarly, Kartik Nair's work on the genre also emphasizes the general incompetence of the production apparatus: "The genre's conventions, forced into visibility by the yawning gap between aspiration and accomplishment—when the make-up is under-baked, or the camera doesn't move nearly fast enough, or when the cat looks less like it's jumping into the frame and more like it's being chucked into it by a spotboy—can be moments of unintentional hilarity, as globally circulating 'signs' of horror are shriveled to an embarrassingly inchoate generic language that cannot conceal its own manufacturedness." Kartik Nair, "Fear on Film: The Ramsay Brothers and Bombay's Horror Cinema," *Sarai Reader* 8 (2008), 258.

11. The state-sponsored Film Finance Corporation (FFC) was a product of this era as well, established to encourage new filmmakers and the dissemination of "good" cinema. Mrinal Sen's *Bhuvan Shome* (1969) was one of the first films produced by the FFC, which eventually became its current avatar NFDC (National Film Development Corporation). So, the 1970s also saw the flowering of different kinds of cinema in India, and only some of these have been considered worthy of serious consideration until recently.

12. Describing the reception of action-adventure-fantasy genres of the silent period, Kaushik Bhaumik writes: "The stories and performers were all seen as rising from a disreputable quarter of popular performances, from a space that . . . I have called the *bazaar*, serving the rude and simple desires of the unlettered folk of the subcontinent. Dirty bodies, then, in and for a sordid cultural universe . . . The solution to this problem was a universally endorsed one—bring in the literate middle class and one would get a better cinema." Kaushik Bhaumik, "Querying the 'Traditional' Roots of Silent Cinema in Asia," *Journal of the Moving Image* (2008), accessed December 23, 2015, at www.jmionline.org/articles/2008/querying_the_traditional_roots_of_silent_cinema_in_asia.pdf.

13. See Kartik Nair, "Taste, Taboo, Trash: The Story of the Ramsay Brothers," *Bioscope: South Asian Screen Studies* 3 (2) (2012); and Sangita Gopal, *Conjugations: Marriage and Form in New Bollywood Cinema* (Chicago: University of Chicago Press, 2011).

14. Nair, "Fear on Film," 255.

15. Tulsi Ramsay, interview by Meheli Sen, July 8, 2009.

16. Nair has therefore understood the Ramsay enterprise as a "cottage industry of horror." See Nair, "Fear on Film," 254.

17. Sangita Gopal, for example, has argued persuasively that the Ramsay horror film was in fact a perfect fit for B circuits in India at this time:

> Because it could not capture the mainstream market, the genre got plugged into what was known in India as the B circuit. This vast sector of the film

> industry consisted of small distribution companies dealing in low-budget products, reruns, soft porn, down-market imports, dubbed films from other languages, and other marginal products. B movies typically played in decrepit movie theaters that operated on razor-thin margins, in lower-income urban and suburban neighborhoods, small towns, and the semirural hinterlands. . . . Horror as a genre possessed attributes—sensationalism, action-oriented plot line, simplistic structure, low production cost—that made it ideal for this improvised and ramshackle circuit of exhibition and reception. (Gopal, *Conjugations*, 95–96)

18. In a recent interview, Shyam Ramsay claimed that some of their films performed poorly because they were too far ahead of their time and much too advanced for the target audience:

> I made a film called *Andhera* (1975). It was a very well made film, and ahead of its time.
>
> It was based on the Hollywood film *Boston Strangler*. In my film, a killer loses both his limbs and he starts killing with his artificial limbs. The police don't suspect him because he has no hands.
>
> The audience was not prepared for that. If the film was made today, it would do good business because now people understand robots.
>
> Another film, *Guest House*, also flopped. In the film, four men cut a person's hand and the amputated hand murders people.
>
> There was no ghost, just a creepy hand that keeps killing people. This movie was not accepted at all.
>
> People in small centres still want to watch horror films that have witches and feet turned backwards; in fact people in B and C centres still believe in such things. ("Shyam Ramsay: People Say the Ghosts in My Films Were Not Scary," *Rediff*, last modified March 13, 2014, accessed June 25, 2015, at www.rediff.com/movies/report/slide-show-1-shyam-ramsay-people-say-the-ghosts-in-my-films-were-not-scary/20140313.htm?print=true)

19. Tulsi Ramsay, interview by Meheli Sen, July 8, 2009. Although initially reluctant to gender his projected audiences, Tulsi Ramsay finally conceded that "perhaps only 30 percent of [our] audiences were female." Ibid.

20. It ought to be noted that the notion of spectatorship in cinema studies does not necessarily refer to actual people who buy tickets and form audiences of any given film. Modes of address and formal particularities posit an "ideal spectator," a position that the film most effectively speaks to.

21. "But time is not the only factor that explains the silence surrounding this brief period. This silence can also be explained in terms of the unsettling nature of what went on during those 21 months when democratic rights were suspended under Indira Gandhi and coercive measures brought into play. Press censorship, arrests, torture, the demolition of slums and tales of forcible sterilization have all

made the Emergency fertile food for fiction, but uncomfortable ground for historical, political or sociological analysis. . . . The silence that surrounds the Emergency 'as fact' is not entirely accidental." Emma Tarlo, *Unsettling Memories: Narratives of the Emergency in Delhi* (Berkeley: University of California Press, 2003), 2.

22. Ibid., 10.

23. Ibid., 52.

24. Ibid.

25. In the editorial of a special issue devoted to the Emergency and its cinemas, the authors continue:

> The legacies for the 1970s for cinema remain palpable today. The parallel cinema, documentary filmmaking, and film industries outside Bombay thrive because of talent and institutional initiatives originating in the 1970s. Likewise, the "New Bollywood" cinema of the 1990s and beyond continues to reckon with political commitments made two decades earlier. The expansion of India's media culture that is so palpable today must likewise recon with the dramatic expansion that occurred in that culture during the 1970s. (Rajinder Dudrah and Priya Joshi, "Editorial: The 1970s and Its Legacies in India's Cinemas," *South Asian Popular Culture* 10 [1] [2012]: 1–5)

26. Priya Joshi, *Bollywood's India: A Public Fantasy* (New York: Columbia University Press, 2015), 64.

27. M. Madhava Prasad, *Ideology of the Hindi Film: A Historical Construction* (New Delhi: Oxford University Press, 2001), 118.

28. It is instructive to recall that risking the historical alliances of the Congress, Indira Gandhi's brand of populism was specifically aimed at the lower and lower-middle classes, and as Vitali reminds us, "the very same populism had the effect of alienating the layers upon which Congress had so far relied for its legitimacy." Valentina Vitali, "The Evil I: Realism and Scopophilia in the Horror Films of the Ramsay Brothers," in *Beyond the Boundaries of Bollywood*, ed. Rachel Dwyer and Jerry Pinto (New Delhi: Oxford University Press, 2011), 80. In an astonishing moment in the Ramsay film *Dak Bangla*, a minister—a comic buffoon played by Rajendra Nath—invokes Indira Gandhi's famous battle cry, *Garibi hatao* (abolish poverty): "*Main soch raha hoon, ki garibi hatayi jay, ya garibon ko hataya jai? Na rahega baans, na bajegi bansuri*" (I have been thinking, should we abolish poverty, or just get rid of the poor? That would do away with the root of the problem). Although satirizing politicians is not new to the cinema of the 1980s, the direct reference to the Emergency discourse—of helping the poor while rendering them homeless—does lend a certain subversive charge to the humor of this sequence. This is not the only way the Ramsay film would reference the Emergency, as I show in this inquiry, but this moment stands out for its audacity.

29. Gopal, *Conjugations*, 95.

30. "With an estimated five million TV sets, and a nightly audience of more than 50 million, a soap opera in a single night has a viewership larger than the *entire* audience of a hit movie! Film revenues have shot down by 40 percent from what

they were two-and-a-half years ago while unreleased films pile on the shelves. . . . All the classic symptoms . . . are here: Falling audience figures, the bulldozing of theatres, and a series of flops of 'big' movies." I. Masood, "The Not So Popular Cinema," *Utsav 1985–1986* (New Delhi: DIFF, 20–25), 22, as quoted in Nair, "Taste, Taboo, Trash," 132.

31. Here, I am gesturing toward a general lumpenization and criminalization of the public sphere in the 1980s—a process that began with the Emergency and continued well after it was officially called off. Hindi cinema in general and the Ramsay film in particular makes meaning within this rapidly transforming social and political imaginary.

32. According to Nair:

> The fact is that the brothers had struck gold in the dead of night, scoring their biggest hit in the dark corridor of Bombay film history, a corridor reverberating with the doom-and-gloom of falling admissions and the footfalls of film pirates.
>
> *Purana Mandir* had in fact been diverted to the black market during the very week of its release. From a Bombay video-parlor, police recovered videotape copies of the film, along with the rudimentary technology being used for exhibition: "Video cassettes of *Purana Mandir* which was being shown to about 75 persons was seized from the parlour. . . . The police also seized a Nelco VCR, Weston TV, and Rs 105 in cash. Mohd. Rafiq and Mohd. Shafi were arrested. *Film Information*, October 27, 1984." (As quoted in Nair, "Taste, Taboo, Trash," 132)

33. Linnie Blake, *The Wounds of Nations: Horror Cinema, Historical Trauma and National Identity* (Manchester, UK: Manchester University Press, 2012), 2. She further suggests that "the ways in which the generic and sub-generic conventions of horror allow for a decoding of traumatic memories already encoded at the cultural, social, psychic, and political life of the nation's inhabitants by shocking historical events." Ibid., 5.

34. Adam Lowenstein, *Shocking Representation: Historical Trauma, National Cinema, and the Modern Horror Film* (New York: Columbia University Press, 2005), 9.

35. Dudrah and Joshi, "Editorial," 3.

36. A possible reason for this reluctance to connect the Ramsay film to the earlier Gothic genre may be a cinephiliac resistance to discuss the older films—much cherished by audiences and scholars alike—in the same terms as the debased Ramsay product.

37. I do not mean to imply an indexical or "reflectionist" reading of the genre in question; the relationship between the social and the cinematic is far more complex than this. However, I am suggesting that the Ramsay film makes meaning in an intersecting web of determinants—social and industrial, as well as technological.

38. An exception is the big-budget *Ghungroo Ki Awaz* (also directed by Shyam and Tulsi Ramsay, 1981) that featured Rekha and Vijay Anand as stars and was pro-

duced by the prestigious production house Navketan. In tone, style, iconography, and narrative, *Ghungroo* is very close to the ghost films of the 1950s, including a mysterious woman who haunts the hero through her phantom song. Perhaps all of these exceptions explain why this particular film text is rarely mentioned in any discussion of the Ramsay genre.

39. This, again, is Chion's "acousmatic" sound, wherein the film stubbornly refuses to show us what body the voice we hear normally inhabits. It is also crucial to remember that the voice-over is a point of authority in the narration, the omniscient "truth-telling" voice, as it were. In the Ramsay context, it is used in a markedly different manner than the spectral songs in the older Gothic texts.

40. Madhava Prasad, for example, has argued that the customary late arrival of the police in Hindi cinema, after the villains have been decisively defeated by the hero, "attests not only to the endorsement of a feudal system of justice by the representatives of the modern state, it also enacts the formal alliance between these two sites of power which retain their separate identities." Prasad, *Ideology of the Hindi Film*, 96.

41. Ravi Vasudevan, "Disreputable and Illegal Publics: Cinematic Allegories in Times of Crisis," *Sarai Reader* 4 (2004), 73.

42. These characters share the names of Shyam and Kumar Ramsay, perhaps as the insertion of an "in-joke" in the film.

43. Interestingly, the zombie as a figure is actually mentioned in Rajvash's diary in this film, more than four decades before Bollywood's first "official" zombie films released in 2013.

44. Vitali, "The Evil I," 86.

45. Describing the delirious inchoateness of the Ramsay Film, Shubhajit Chatterjee writes, "In fact the random assortments of mise en scene and thematic motifs (ranging from Islamicate mansions, Tantric backdrops, quasi Gothic decors and Christian graveyards, to sporadic references to indigenous spiritual cults) endow them with a conflicted and hesitant ideological texture that resists any easy mapping within the grid of communal and decentralizing political forces accumulating through the 1980s." Shubhajit Chatterjee, "On Disreputable Genres: B Movies and Revisionary Histories of Bombay Cinema," *Marg* 64 (4) (2013): 32–41.

46. See Gopal, *Conjugations*, Chap. 1.

47. The extremely popular song "Jawaani Jaaneman Haseen Dilruba" from *Namak Halal* (1982) is only one of the many memorable disco songs of this era.

48. Geeta Dayal, "Studio 84: Digging into the History of Disco in India," *The Original Sound Track*, last modified August 29, 2010, accessed June 25, 2015, at www.theoriginalsoundtrack.com/2010/08/29/studio-84-the-history-of-disco-in-india/.

49. Gopal, *Conjugations*, 40.

50. The Ramsay film's romancing of contemporary global pop music does not end with disco. Michael Jackson's music—especially the video of *Thriller* (1983)—had an enormous influence on the genre, and Indian pop culture more broadly. In *3D Saamri*, the comic chef Changez Khan (Jagdeep) sings and dances in a cemetery

with a large crowd of un-dead, both replicating and paying tribute to the global chartbuster. I suspect this is also how the Ramsays were hoping to address a different audience segment than their standard spectators.

51. Kartik Nair, "Temple of Womb," *New Inquiry*, last modified July 23, 2013, accessed January 2015, at http://thenewinquiry.com/essays/temple-of-womb/.

52. Nair argues that the terror that gathers around procreation and fertility in *Punara Mandir* "ventilates the Emergency-era imagination of the urban-underclass male as a figure of threatening virility that must be checked. In classic ideological fashion, the film gives him an action-hero narrative and a villain to emasculate. But it also confusingly recirculates the figure of the urban-underclass male as traumatized by the technologies of the Emergency." Ibid.

53. Given the parameters that the Indian censor board operates within, full nudity or sex could not be represented. However, female bodies are foregrounded primarily for voyeuristic titillation of the spectator in the Ramsay film.

54. Tulsi Ramsay is very clear about the advantages of having an A certificate. He insists that a milder rating would have harmed his commerce because audiences would have assumed that "there's nothing to see" in films rated U/A. Tulsi Ramsay, interview by Meheli Sen, July 8, 2009.

55. Men, for the most part, remain decorously clothed in the genre. However, B actors such as Puneet Issar and Hemant Birje occasionally strip down to display rippling muscles, especially in the action sequences and fight scenes of the genre. It is worthwhile to keep in mind that heroes did not often display their bodies in this manner in the 1980s; the pleasures and sensations offered by the genre are, thus, transgressive on multiple levels.

56. Although the Ramsay horror film's notoriety can partially be linked to this consistent inclusion of rape and sexual violence, it is instructive to recall that violence in the mainstream Hindi cinema also escalated significantly at this time. The rape-revenge genre, as mentioned in the last chapter, congeals as a genre in the 1980s. Sexual violence was not exclusive to horror cinema at this time.

57. Barbara Creed, *The Monstrous-Feminine: Film, Feminism, Psychoanalysis* (New York: Routledge, 1993), 31. Creed also suggests that the figure of the witch (although Nakita is a *chudail* who displays vampiric tendencies in the garbled Ramsay grammar) challenges the patriarchal symbolic order in a special way: "The witch is defined as an abject figure in that she is represented within patriarchal discourses as an implacable enemy of the symbolic order. She is thought to be dangerous and wily, capable of drawing on her evil powers to wreak destruction on the community. The witch sets out to unsettle the boundaries between the rational and irrational, symbolic and imaginary." Ibid., 76.

58. In a recent interview with Shyam Ramsay, Jasmine's indiscretions continue to be a topic of conversation: "'Jasmine (the heroine of the cult Ramsay film *Veerana* in the '80s) would lure young boys to bed. That's bad, no?' he asks. 'She was possessed by evil spirits . . . But I exposed her decently.'" Shyam Ramsay, interview by Paramita Ghosh, "King of Creeps," *Hindustan Times*, last modified Septem-

ber 11, 2010, at www.hindustantimes.com/entertainment/king-of-creeps/article1-599031.aspx.

59. For a reading of non-normative sexual behaviors, especially incest and necrophilia in the Ramsay film, see also Mithuraaj Dhusiya, "The Ramsay Chronicles: Non-Normative Sexualities in *Purana Mandir* and *Bandh Darwaza*," in V. Kishore, A. Sarwal, and P. Patra, eds., *Bollywood and Its Other(s): Towards New Configurations* (London: Palgrave Macmillan UK, 2014), 174–185.

60. Aditi Sen, "'I Wasn't Born with Enough Middle Fingers': How Low-Budget Horror Films Defy Sexual Morality and Heteronormativity in Bollywood," *Acta Orientalia Vilnensia* 12 (2) (2011): 75–90.

61. Harry M. Benshoff, *Monsters in the Closet: Homosexuality and the Horror Film* (Manchester, UK: Manchester University Press, 1997).

62. Shyam Ramsay, "King of Creeps."

CHAPTER THREE: RAVISHING REPTILES

1. Rachel Dwyer, who mentions the snake film in passing, notes this gap in Indian cinema studies when she writes, "[T]he low status of these films is underlined by the fact that *An Encyclopedia of Indian Cinema* (Rajadhyaksha and Willemen 1999) lists over fifty films with '*naag*' and related 'snake' words in their titles but discusses only two, the Kannada film *Nagakannika* (1949, dir. G. Vishwanathan), only because it is a folklore film on the lines of the Telegu *Patala Bhairavi*, and *Nagin* (1954, dir. Nandlal Jaswantlal)." Rachel Dwyer, *Filming the Gods: Religion and Indian Cinema* (London: Routledge, 2006), 49.

2. Amanda A. Klein, "Introduction: Love at First Sight," in *American Film Cycles* (Austin: University of Texas Press, 2011), 3–4.

3. Films involving magical snakes exist in other countries, too, such as Tsui Hark's sumptuous fantasy *Green Snake* (1993), which is based on Chinese myths involving shape-shifting serpents.

4. Films like *Nagin* (1954) revolve around tribes of warring snake charmers, but the supernatural snake film that I discuss here is a somewhat distinct generic form. *Vishkanya* (1991), which was a late entrant into the snake-film genre, was not a commercial success, but it launched the career of Pooja Bedi, who thereafter gained notoriety for modeling for a condom brand.

5. The presence of snakes in mythic narratives is, of course, not specific to South Asia. The serpent in Eden and Quetzalcoatl are only two famous figures in a global tapestry of mythic snakes. But the sheer profusion of snakes in Indian mythology is noteworthy: Shesh-naag, Vasukhi, Nagaraja, goddess Manasa's pet snakes, and various snake goddesses in the southern Indian states are only some of the magical-fantastical serpents that populate the subcontinent.

6. Whereas snakes in Judeo-Christian traditions remain largely phallic—a notion furthered by Western psychoanalytic readings—the gendered associations of

the serpent remain far more complex in South Asian narratives; if anything, snakes are more often associated with feminine power and female deities, such as Manasa in Bengal and a number of South Indian goddesses, rather than masculine ones.

7. Amy Allocco writes in "Fear, Reverence and Ambivalence: Divine Snakes in Contemporary South India," in *Charming Beauties and Frightful Beasts: Non-Human Animals in South Asian Myth, Ritual and Folklore*, ed. Fabrizio M. Ferrari and Thomas Dähnhart, 217–235 (Sheffield, UK: Equinox Publishing, 2013): "It is likely that fear of snakes (*nāgas*) and their poison was an early motivation for their propitiation, or that some of snakes' unique characteristics, such as the periodic shedding of their skin, led to their being ascribed magical powers and eventually being deified. Whatever initially catalysed religious and ritual interest in snakes, it is clear that Indic traditions have long regarded them as divinities linked with water, fertility and anthills" (p. 217). She further notes that

> similar ideas persist in South India, where the karmic consequences of one's conduct toward snakes continue to be understood as truly literal. Snakes are believed to retaliate in kind for sufferings endured; for example, farmers who kill snakes in their fields, householders who disturb mating snakes, or those who knock down anthills wherein snakes were living will be similarly deprived of livelihood, progeny, and shelter. . . . There are significant homologies between the beliefs about *nāgas*' curses chronicled in . . . early- and mid-twentieth-century sources and those that circulate in contemporary South India. Maligned snakes are most commonly thought to curse their antagonists with childlessness while diseases and conditions affecting the skin and eyes are counted among their secondary set of afflictions. (p. 218)

See also Amy Allocco, "Snakes in the Dark Age: Human Action, Karmic Retribution, and the Possibilities for Hindu Animal Ethics," in *Asian Perspectives on Animal Ethics: Rethinking the Nonhuman*, ed. Neil Dalal and Chloe Taylor, 179–201 (London: Routledge, 2014).

8. Anat Pick, *Creaturely Poetics: Animality and Vulnerability in Literature and Film* (New York: Columbia University Press, 2011), 106.

9. Ferrari and Dähnhardt, "Introduction," in *Charming Beauties and Frightful Beasts*, ed. Ferrari and Dähnhardt, xii–xiii.

10. Temporality is an especially interesting coordinate of the snake film, as both enchanted/messianic and secular/homogenous temporal structures often inhabit the same films. Although the mythic or folkloric themes of these films often invoke "time immemorial," the rest of the narrative often unfolds in the contemporary here and now. Anustup Basu calls this the "curvature of time in which a linear temporal imagination combines with a cyclical one." Anustup Basu, "The Eternal Return and Overcoming 'Cape Fear': Science, Sensation, Superman and Hindu Nationalism in Recent Hindi Cinema, *South Asian History and Culture*, special issue, *South Asian Transnationalisms: Cultural Exchange in the Twentieth Century* 2 (4) (2011), 561.

11. Rachel Dwyer, "The Biggest Star of All: The Elephant in Hindi Cinema," in *Charming Beauties and Frightful Beasts*, ed. Ferrari and Dähnhardt, 190.

12. Interestingly, in the mid-1960s, *Filmfare* ran a feature on Vinod Desai, producer-director of several films featuring snakes that were considered to be "mythologicals" in generic terms. The article proclaims that the 1953 film *Nag Panchmi*, produced by Desai, was a huge commercial success:

> The first film of Vinod Desai to feature snakes was "Nag Panchmi." Directed by Raman B. Desai, the picture became a big hit of 1953, enjoyed silver jubilee runs in a number of cities and yielded as many as 150 prints which is something of a record for a mythological film. With his next film, "Raj Kanya," which again featured snakes, Vinod Desai himself turned director. The three other snake-infested films he has since produced and directed are "Gouri Puja," "Nag Champa" and "Nag Devta." ("Behind the Scenes," *Filmfare*, November 27, 1964, 45)

See also Rosie Thomas, who has argued that the *masala* film of the 1970s and 1980s cannot be understood except in relation to the magic-fantasy-action films of the silent era: "The importance of a history of Bombay cinema told 'from below'—through the frame of the magic and fighting films—is that it brings to our attention the crucial role played by these lower-brow forms in the rise of the big-budget masala film in the 1970s. The spectacle, action and special effects magic of the B-movies were all greedily incorporated within the conventions of the mega-masala films that ruled the box office of that decade. . . . " Rosie Thomas, *Bombay Before Bollywood: Film City Fantasies* (Albany: SUNY Press, 2013), 15.

13. As Amanda Klein notes in *American Film Cycles*, 20: "We can . . . view film cycles as a mold placed over the zeitgeist, which, when pulled away reveals the contours, fissures, and complicated patterns of the contemporary moment. By revisiting the sites of their release, promotion, and reception, we can not only understand how and why these films fell to the margins (and the ideology and politics behind their outlaw status), but also expand the way film studies documents and theorizes the history of cinema."

14. Juwen Zhang, "Filmic Folklore and Chinese Cultural Identity," *Western Folklore* 64 (3–4) (2005): 263–280.

15. The endurance and power of these discourses are so significant that animal-activist-turned-politician Maneka Gandhi regularly writes columns debunking myths about snakes that are irresponsibly disseminated by Hindi movies. She seems especially outraged by the recursive cinematic trope of snakes drinking milk on Nag Panchami, a falsification of serpentine physiology, she argues. See, for example, Maneka Gandhi, "Tell It to the Birds," *Hindu*, last modified February 24, 2013, at www.thehindu.com/todays-paper/tp-features/tp-sundaymagazine/tell-it-to-the-birds/article4448002.ece.

16. Suchitra Mathur's work on the *Nagraj* comic series offers a valuable summary of snake myths and popular culture:

> "Hindutva" has invented an Indian tradition that is a curious amalgamation of Hindu scriptures and mythologies along with popular legends that are given a specifically Hindu spin. It is this last set that is particularly relevant to *Nagraj*, which draws upon the folklore of *ichchadhari nagas*—shape-shifting snakes—and combines it with the Naga cult of Hinduism. In Hindu mythology, snakes, especially the *nag* (cobra), are revered as protectors and worshipped as symbols of prosperity and fertility. The festival of Naag-Panchami, for instance, is dedicated to the snake goddess and is celebrated across India by feeding snakes on the fifth day of the month of Shravan. But in addition to this specifically Hindu mythology regarding snakes, there also exist legends about *ichchadhari nagas* that have no direct relationship with the idea of the naga as a divinity. These legends tell the tale of a breed of snakes that over millennia have developed the power of shape-shifting and can thus exist in the form of both humans and snakes. Romantic stories about the mutual loyalty of *ichchadhari naga* couples (who always avenge the unlawful death of their partners) and the precious magical "*mani*" (jewel) set in the hood of the male *nagraj* (king cobra) permeate the popular imagination and have found frequent expression in the world of Hindi cinema. Significantly, in all such myths and legends, snakes are viewed positively, which completely inverts the Western Judeo-Christian association of snakes with evil, an association that is qualitatively different from the mundane negative feelings (found as much in India as in the West) aroused by a potentially life-threatening creature. (Suchitra Mathur, "From Capes to Snakes: The Indianization of the American Superhero," in *Comics as a Nexus of Cultures: Essays on the Interplay of Media, Disciplines and International Perspectives*, ed. Mark Berninger, Jochen Ecke, and Gideon Haberkorn [Jefferson, NC: McFarland, 2010], 180)

Although Nagraj with his impressive pectorals and knee-high boots is clearly more a Marvel-style superhero than a mythological creature, the same cluster of popmyth narratives that informed the comic-book series fertilizes the snake film: in many of the films, the serpents' magical powers are also bestowed by divine agency.

17. Describing *Jai Santoshi Ma*'s popularity, Philip Lutgendorf writes,

> This low-budget film with unknown actors unexpectedly emerged as one of the highest-grossing releases of 1975—sharing the spotlight with the likes of SHOLAY and DEEWAR. This bewildered critics and intrigued scholars (resulting in a modest literature on the film as a religio-cultural phenomenon), but made perfect sense to millions of Indian women, who loved its folksy story about a new "Goddess of Satisfaction," easily accessible through a simple ritual (which the film also demonstrates). A classic example of the "mythological" genre—the original narrative genre of Indian-made films—and one of the most popular such films ever made, it gave a new (and characteristically Indian inflection) to the American pop-critical term "cult film," for viewers often turned cinemas into temporary

temples, leaving their footwear at the door, pelting the screen with flowers and coins, and bowing reverently whenever the goddess herself appeared (which she frequently did, always accompanied by a clash of cymbals). (Philip Lutgendorf, "*Jai Santoshi Ma*," *Indian Cinema: Philip'sfil-ums*, at www.uiowa.edu/indiancinema/jai-santoshi-maa)

18. Geeta Kapur, "Mythic Material in Indian Cinema," *Journal of Arts and Ideas* 14–15 (1987): 79–108.

19. *Sheshnaag* tells the story of two distinct realms—the quotidian realm of the here and now, and the mythic realm of Sheshnaag the god, and his *ichhadhari nag* and *nagin* named Pritam and Bhanu (Jeetendra and Madhvi, respectively). In the human story, the protagonists include Champa (Rekha), a good Hindu wife; Bhola (Rishi Kapoor), her simpleton brother; and her greedy, abusive husband (Anupam Kher). These two narrative orders are braided together via the figure of the villainous (and venomous) Aghori (Danny Denzongpa), who desires to be more powerful than the gods. He relentlessly pursues the snake-couple, who can perform the miracle that would enable this augmentation of his powers. Interestingly, even the story of the "natural" world is shot through with mythological and epic references: Champa's husband gambles her away after staking all other material possessions; she, like Draupadi, invokes the protection of Krishna as she is disrobed and almost gang-raped. Bhola (whose name invokes Shiva and innocence simultaneously) is a Krishna surrogate whose melodious flute charms animals and women alike; in his innocence he is also a composite figure of child-gods like Ram and Krishna. In the supra-human domain, Bhanu repays Bhola's kindness—he had saved her from the Aghori—by masquerading as his sister, Champa, and nurturing him lovingly. The film is also replete with mythic female types—from the devoted Champa, who replicates the Sita-Savitri archetype, to Bhanu, who, as the shape-shifting snake, runs the gamut from avenging goddess to seductive temptress.

20. One of the most curious aspects of the reception of the cycle in that period can be seen in its insistent comparison to foreign films in English-language publications. Despite the snake film's robust local moorings, critics in multiple publications, more often than not, drew arguably tenuous parallels with Western films; perhaps this tells us something about the tenor of English-language film criticism in India then. For example, the critic at *Screen* proclaimed, "The genre of fantasy, weird and awe-arousing in its own way, has seldom been tried in Hindi cinema, especially linked with a modern social background, as done so well by foreign films like the East European ones. To that extent 'Nagin' (Eastman Color) breaks some new ground, by tying up traditional Indian beliefs and legends about snakes and their human forms with present-day characters, the conflict being that of hostility and revenge between the two sides." Review of *Nagin*, in *Screen*, February 6, 1976, 6. Even more audaciously, in a review of *Nagin*, Truffaut was invoked by the critic at *Nagpur Times*: "The story smacks of a French film odour—Truffaut's 'The Bride Wore Black'—where a woman's husband was shot dead on their wedding day. Furious like a snake, the woman hunts out each of them and destroys. Similar

snake themes were attempted in earlier Hindi films like *Milap*, *Sapera* and *Nagin* but they had a garbled and confused form. Not one reached the perfection of weirdness and suspense as is achieved by this film." "*Nagin*—Our Review," *Nagpur Times*, March 28, 1976.

In most of these reviews, unsurprisingly, the locally produced snake film did not compare favorably to whatever foreign film was being invoked as a frame of reference. *Nagina* was likened to *Splash* (Ron Howard, 1984) a decade later:

> Going by the 1984 Hollywood hit *Splash* in which actress Daryl Hannah transforms herself into mermaid in a New York hotel, Sri Devi's exercise does not look an impossibility altogether except that a mermaid is far more seductive than the deadly reptile which to many makes a repulsive sight. But, unlike mermaid, snake is a part of Indian religion and mythology and in tune with it. Harmesh Malhotra's movie finds Sri Devi singing in a dilapidated mansion in the presence of Lord Shiva around whose image the reptiles go about playfully and whenever thugs and eve teasers chase Sri Devi a battalion of snacks [*sic*] with hoods raised obstruct their path. (Debu Mazumdar, "Snaky Sri Devi in *Nagina*," *Indian Express*, November 24, 1986)

What these types of reviews alert us to is also the kinds of films that urban critics could assume their readers' familiarity with. It would appear that even in the 1970s and 1980s, urban, presumably middle-class, English-reading viewers, who had largely abandoned the cinema in favor of television, were watching at least Hollywood and other Western films in the theaters.

21. Gunning's now classic formulation of the aesthetic of attraction snugly fits the types of pleasures and curiosities that the snake film offers to its viewers:

> The aesthetic of attraction addresses the audience directly, sometimes . . . exaggerating this confrontation in an experience of assault. Rather than psychology, the cinema of attractions solicits a highly conscious awareness of the film image engaging the viewer's curiosity. The spectator does not get lost in a fictional world and its drama, but remains aware of the act of looking, the excitement of curiosity and its fulfillment. Through a variety of formal means, the images of the cinema of attractions rush forward to meet their viewers. (Gunning, "An Aesthetic of Astonishment," 121)

22. The figure of the tantric in the Hindi film is one of deep ambivalence. Although his mastery of ritual practices makes him powerful and worthy of respect, the fact that this power/knowledge remains precipitously aligned to the black arts is of key importance. In the snake film, he remains a formidable adversary at the very least; at worst, he is a malevolent, power-hungry monster like Aghori in *Sheshnaag*. For an interesting reading of the tantric in the Ramsay horror film, see Usha Iyer, "Nevla as Dracula: Figurations of the Tantric as Monster in the Hindi Horror Film," in *Figurations in Indian Film*, ed. Meheli Sen and Anustup Basu, 101–115 (Hampshire, UK: Palgrave Macmillan, 2013).

23. *Sheshnaag*, in fact, uses these effects in abundance, and far more frequently

than other films of the cycle. Perhaps because it comes later in the cycle, the makers felt it necessary to crank up the technology ante.

24. Sean Cubitt, "Phalke, Melies, and Special Effects Today," *Wide Angle* 21 (1) (1999): 115–130.

25. There are numerous blogs where enthusiastic fans review, ridicule, but also display considerable enthusiasm for the snake film. The Internet has spawned a new form of cinephilia, and the camp propensities of the snake film have garnered it significant visibility online. See, for example, "Filmi Snake Spotter's Field Guide," *Cinema Chaat: Masala, Movies, Moustaches, and More!*, last modified July 31, 2011, at http://cinemachaat.com/2011/07/31/filmi-snake-spotters-field-guide/; "An Open Letter on the Subject of Filmi Snake Identification and Research," *Cinema Chaat: Masala, Movies, Moustaches, and More!*, last modified August 10, 2011, at http://cinemachaat.com/2011/08/10/an-open-letter-on-the-subject-of-filmi-snake-identification-and-research/; and Beth Watkins, "Adventures in a Subtitleless and Otherwise Wild and Woolly Land: *Sheshnaag*," *Beth Loves Bollywood*, last modified October 31, 2010, at http://bethlovesbollywood.blogspot.com/2010/10/adventures-in-subtitleless-and.html.

26. For example, *Filmfare* ran a viewer's review section in which entries were judged for a prize during a period of time called "View from the Gallery." In it, a certain K. Gopalan from Bombay described his experience of viewing *Nagin* with a great deal of wit and skepticism and not a bit of credulity:

> Reena takes the form of Hina Kausar and brings Sanjay's end. There follows "dishum dishum" between Feroz and Sunil, and I know Feroz cannot die immediately since Mumtaz is cast opposite him and a duet is due. But I can't understand how the "Saap" also manages to reach Kashmir.
>
> By now I know the end. Either Sunil or the "Saap" would die. Sunil, unlike the Rajesh Khannas and the Dharmendras, does not mind dying on the screen. Rekha's sexy image has no appeal to me. But what appeals to me is the thrilling climax.
>
> The film comes to an end with Reena's death. While leaving the theatre I recollect the cast: Premnath, Jagdeep, Sulochana, Komilla Wirk, Aruna Irani and above all, "Jai Santoshi Maa" Anita Guha. I wondered why the director had left out the remaining few artistes in the film industry. Maybe, like "Godfather II" and "Exorcist II," Raj Kumar Kohli plans to make "Nagin II" with them. ("View from the Gallery: *Nagin*," K. Gopalan, Bombay, *Filmfare*, March 5–18, 1976)

27. Tom Gunning has reminded us that early cinema's terrified, "enthralled spectator" is largely a fiction devised by film theorists, who remain strangely unanchored from space and time. Gunning, "An Aesthetic of Astonishment." Similarly, there is no evidence to suggest that audiences watched these films with any degree of gullibility. However, the films themselves expend considerable energy in creating a visual/narrative realm where the fantastic needs no logic to exist.

28. Contemporary reviews of snake films, especially in the English-language

press, provide a fascinating window into the public perception of these films and especially the elitism that tinged their reception in certain quarters. For example, *Statesman*'s sneering review of *Nagin*:

> All that mumbo-jumbo about nags and nagins and the she-cobra's terrible revenge might seem a little passé to cinema audiences in metropolitan cities brought up on spaghetti and karate westerns, but one never knows what audiences in smaller cities might think of it. This very long film therefore meanders through an elaborate succession of revenges by the grieved [*sic*] nagin who can take any form and get rid of her husband's killers. Personally, this critic found it all very unconvincing, the songs very ordinary and the performances contrived. But for those who do not mind this kind of theme, it is no better or worse than any Bombay film. ("A Nagin Without the Bite," *Statesman*, January 25, 1976)

A decade later, *Nagina* inspired very similar sentiments in this newspaper: "One could never imagine that a producer-director of the caliber of Harmesh Malhotra, who has made some taut and gripping dacoit films, would stoop to snake lore. Maybe some of his films have bombed and in sheer desperation he is clutching at straws. But then if he is banking upon this film to retrieve his talks then by now he should already have been neck deep. For this washout film never manages to generat [*sic*] any interest or make sense." *Statesman*, November 24, 1986. But this type of elitism and scorn was not limited to a single newspaper or publishing house. By and large, the English-language press was united in its derision of the snake film. The film critic at *Indian Express*, another major newspaper, had the following to say about *Nagina*: "Whether the idea of Sri Devi being made to crawl clicks, or not, there is little doubt that such mythological enactments still have a pull, at least, with the front benchers who if disappointed, can still console themselves of having witnessed the miracle not to mention the last trishul fight between Amrish and Rishi with Sri Devi pondering whether to use magical powers or not." Debu Mazumdar, "Snaky Sri Devi in *Nagina*," *Indian Express*, November 24, 1986.

29. Carlo Nardi writes:

> The first time Kalyanji used the Clavioline to recreate the sound of the *been* was in S. N. Tripathi's *Naag Panchami* (1953). Tripathi then recommended Kalyanji to Hemant Kumar, who was able to take advantage of the novelty effect that the synthesised snake charmer's sound could still achieve, due to the relative lack of success of *Naag Panchami*—at least as compared to *Nagin*. What is worth noting here is that the introduction of the Clavioline played such a major role not only in Kalyanji's career but also in those of Hemant Kumar and Ravi as music directors (Lata Mangeshkar at the time was already a successful star). (Carlo Nardi, "Reinventing Technology in Indian Popular Cinema," *Journal on the Art of Record Production* 5 [2011])

30. Amita Nijhawan, "Excusing the Female Dancer: Tradition and Transgression in Bollywood Dancing," *South Asian Popular Culture* 7 (2) (2009): 99–112.

31. Rachel Dwyer describes the style quite accurately as "wiggling" dances in her brief discussion of the snake film. Dwyer, *Filming the Gods*, 49.

32. See https://twitter.com/hashtag/nagin, accessed June 27, 2015.

33. In this sense, one might even argue that the snake-dance sequences are "item numbers" ahead of their time—spectacular and single-mindedly sexual in texture and intent—much like the cabaret or nightclub songs that routinely featured Helen and provided sexualized spectacles in the Social and, later, *masala* films. But, it is important to note that for the most part, Helen dances alone with minimal participation by the male protagonists, with the exception of Shammi Kapoor. Men in Helen's nightclubs are either leering villains or heroes who remain splendid figures of temperance and rectitude, who would never dance with the vamp; even in private settings, they rarely join her—for example, in the song "Yeh Mera Dil" in *Don* (Barot, 1978). The snake film, by contrast, allows male stars to participate in sexualized dance sequences in a way that destabilizes these unspoken rules of Hindi cinema. See, for example, Anustup Basu, "'The Face That Launched a Thousand Ships': Helen and Public Femininity in Hindi Film," in *Figurations in Indian Film*, ed. Meheli Sen and Anustup Basu, 139–157 (Hampshire, UK: Palgrave Macmillan, 2013).

34. It is no surprise that the most emblematic stars of the snake film—Reena Roy, Sridevi, Rekha, Meenakshi Sheshadri, and Jeetendra—are accomplished dancers; their dancing skills remain important components of their star personas.

35. See Anandam P. Kavoori and Christina Joseph, "*Nagina*: Conversations with a Snake," *Jump Cut* 43 (2000): 86–91. Interestingly, this essay primarily focuses on how young people in the diaspora use the *nagin* dance as a form of sexual expression as well as cultural belonging.

36. Mithuraaj Dhusiya offers an interesting reading of how this song, in fact, overturns many of the elements of the typical *mujra*:

> Where in most Hindi film mujra songs the camera shows the dancer's steps as limited to the imaginary circle made by her male audience, here it begins with a low angle shot of a visibly angry Sridevi descending the staircase in a zigzag manner that broaches and challenges the traditional limits of the artificial circle that proscribes and enjoins stasis of the female "performer." The song's composition, edited using the continued [*sic*] editing format, never for once shows a full circle of limitation or proscription that the heroine is enjoined to stay within. Instead of the circle in entirety, the song's shots instead reveal arcs of men sitting with their flutes. Then the camera shows her transgressing this putative circle of men, first by medium close-up crane shots which suggest that she is moving above those sitting men, second, when the camera pans right to left showing her moving in and out of the circle made by men. (Mithuraaj Dhusiya, "Bestiality, Com-

passion and Gender Emancipation: The Snake Woman in Hindi Horror Films," *Cineforum* 15 [2012], 121)

37. Lalitha Gopalan, *Cinema of Interruptions: Action Genres in Contemporary Indian Cinema* (London: British Film Institute, 2002), 34.

38. Posters of the film that were used on hoardings (poster billboards) and walls and advertisements placed in the print media bear testament to the fact that it was marketed for its impressive star cast, as well as the snake erotics discussed above.

39. All of the men die with the knowledge that despite their best efforts—including a talismanic pendant furnished by a tantric, a seventh male figure—they have, in fact, lost to the *nagin*.

40. Incidentally, Vijay, the only one who survives her relentless pursuit, insists on seeing her dying as woman, rather than as snake. She dutifully complies, and we get a gruesome image of a suffering woman impaled on phallic spikes, a scene that many contemporary reviewers of the film found particularly odious. The critic at *Screen* made her/his displeasure clear: "The routine climax is too long-drawn and absurdly placed (the main hero and a child sliding on a rope between two buildings with the snake in hot but slow pursuit) and there was no need for the dying reptile to take the human form to express her feelings near an aghast crowd. This also breaks the fantasy spell, which should be always restricted to a few characters getting such an experience and remain on a believe-it-or-not level." Review of *Nagin*, in *Screen*, February 6, 1976, 6. Almost echoing this sentiment word for word, the reviewer at *Nagpur Times* wrote, "The last scene, where Sunil with one of the victim's child [*sic*] clasped behind him slides along a rope between the two skyscrappers [*sic*] with the cobra in hot pursuit, is too long-drawn though it does bring realistic effect. There was also no need to show the female cobra at the end of her tether assuming human form in the midst of a crowd of spectators just to say 'revenge has its limit.' This is more like a miracle spectacle." "*Nagin*—Our Review," *Nagpur Times*, March 28, 1976.

41. This hit song was sung by Anuradha Paudwal, whose popularity was beginning to contest Lata's absolute hegemony in playback in the 1980s.

42. In fact, it is the unsympathetic mother—a key antagonist—who introduces this unseemly truth in a conversation with Rajni.

43. Quite suitably, several posters of *Nagina* feature the human cast, but not the reptile performers.

44. One of the first supernatural favors Rajni bestows on the family involves securing Rajiv's feudal patrimony, which was being usurped by Thakur Ajay Singh (Ajit Vachchani), yet another villainous character whose daughter Rajiv had earlier spurned.

45. She declares as much in a momentous confrontational encounter to Bhairavnath; it is her power as a *sati* and a *pativrata* (devoted wife) that will enable her to thwart his evil designs.

46. Although *Nagina* catapulted Sridevi into superstardom in 1986, contem-

porary reviews of the film were almost uniformly dismissive of her performance. Mazumdar's take in *Indian Express* seems especially harsh in retrospect:

> Money is said to make mare go [*sic*] and no wonder Sri Devi takes to her "reptile" role as if it was the only right thing to do and enacts the relevant scenes with appropriate convulsive [motions]. In fact, when the time comes to slip into her "other" role which she must once in 24 hours as predicted by tantric Amrish Puri to her mother-in-law Sushma Seth, Sri Devi's eyes start emitting extra-terrestrial rays with the hooded reptile dancing over her face and the next minute the hale and hearty Sri Devi slips through the crack in the door. (Debu Mazumdar, "Snaky Sri Devi in *Nagina*," *Indian Express*, November 24, 1986)

Even Iqbal Masud, noted film journalist, was far from complimentary:

> I suppose Sridevi had to play a she-cobra someday. At least it makes her potentially more interesting than the retarded woman-child of *Sadma*. Pity, she is amply sensuous rather than sinuous so one can't take her seriously as a "Naagin." But then you are meant to take her as one of the benevolent variety. . . . At a nearby ruin, Rajeev is spellbound by a voice. A "Mahal-like" apparition flits through the ruin and materialise [*sic*] as Rajani (Sridevi) in solid flesh. . . . Rajiv falls swooningly under Rajani's spell—though Sridevi's hip-wiggling and liquid gaze are standard offerings." (Iqbal Masud, "*Nagina*—Passable as Fable," *Indian Express*, November 30, 1986)

The degree of misogyny these types of reviews exhibit also gives us a sense of the tenor of film journalism in India in the 1970s and 1980s, which works perfectly in tandem with the ethos of the *masala* film generally.

47. In fact, snake films continue to be made in Telegu, Tamil, and other South Indian languages. Some soft-core porn films also include shape-shifting snake women in them, attesting to the erotic and spectacular possibilities inherent in the formation.

48. Lynch says in an interview, "*Hisss* was taken away from me in the edit. I have no idea what the film looks like. I came close to a directors' cut, which Mallika, Venus and producers referred to as 'European, languid and sensual' all the things I thought were compliments. Apparently, that did not make them happy. I have no idea what is out there. Good or bad, I cannot take credit for it. Aside from shots and performances that I pray have not been butchered." Subhash K. Jha, "I Didn't Make *Hisss*: Jennifer Lynch," *Times of India*, last modified October 25, 2010, at http://articles.timesofindia.indiatimes.com/2010-10-25/news-interviews/28248678_1_hisss-govind-menon-mallika-sherawat. A behind-the-scenes documentary titled *Despite the Gods* was released in 2012, which records Lynch's trials and tribulations during the shoot of *Hisss*.

49. "Review: Mallika's 'Hisss' Fails to Charm the Box Office," *Zee News*, last

modified October 22, 2010, at http://zeenews.india.com/entertainment/movies/review-mallika-s-hisss-fails-to-charm-the-box-office_73701.html.

50. Isabel Cristina Pinedo, *Recreational Terror: Women and the Pleasures of Horror Film Viewing* (Albany: SUNY Press, 1997), 61. In this sense, *Hisss*, like some of David Cronenberg's films, mobilizes pure affect, wherein "[t]he body is the site of the most violent alternations and of the most intense affects. It is continually subjugated and remade, and in this process it experiences extremities of pleasure, pain, and horror. The flesh is less rigidly determined, more fluid and open to metamorphosis, than we generally like to think." Steven Shaviro, *The Cinematic Body* (Minneapolis: University of Minnesota Press, 1993), 128.

51. Ibid., 133.

52. It is important to note that the female snake remains completely mute in *Hisss*. Although this certainly buttresses her animal/reptile ontology, it further alienates the creature from the older iterations of the snake film, where the snake woman was more human than animal.

53. See, for example, Charukesi Ramadurai, "Bollywood's Foreign Appeal Finds Online Expression," *Sunday Guardian*, last modified February 16, 2013, at www.sunday-guardian.com/masala-art/bollywoods-foreign-appeal-finds-online-expression; Ashwin Ahmad, "Bollywood Goes Global! Meet the Fans of Indian Cinema Across the World Who Know Their Shammi from Their Ranbir," *Daily Mail India*, last modified April 26, 2014, at www.dailymail.co.uk/indiahome/indianews/article-2613971/Bollywood-goes-global-Meet-fans-Indian-cinema-world-know-Shammi-Ranbir.html; and Ashwin Ahmad, "Memsaab: Bollywood's Phoren Fan Brigade," *Economic Times*, last modified June 1, 2008, at http://articles.economictimes.indiatimes.com/2008-06-01/news/27698718_1_indian-cinema-hindi-film-bollywood.

54. Review of *Nagin*, in *MemsaabStory*, http://memsaabstory.com/2012/01/15/nagin-1976/; for another humorous review of *Nagin*, see, "*Nagin*: Don't Mess with the Ladies," http://indiequill.wordpress.com/2009/05/19/nagin-dont-mess-with-the-ladies/.

55. Watkins, "Adventures in a Subtitleless and Otherwise Wild and Woolly Land," www.bethlovesbollywood.com/2010/10/adventures-in-subtitleless-and.html.

56. New fans of the formation are also incredibly creative with what they "do" with these camp-texts on the Internet. Consider, for example, the recent fan-created video in which Sridevi's snake dance from *Nigahen* is synchronized with "Lean On," Major Lazer and DJ Snake's chart-topping EDM song: www.huffingtonpost.in/2015/09/09/sridevi-major-lazer_n_8107932.html.

57. The snake film's special affinity for queer camp is also signaled by the fact that Sridevi has come to be a huge queer icon, and her dance performance in the snake film accounts for this other kind of stardom. See "Why All Gay Guys Love Sridevi," *Santa Banta: The Never Ending Show . . .*, last modified October 12, 2012, accessed June 1, 2015, at www.santabanta.com/bollywood/59916/why-all-gay-guys-love-sridevi/.

1. Meraj Ahmed Mubarki correctly notes that there is something unmistakably "Hindu" about Arjun's physical appearance as well:

> Arjun's physical attributes: tall height, wide chest and broad shoulders, coupled with his fearlessness, symbolise an assertive Hindu virility. Arjun's God becomes merciful, all-embracing, over-arching, dominant, ever-forgiving and non-exacting unlike the God of Father Thomas. Finally, the spirit itself shows where its allegiance lies, for it is through its machinations that the play of opportunities is set in motion where Father Thomas and his faith stands totally disgraced and discredited. The evil in *1920* allows Arjun to recover his Hindu faith and assert his spiritual superiority. The Hindutva ideologic lays exclusive claim over the possessed. (Meraj Ahmed Mubarki, "Mapping the Hindi Horror Genre: Ghosts in the Service of Ideology," *History and Sociology of South Asia* 7 [1] [2013]: 60)

2. Ibid.

3. See, for example, Christine Brosius, *India's Middle Class: New Forms of Urban Leisure, Consumption and Prosperity* (New Delhi: Routledge India, 2014).

4. Leela Fernandes, "The Politics of Forgetting: Class Politics, State Power and the Restructuring of Urban Space in India," *Urban Studies* 41 (12) (2004): 2415–2430.

5. William Mazzarella, *Shoveling Smoke: Advertising and Globalization in Contemporary India* (Durham, NC: Duke University Press, 2003).

6. Mazzarella reminds us that

> [t]he tension between individualism and standardization was justified in terms of *equity*: equal access to the dream of self-transformation . . . The new advertising, then, positioned itself as a democratizing force, theoretically opening the infinite transformations of consumption to all comers. In concert with the drive towards "liberalization" of markets that was initiated by Indira but most strongly identified with her son Rajiv, it figured itself as an expansive gesture of inclusion—a field of possibilities finally opened for those previously excluded. (Ibid., 89)

7. "[T]he efficacy of the commodity image was the same whether its task was realizing 'social' or 'commercial' value. But the problem of pleasure remained a formidable aporia to the linkage between consumption and public service. The pleasures of seduction and the indulgence of desire that drove consumer goods advertising were quite simply absent from exhortations to public service, much as the latter might otherwise demonstrate the ability of the well-deployed image to harness self-interest productively." Ibid., 95.

8. Arvind Rajagopal, *Politics After Television: Hindu Nationalism and the Reshaping of the Public in India* (Cambridge, UK: Cambridge University Press, 2001), 77.

9. For example, *Krishi Darshan*, a program on which farmers and other experts

discussed insights on agriculture, was one of the longest-running programs on Doordarshan. This type of content—of no interest to urban viewers who owned the majority of television sets—is a measure of the disconnect between urban, middle-class audiences and the institutions that were entrusted with creating and managing television content in this era.

10. Both Purnima Mankekar and Arvind Rajagopal look to the broadcast of the Sanskrit epics Ramayana and Mahabharata on Doordarshan as especially indicative of the multiple discourses that transformed the cultural arena at that time. See Mankekar's *Screening Culture, Viewing Politics: An Ethnography of Television, Womanhood, and Nation in Postcolonial India* (Durham, NC: Duke University Press, 1999).

11. Rajagopal, *Politics After Television*, 34.

12. Ibid., 42.

13. For example, there was a section of the Hindu right that promulgated *swadeshi* and rejection of all things "foreign," however the twin energies of consumption and religiosity managed to co-opt and subsume these dissonant voices quite seamlessly and successfully.

14. For an analysis of the nomenclature and its larger implications, see M. Madhava Prasad, "This Thing Called Bollywood," *Seminar* 525 (May 2003), at www.india-seminar.com/2003/525/525%20madhava%20prasad.htm.

15. Ashish Rajadhyaksha, "The 'Bollywoodization' of the Indian Cinema: Cultural Nationalism in a Global Arena," *Inter-Asia Cultural Studies* 4 (1) (2003): 25–39.

16. Describing the postcolonial state's apathy—if not outright hostility—to the film industry, Ganti writes:

> [T]he Indian state did not accord filmmaking much economic significance, even though shortly after independence, India became the second largest filmproducing country in the world. . . . Entertainment was not viewed as a necessity in a country that at the time of independence had a literacy rate of 18 percent, had an average life expectancy of 26 years, was suffering from a food crisis, and had over one million refugees to resettle. (Tejaswini Ganti, *Producing Bollywood: Inside the Contemporary Hindi Film Industry* [Durham, NC: Duke University Press, 2012], 53)

17. Ibid., 63.

18. See, for example, Patricia Uberoi, "The Diaspora Comes Home; Disciplining Desire in DDLJ," *Contributions to Indian Sociology* 32 (1998): 305–336. As I write this, Bollywood is poised to explore newer markets overseas. Prominent critic Anupama Chopra writes that

> [t]he French and Chinese are among the many converts to Bollywood's rapidly growing following. Hindi films have long had devoted fans among the 21 million Indians living overseas, and in the 1950s and '60s, the actor-director Raj Kapoor became a household name in Soviet Russia, while Hindi films traveled to the Middle East and Africa. But in the last decade, Bollywood's unique cocktail of emotion, song, dance and melodrama has

> found takers in several new markets. According to the box office tracking company Rentrak, revenues for Indian films across 36 territories rose from $66.2 million for 69 titles in 2009 to $289 million for 170 titles in 2013. The new fans are in countries as diverse as Turkey, Peru, Panama and Iraq. Hindi films first reached Japanese theaters in 1952, but regular releases began only last year.

Chopra lists Germany as a potential new market and notes that non-Indian audiences in the United States and the United Kingdom—which Bollywood has been struggling to reach—may be the final frontier. See Anupama Chopra, "Bollywood Is Prancing Far Abroad: Shah Rukh Khan and Bollywood's Global Fortunes Advance," *New York Times*, last modified September 26, 2014, at www.nytimes.com/2014/09/28/movies/shah-rukh-khan-and-bollywoods-global-fortunes-advance.html?hpw&rref=movies&action=click&pgtype=Homepage&version=HpHedThumbWell&module=well-region&region=bottom-well&WT.nav=bottom-well&_r=1. So far I have been tracing the Bombay-made film's global aspirations and trajectories. What is called "diasporic cinema," however—transnational filmmaking practices which "straddle and traverse multiple film cultures"—is not reducible to Bollywood per se. See, for example Jigna Desai, "The Scale of Diasporic Cinema: Negotiating National and Transnational Cultural Citizenship," *Routledge Handbook on Indian Cinema*, Routledge, 206–217, 2013.

19. Aswin Punathambekar, *From Bombay to Bollywood: The Making of a Global Media Industry* (New York: New York University Press, 2013), 38.

20. The PVR Anupam in New Delhi is considered to be India's first bona fide multiplex, and it opened in 1997.

21. Amit Rai, for example, calls these types of venues "malltiplexes":

> The first wave of multiplex construction swept through the major metros in the late 1990s, accompanied by a boom in mall construction: the mall and the multiplex, the twin arcades of postmodernity, thus emerge from one technology. . . . The retail boom unleashed by the economic liberalization policy sustains the malltiplex, and it is thus aligned with and extends the transformations of India's urban milieus within the framework of globalized consumerism. The mallplex's steady proliferation in the metropolis and simultaneous penetration into some smaller cities and towns testifies to its close association with a globalized modernity, which coincides with the rise of disposable incomes in the hands of the urban Indian family. (Amit Rai, *Untimely Bollywood: Globalization and India's New Media Assemblage* [Durham, NC: Duke University Press, 2009], 142)

See also Adrian Athique, "Leisure Capital in the New Economy: The Rapid Rise of the Multiplex in India," *Contemporary South Asia* 17 (2) (2009): 123–140.

22. Sangita Gopal, *Conjugations: Marriage and Form in New Bollywood Cinema* (Chicago: University of Chicago Press, 2011), 135.

23. Ibid., 133.

24. Carol J. Clover, *Men, Women, and Chainsaws: Gender in the Modern Horror Film* (Princeton: Princeton University Press, 1993), 23.

25. As Sangita Gopal puts it, "[T]he movement between Bandh Darwaza and Raat is more than the shift from horrifying masala to horror as a distinct genre; it is simultaneously an index of the radical differences between Nehruvian and post-liberalization India. By constructing the couple-form as middle-class in its very essence, the horror film enables us to inhabit and travel in the spaces and pathways that make up twenty-first-century India." Gopal, *Conjugations*, 114.

26. Interestingly, for Ram Gopal Varma, the two most influential horror films remain the Ramsays' *Do Gaz Zameen Ke Neeche* and *The Exorcist*. The former allegedly scared him so much that he took long detours from his local bus stop, simply to avoid a graveyard in between the bus stop and his house; he revisits this experience in his 2006 portmanteau horror film *Darna Zaroori Hai*. Ram Gopal Varma, interview by Meheli Sen, Mumbai, India, July 29, 2009.

27. Shubham Roy Choudhury, "Sound of Horror: Sound and Dread in Hindi Cinema," *Journal of the Moving Image* (2007).

28. The fact that so many of the new horror films are "inspired by" other sources also means that Western theoretical models can be usefully mobilized to read and unpack these texts. However, as Moreland and Pervez note in their exploration of *Bhoot*, *1920*, and *Raaz 2* in light of Carol Clover's work, notions of "imitation" or "plagiarism" rarely furnish useful answers when dealing with the manner in which Bollywood adapts and translates this arguably foreign material: "Through exploring the telling parallels between the narrative and identificatory structures of *Bhoot*, *1920* and *Raaz 2* and those of some of their Western counterparts, it becomes immediately apparent that these Bollywood films, like the films Clover considers, follow a 'standard scheme [that] puts, or at least seems to put, the female body on the line only in order to put the male psyche on the line,' using the female body as a locus for cultural crises in masculinity. However, despite the considerable stylistic allusions and pastiches presented by each of these films, we argue that the structural parallels they share with earlier Western possession films are often not so much the result of direct influence or imitation as they are the result of a shared ancestry in pre-cinematic cultural, and especially religious, narratives." Sean Moreland and Summer Pervez, "Acts of Repossession: Bollywood's Re-Inventions of the Occult Possession Film," in *Fear and Learning: Essays on the Pedagogy of Horror*, ed. Aalya Ahmad and Sean Moreland (Jefferson, NC: McFarland, 2013), 76.

29. Bishnupriya Ghosh, "The Security Aesthetic in Bollywood's High-Rise Horror," *Representations* 126 (1) (2014), special issue, *Financialization and the Culture Industry*: 58–84.

30. Gopal, *Conjugations*, 113.

31. Ghosh, "The Security Aesthetic," 8.

32. Bishnupriya Ghosh, lecture description for "The Security Aesthetic in Bollywood's High-Rise Horror," at http://web.international.ucla.edu/southasia/events/10334.

33. Meheli Sen, "Terrifying Tots and Hapless Homes: Undoing Modernity in Recent Bollywood Cinema," *Literature Interpretation Theory* 22 (2011): 197–217.

34. For example, Roy Choudhury in an essay that focuses primarily on the use of sound effects in new horror writes, "The transition from sleazy 'B' circuit horror flicks to the sleek multiplex films is therefore a journey from spectacle to anxiety. Rather than showing a scary figure directors are using the psychological impact of a shock and to creating [*sic*] the 'atmosphere' of fear." Roy Choudhury, "Sound of Horror: Sound and Dread in Hindi Cinema," *Journal of the Moving Image* (2007), 7.

35. Similarly, in both *Raaz* and *Raaz 2*, one half of the couple falls victim to malevolent supernatural forces and endangers the other person.

36. Films like *Hawa* and *Haunted 3D* (which I discuss later in the chapter) remind us that rape and violence to the female body, for which the B/C horror film was so resoundingly condemned, remain alive and well in Bollywood horror. This provides yet another point of entry into the disquieting series of continuities that accompany the genre.

37. Robin Wood, "An Introduction to the American Horror Film," in *Planks of Reason: Essays on the Horror Film*, ed. Barry Keith Grant and Christopher Sharret, 146–192 (Blue Ridge Summit, PA: Scarecrow Press, 2004).

38. Vikram Bhatt, interview by Meheli Sen, Mumbai, India, July 6, 2009.

39. It is instructive to recall that Tulsi Ramsay had used metaphors of food to describe a very similar appetite for a more holistic experience to characterize Indian audiences. Shyam Ramsay also notes the similarities between their cinema and Bhatt's updating of that aesthetic in the epigraph included in this chapter.

40. In his own estimation, horror in India has to be kept "very basic." *Raaz* is a film about a husband and wife: "*mangalsutra* (holy thread of Hindu matrimony), *sauten*, (co-wife), and *biwi* (wife)." The film *1920* is similarly a "basic" story of a couple, "1857, Mutiny, dying for your country . . . but shot in Yorkshire." In other words, Bhatt remains well aware of the continuities that attend to his cinema. Bhatt, interview by Meheli Sen, July 6, 2009.

41. In multiple interviews, Bhatt has referenced the Gothics like *Woh Kaun Thi?* as natural forebears to horror, and to his own work as well.

42. Marcia Landy, *Cinematic Uses of the Past* (Minneapolis: University of Minnesota Press, 1996), 15.

43. Sue Harper, "Historical Pleasure: Gainsborough Costume Melodrama," in *Home Is Where the Heart Is: Studies in Melodrama and the Woman's Film*, ed. Christine Gledhill (London: British Film Institute, 1987), 181. Quoted in Landy, *Cinematic Uses of the Past*, 15.

44. Fredric Jameson, *Postmodernism, or, the Cultural Logic of Late Capitalism* (Durham, NC: Duke University Press, 1991).

45. According to Boym, in fact, a certain kind of nostalgia is immanent to the modern condition: "[I]t can be called 'off-modern' . . . it makes us explore side shadows and back alleys, rather than the straight road of progress; it allows us to

take a detour from the deterministic narratives of history. Off-modernism offers a critique of both the modern fascination with newness and the no-less modern invention of tradition." Svetlana Boym, "Nostalgia and Its Discontents," *Hedgehog Review* 9 (2) (2007): 9. See also Svetlana Boym, *The Future of Nostalgia* (New York: Basic Books, 2002).

46. This is exactly the kind of affect that Arjun Appadurai describes as "imagined nostalgia," invoked powerfully in, for example, advertising: "[S]uch nostalgia . . . does not principally involve the evocation of a sentiment to which consumers who have really lost something can respond. Rather, these forms of mass advertising teach consumers to miss things they have never lost. . . . In thus creating experiences of losses that never took place, these advertisements create what might be called 'imagined nostalgia,' nostalgia for things that never were." Arjun Appadurai, *Modernity at Large: Cultural Dimensions of Globalization* (Minneapolis: University of Minnesota Press, 1996), 77.

47. Jameson, *Postmodernism*, 9.

48. For example, both Ghosh and Gopal comment on the sense of "realness" that the new horror film invokes. For Ghosh, this horror resonates with the real impact of large-scale urbanization—land grabs, evictions, squatter colonies, and so on. For Gopal, as quoted above, the profusion of domestic objects and technologies within diegetic worlds enhances a sense of real space/place, and so forth.

49. Although not actually a manor house, the sprawling bungalow does stand in for colonial grandeur in this context.

50. As in the Ramsay horror films, nontraditional and multiple forms of religious authority often come to the aid of Bhatt's protagonists.

51. Mark Fisher, *Ghosts of My Life: Writings on Depression, Hauntology and Lost Futures*. (Winchester, UK: Zero Books, 2014), 6.

52. Following Jameson, he describes this as "a formal attachment to the techniques and formulas of the past, a consequence of a retreat from the modernist challenge of innovating cultural forms adequate to contemporary experience." Ibid., 11–12.

53. Frederic Jameson, "Postmodernism and Consumer Society," lecture at the Whitney Museum of American Art, New York City, Fall 1982.

54. Ibid.

CHAPTER FIVE: THE PLANETARY PARANORMAL

1. Ali Khan and Ali Nobil Ahmad, "From Zinda Laash to *Zibahkhana*," *Third Text* 24 (1) (2010): 149–161.

2. Omar Khan, a self-confessed horror film buff, has elaborated on these influences and allusions in several interviews:

> *Zibahkhana* was designed not only as a standalone film but also very much as a tribute to the great horror films of years gone by. Slasher elements are

to the front but there are nods along the way to films as diverse as *Pink Flamingos*, *Psycho*, most obviously *Texas Chainsaw Massacre* but also *Friday the 13th* part two and definitely Fulci and Romero zombie films as well. All sorts of nods, nudges and winks are laden for horror movie fans to pick up on throughout *Zibahkhana*, including the name of our hero: "Ash" (from Ayesha), as in the legendary Ash from *Evil Dead*. (Fatima Shakeel, "Q&A with 'Zibahkhana' director Omar Khan on the Popularity of Zombies," *The Final Frolics of Fatima Shakeel*, accessed February 8, 2015, at https://eelshake.wordpress.com/2013/04/13/qa-with-*zibahkhana*-director-omar-khan-on-the-popularity-of-zombies/)

See also "Omar Khan Interview," accessed February 8, 2015, at www.horrorchronicles.com/interviews/omar-khan-interview.html.

3. Aryn Baker, "A Horror Movie on the Doorstep of the Taliban," last modified June 12, 2007, accessed February 7, 2015, at http://content.time.com/time/world/article/0,8599,1632168,00.html.

4. Khan and Ahmad, "From Zinda Laash to *Zibahkhana*."

5. Gwendolyn S. Kirk, "Working Class Zombies and Men in Burqas: Temporality, Trauma, and the Specter of Nostalgia in *Zibahkhana*," *BioScope* 5 (2) (2014): 141–151.

6. For a detailed discussion of how Hollywood production companies interact with the Bollywood industry and market in the new millennium, see, for example, Nitin Govil, *Orienting Hollywood: A Century of Film Culture Between Los Angeles and Bombay* (New York: New York University Press, 2015), 77–114.

7. M. Madhava Prasad, "Surviving Bollywood," in *Global Bollywood*, ed. Anandam P. Kavoori and Aswin Punathambekar, 41–51 (New York: New York University Press, 2008).

8. Ibid.

9. Ibid.

10. As Sangita Gopal has argued, the process of generic differentiation began with the advent of the multiplex, and what she calls "new Bollywood." Nevertheless, I would argue that the last decade and a half have been radically transformative for the supernatural and in ways that are not addressed in Gopal's analysis.

11. Tejaswini Ganti, "No Longer a Frivolous Singing and Dancing Nation of Movie-Makers: The Hindi Film Industry and Its Quest for Global Distinction," *Visual Anthropology* 25 (4) (2012): 340–365. Ganti additionally argued that "the contemporary moment of Hindi filmmaking is marked by efforts to erase, rather than highlight, the signs of cultural difference in order to circulate and accrue distinction globally." See also Sangita Gopal, "When the Music's Over: The History of the Romantic Duet," Chap. 1 of *Conjugations: Marriage and Form in New Bollywood Cinema* (Chicago: University of Chicago Press, 2011).

12. The recently released *Badlapur* (Sriram Rhagavan, 2015) and *NH 10* (Navdeep Singh, 2015), both reminiscent of the hyper-violent "Asia extreme" films, are excellent instantiations of the tendency I am describing here.

13. Prasad, "Surviving Bollywood."

14. Bhaskar Sarkar, "Metafiguring Bollywood: Brecht after *Om Shanti Om*," in *Figurations in Indian Film*, ed. Meheli Sen and Anustup Basu, 205–235 (Hampshire, UK: Palgrave Macmillan, 2013).

15. Gopal, for example, notes, "Indeed, post-liberalization cinema's obsession with remakes—*Om Shanti Om* is a perfect case in point—shows a pervasive tendency to cite, exaggerate, and historicize *masala* aesthetics, thus announcing its break from lineage." Gopal, *Conjugations*, 14.

16. Ganti, "No Longer a Frivolous Singing and Dancing Nation."

17. According to one source, the Internet was still accessed by 19.19 percent of the total population in India in 2014. See Internet Live Stats, accessed July 18, 2015, at www.internetlivestats.com/internet-users/india/.

18. Henry Jenkins, *Convergence Culture: Where Old and New Media Collide* (New York: New York University Press, 2006), 3.

19. Shaviro describes the digital moment thusly: "I think it is safe to say that these changes have been massive enough, and have gone on for long enough, that we are now witnessing the emergence of a different media regime, and indeed of a different mode of production, than those which dominated the twentieth century. Digital technologies, together with neoliberal economic relations, have given birth to radically new ways of manufacturing and articulating lived experience." "Introduction," *Post-Cinematic Affect* (Ropley, UK: Zero Books, 2010), 2.

20. "In contrast to the earlier decades, the 1990s generated fast-moving, tactile media. Low-cost computers, advertising, mobile phones and digital images have transformed urban life. The experience is now a more global one, incorporating design, telecom networks, architecture, software and media industries, service workers, personal media objects and multiple sensory environments." Ravi Sundaram, *Pirate Modernity: Delhi's Media Urbanism* (New York: Routledge, 2010), 6.

21. Shaunak Sen, "Spectral Pixels: Digital Ghosts in Contemporary Hindi Horror Cinema," *Wide Screen* 5 (1) (2015), 3.

22. Shaviro, "Introduction," 3.

23. See Bishnupriya Ghosh, "The Security Aesthetic in Bollywood's High-Rise Horror," *Representations*, special issue, *Financialization and the Culture Industry* 126 (1) (2014): 58–84; or Sen, "Spectral Pixels."

24. Arjun Appadurai, *Modernity at Large: Cultural Dimensions of Globalization* (Minneapolis: University of Minnesota Press, 1996).

25. The temporality of digital worlds has been variously theorized by scholars in recent years. See, for example, *Time and the Digital*, in which Timothy Scott Barker argues that a new order of temporality is *produced* by the digital, such that "new types of temporal experience may emerge in our interactions with objects and processes such as the Internet, the archive of the data-base, and the particular programming language and software processes enacted by digital systems." Timothy Scott Barker, *Time and the Digital: Connecting Technology, Aesthetics, and a Process Philosophy of Time* (Hanover, NH: Dartmouth College Press, 2012), 7. Re-

sponding to the largely spatialized readings of digital media ("sites," "cyberspace," and so forth), Barker argues that

> [w]e need to think of digital communication in terms of the new times that it produces as well as the new spaces. After all, the data in data-bases, our online history, and the things that we input onto social media sites don't just exist in a digital space somehow sitting outside time. Digital information exists in time and thereby in continuous contact with our experiences in time. In other words, the time produced by digital preservation overlays the time that we experience in our day-to-day lives. (Ibid., 19)

In this philosophy of time, the human subject is likewise refashioned as a far more contingent and emergent entity: "[T]he meaning of data emerges from an aesthetic process in which multiple actors are involved. In these occasions, there is no "subject" or "user," as a discrete "knower" apprehending reality from a privileged vantage point as the sole possessor of agency. Interaction is rather an active involvement with the changing processes of the encounter, as our perception of the world is continually remade and reordered by technology." Ibid., 109.

26. Mayank Tewari, "Indian Youth Is Not Just Ready for a Zombie Film, It Is Demanding One," *Tehelka*, last modified September 12, 2011, accessed May 12, 2015, at http://archive.tehelka.com/story_main50.asp?filename=Ws120911Cinema.asp.

27. Among many others, Jeffrey Jerome Cohen describes the sheer abundance of recent zombie media with an air of bewilderment:

> Peter Dendle's *The Zombie Movie Encyclopedia* (2001) lists over two hundred films. Jamie Russell's *The Book of the Dead: The Complete History of Zombie Cinema* (2005) adds many more to that list. Yet conventional media are not the zombie's only habitat. Those of us with an iPhone know that the undead takeover is in its last stages when it comes to the Mac iOS. Among the hundreds of zombie downloadables in the App Store are Zombie Crisis 3D, Zombie Drop, Zombie Assault, Burn Zombie Burn, Zombie Soccer, Zombie Biker, ZFL ("Zombie Football League"), Stupid Zombies (seems redundant), Zombie Pond, Zombie Heads, Zombiepox, Plants vs Zombies, Girl vs Zombies, Jason vs Zombies, Commando vs Zombies, Robots vs Zombies. Those with an X-Box know that zombie mode is a frequent option no matter the game." (Jeffrey Jerome Cohen, "Undead (A Zombie Oriented Ontology)," *Journal of the Fantastic in the Arts* 23 [3] [2012]: 397–412, 401)

28. Ali S. Khan, "Preparedness 101: Zombie Apocalypse," *Public Health Matters Blog*, posted on May 16, 2011, accessed, March 14, 2015, at http://blogs.cdc.gov/publichealthmatters/2011/05/preparedness-101-zombie-apocalypse/.

29. Jennifer Schuessler, "Academic Zombies Attack! (Again)," *New York Times*, last modified October 31, 2014, at http://artsbeat.blogs.nytimes.com/2014/10/31/academic-zombies-attack-again/?_r=0; Erica E. Phillips, "Zombie Studies Gain Ground on College Campuses," *Wall Street Journal*, last modified March 3, 2014,

at www.wsj.com/articles/SB10001424052702304851104579361451951384512; and Steve Kolowich, "A Brief History of Academics Writing Seriously About Zombies," *Chronicle of Higher Education*, last modified October 41, 2014, at http://chronicle.com/article/A-Brief-History-of-Academics/149755.

30. For example, the authors of "A Zombie Manifesto" observe:

> This figure, simultaneously slave and slave rebellion, is a more appropriate reflection of our capitalist moment, and even if it holds less promise than a cyborg future, its prophesy of the posthuman is more likely to come to fruition. The zombie, we feel, is a more pessimistic but nonetheless more appropriate stand-in for our current moment, and specifically for America in a global economy, where we feed off the products of the rest of the planet, and, alienated from our own humanity, stumble forward, groping for immortality even as we decompose. (Sarah Juliet Lauro and Karen Embry, "A Zombie Manifesto: The Nonhuman Condition in the Era of Advanced Capitalism," *boundary 2, an international journal of literature and culture* 35 [1] [2008]: 93)

31. David McNally, *Monsters of the Market: Zombies, Vampires and Global Capitalism* (Leiden, The Netherlands: Brill, 2011).

32. Deborah Christie and Sarah Juliet Lauro, eds., *Better Off Dead: The Evolution of the Zombie as Post-Human* (New York: Fordham University Press, 2011).

33. Sean Posey, "A Country Walking Dead: The Zombie as Metaphor in American Culture and Film," *The Hampton Institute*, last modified February 27, 2014, at www.hamptoninstitution.org/country-walking-dead.html#.VSxAuNzF_oU.

34. Cohen, for example, muses, "*Un-dead* is not the same as alive, nor does it allow for the quiescence of mortality. *Undead* names the zone of restless and perplexing activity from which monsters arrive, a gap in the fabric of the known world that opens a space neither real nor chimerical, a breach in which everything familiar loses its certainty—including what constitutes life." Cohen, "Undead," 398.

35. Peter Dendle, "Zombie Movies and the 'Millennial Generation,'" in *Better Off Dead*, ed. Christie and Lauro, 175.

36. For example, in the hit television show *The Walking Dead*, the zombie pandemic is caused by a virus, bacteria, or microorganism.

37. In fact, *ROTZ* was widely promoted in colleges in Bombay, an indication that the producers were quite clear about the target demographic. Part of the promotional strategy was the organization of a "zombie walk," in which students of local colleges participated in large numbers in full makeup and appropriately post-apocalyptic regalia.

38. Recall that the Ramsay horror film generated an impressive array of monsters, many of which certainly shared a kinship with the zombie. However, the media environment in the 1970s and 1980s and the target audience of the Ramsays hardly necessitated that the creature be named as such.

39. Luke Kenny is an actor, musician, and television video jockey who remains

strongly associated with Western music. In 2008, he portrayed a keyboard player in the hit film *Rock On!*, based on the trajectory of a rock band in Bombay, further reinforcing the association.

40. Kenny has declared in several interviews that an "international" look was conceptually important for *ROTZ*: "Kenny said the film was made for 'less than the song and dance sequence of a Bollywood film,' with the filmmakers relying mainly on makeup and camera effects rather than more costly computer graphics used in Hollywood horror films. 'It's a Hindi film with international sensibilities . . . The effort on my part was to make a film that anybody in the world can watch,' he said." Shilpa Jamkhandikar, "Bollywood Launches Its First Zombie Films to Win Back Viewers," *Reuters*, last modified April 6, 2013, accessed May 3, 2015, at http://in.reuters.com/article/2013/04/05/bollywood-film-zombies-idINDEE93405L20130405.

41. Stephen Harper, "*Night of the Living Dead*: Reappraising an Undead Classic," *Bright Lights Film Journal* (November 2005), http://brightlightsfilm.com/night-living-dead-reappraising-undead-classic/#.V84H5_krLIV.

42. However, one has to look closely at the closing credits of the film to unearth the fact that it was shot in Lansdowne in the Kumaon region of Uttarakhand.

43. One is reminded of Marc Auge's conceptualization of "non-places" that congeal as the byproducts of "supermodernity": "[I]f a place can be defined as relational, historical and concerned with identity, then a space which cannot be defined as relational, or historical, or concerned with identity will be a non-place . . . supermodernity produces non-places, meaning spaces which are not themselves anthropological places." Whereas the natural environment of the forest is obviously very different from the built environments and sites of transit that Auge describes, its empty, depersonalized blandness evokes the "world . . . surrendered to solitary individuality, to the fleeting, the temporary and ephemeral" in a striking way. Marc Auge, *Non-Places: Introduction to an Anthropology of Supermodernity*, trans. John Howe (New York: Verso, 1995), 77–78.

44. In the most compelling zombie media—Romero's series, for example, or even AMC's *The Walking Dead*—spatial vectors play an important role in the unfolding drama; rural Pennsylvania, suburban shopping malls, or the city of Atlanta crystallize as real and recognizable participants within the post-apocalyptic, post-infestation scenarios. The overall philosophical bleakness of zombie media remains dependent on the elaboration of recognizable physical spaces and locations. Victor Scalise, the AMC show's supervisor of visual effects, emphasized the importance of verisimilitude in the use of CGI: "We want the audience just to believe everything is real," Scalise said. "And I think that's one of the great things we do on the show is we ride the fine line of practical and digital." See Laura James, "How 'The Walking Dead' Destroyed Atlanta," *Atlanta Journal-Constitution*, last modified February 6, 2015, accessed May 28, 2015, at www.ajc.com/news/entertainment/television/how-walking-dead-destroyed-atlanta/nj585/.

45. Several reviewers commented on the "monotony" of the film; see, for example, Rohit Vats, "'Rise of the Zombie' Review: Monotony Kills the Novelty," *IBN Live*, last modified April 5, 2013, accessed March 5, 2015, at http://ibnlive.in.com

/news/rise-of-the-zombie-review-monotony-kills-the-daring-concept/383409-47-77.html. Similarly, the *Times of India*'s reviewer complained about the sluggish pace of *ROTZ* which "only evokes boredom" in "*Rise of the Zombie* Movie Review," *Times of India*, last modified April 4, 2013, accessed March 5, 2015, at http://timesofindia.indiatimes.com/entertainment/hindi/movie-review/Rise-Of-The-Zombie/movie-review/18589066.cms. Ravina Rawal described the film as "pretty boring," even as she appreciated some of the stylistic innovations: "The camera work is cool, low lit and shaky, with bits reminiscent of *Blair Witch Project* and full credit to the make-up artists who make us want to throw up our popcorn when the gory bits of the movie begin. But I'm afraid there isn't much more." Ravina Rawal, "Movie Review: *Rise of the Zombie* Bites Off More Than It Can Chew," *Firstpost*, last modified April 6, 2013, accessed March 5, 2015, at www.firstpost.com/bollywood/movie-review-rise-of-the-zombie-bites-off-more-than-it-can-chew-688801.html.

46. Shaviro further describes the bodily experience of watching Romero's trilogy thusly: "I watch these films, finally, with an alarming, ambivalent, and highly charged exhilaration. At the end of *Day*, especially I am seduced and transfixed by the joy and the terror—the disgusting, unspeakable pleasure—of the human bodies' exposure and destruction . . . I enjoy this sordid spectacle only at the price of being mimetically engulfed by it, uncontrollably, excitedly swept away." Steven Shaviro, *The Cinematic Body* (Minneapolis: University of Minnesota Press, 1993), 101–102.

47. The bravado of this gesture was not lost on contemporary commentators. Popular film critic Taran Adarsh commented on the film's risks in his review of *GGG*: "But the challenge lies in educating the spectator about zombies, since there's no zombie folklore to enlighten them thus far. Let's face it, making a zom-com means treading into untried, alien territory. It's always a peril if you think out of the box, when you offer something innovative to the spectator." Taran Adarsh, "*Go Goa Gone*," *Bollywood Hungama*, last modified May 9, 2013, accessed May 3, 2015, at www.bollywoodhungama.com/moviemicro/criticreview/id/546910.

48. In a *Salon* interview, the filmmakers insisted that despite its unfamiliar content, *GGG* would be accessible to all audiences: "'We have made it in such a way that all those who know about zombies can sit back and enjoy it, while for those who have no clue about zombies, we have very quickly elucidated what they are,' D. K. explained." Prachi Gupta, "Bollywood Embraces Zombie Culture," *Salon*, last modified March 31, 2013, accessed May 3, 2015, at www.salon.com/2013/03/31/bollywood_embraces_zombie_culture/.

49. It is curious that a film that has 'Goa' in its title would be shot almost entirely elsewhere. Krishna D. K. declared in an interview, "Even though the film is based in Goa, we shot a large portion in Mauritius because we needed an idealistic beach place and Mauritius was perfect." Presumably, the beaches of Goa were not pristine or idyllic enough for the makers. This sleight of hand only serves to make *GGG* seem detached from anything concrete and tangible, insofar as South Asian contexts are concerned. See "Mauritius Bound," *Indian Express*, at http://indianexpress.com/article/entertainment/screen/mauritius-bound/.

50. The song lyrics, written by Priya Panchal, are shockingly racy and transgressive for Bollywood films but fit the overall tenor of *GGG*: "*Raat hai ek whore, hai maange more / Tu lut jaa slowly slowly / Ghaas ka kar jhol, tu karle roll / Magar beta slowly slowly*" ("The night is a whore, she wants more / you surrender slowly slowly / grind some pot, roll yourself a joint / but remember slowly slowly").

51. According to Indian newspaper reports, a Russian mafia is fairly active in Goa. The Boris character, no doubt, draws on the circulation of such stories. See, for example, http://timesofindia.indiatimes.com/city/goa/Russian-mafia-and-not-government-controls-Goa/articleshow/7349882.cms.

52. For example, "Though Illuminati Films have mostly performed well in the overseas market, this time their concept was specifically directed at the Indian multiplex audiences. While the global market found nothing fresh in the zombie comedy idea, Indian audiences are still largely unprepared to receive the premise. Barring a few urban centres, the film performed dismally at the single screens which paved the way for its poor performance at the domestic box office." Mohar Basu, "*Go Goa Gone*: 2nd Weekend Overseas Box Office Collections," *Koimoi*, last modified May 21, 2013, at www.koimoi.com/box-office/go-goa-gone-2nd-weekend-overseas-box-office-collections/.

53. Advertisers for the shows were very clear about their target audience, and Fox Traveler India focused on a series of campaigns that appealed especially to urban youth audiences. See, for example, Vinaya Naidu, "Fox Traveller India Engages with #IndianZombie Memes for the Walking Dead," *Business 2 Community*, last modified March 31, 2014, at www.business2community.com/social-media/fox-traveller-india-engages-indianzombie-memes-walking-dead-0829360; and "Eleven Kinds of Zombies You'll Only Find in India," *Scoop Whoop*, last modified March 28, 2014, at www.scoopwhoop.com/entertainment/11-kinds-of-zombies-youll-only-find-in-india/.

54. Tewari, "Indian Youth Is Not Just Ready for a Zombie Film."

55. Barry Keith Grant suggests that the basic impulses of verité horror "can be traced back to the realistic gore effects of the Grand Guignol, which began in Paris toward the end of the nineteenth century." Barry Keith Grant, "Digital Anxiety and the New Verité Horror and SF Film," *Science Fiction Film and Television* 6 (2) (2013), 155.

56. Describing the use of the found footage aesthetic in *[REC]*, Shelagh M. Rowan-Legg writes, "Postnational genre cinema might be entirely national in production and theme, but it uses semantics that are not nationally specific to tell a story. Alongside these genre semantics are metonymies, which can reflect both the national originating culture, as well as themes relevant to a global audience, making another kind of post-national film." Shelagh M. Rowan-Legg, "Don't Miss a Bloody Thing: *[REC]* and the Spanish Adaptation of Found Footage Horror," *Studies in Spanish and Latin American Cinemas* 10 (2) (2013): 213–223.

57. Acronym for Multimedia Messaging Service, which can send and receive a variety of content—text, audio clips, video clips, or a combination thereof—between mobile phones.

58. Grant, "Digital Anxiety," 161.

59. Sen, "Spectral Pixels," 6.

60. Ibid.

61. Vickey Lalwani, "Delhi's Deepika Is Ekta's Ragini," *Times of India*, last modified May 6, 2011, at http://timesofindia.indiatimes.com/entertainment/hindi/bollywood/news/Delhis-Deepika-is-Ektas-Ragini/articleshow/8166499.cms.

62. Vaibhavi Risbood, "Fifty Percent of 'Ragini MMS' Is True: Ekta Kapoor," *Daily Bhaskar*, last modified March 1, 2011, at http://daily.bhaskar.com/news/ENT-50-of-ragini-mms-is-true-ekta-kapoor-1896512.html.

63. "Ekta has spoilt my image and ruined my life. I want her to come out and clear that the steamy scenes are not about me," she says, adding, "People stop me on the road to ask weird questions . . . it is embarrassing. I never shared (with Kapoor) any experiences of lovemaking. I had only told her that my boyfriend and I had gone for a vacation where he made a video of me, and when we saw it, we sensed some paranormal activity." Neha Sharma, "Ekta Ruined My Life: Real Ragini," *Hindustan Times*, last modified May 13, 2011, at www.hindustantimes.com/tabloid/ekta-ruined-my-life-real-ragini/article1-696679.aspx. See also Smrity Sharma, "Ekta Kapoor Challenges the Real Ragini," *Times of India*, last modified May 13, 2011, at http://timesofindia.indiatimes.com/entertainment/hindi/bollywood/news/Ekta-Kapoor-challenges-the-real-Ragini/articleshow/8293159.cms; and "Real 'Ragini' Speaks Up: BLASTS Ekta Kapoor—Bollywood Hungama Exclusive," last modified May 12, 2011, at www.youtube.com/watch?v=BM-tRhEMVdc.

64. Sen, "Spectral Pixels," 9.

65. Shaviro, "Paranormal Activity: The Ghost Dimension," November 20, 2015, accessed December 29, 2015. at www.shaviro.com/Blog/?p=1345.

66. Cecelia Sayad, "Found Footage Horror and the Frame's Undoing," *Cinema Journal* 55 (2016): 43–66.

67. Jane Roscoe, "*The Blair Witch Project*: Mock-Documentary Goes Mainstream," *Jump Cut* 43 (2000): 3–8, www.ejumpcut.org/archive/onlinessays/JC43folder/BlairWitch.html.

68. For a discussion of the spectrality in digital and analog media, see, for example, Chap. 11 in Cary Wolfe, *What Is Posthumanism?* (Minneapolis: University of Minnesota Press, 2010), 283–299.

69. As Shaunak Sen puts it, "The primordial moral fear now is of the body getting dematerialized and dispersed into a plurality of multiple low-quality images that can travel uncontrollably through the endless annals of the digital world." Sen, "Spectral Pixels," 2.

70. Mayank Tewari, the film's writer, explains the narrative as a cautionary tale:

> In some ways a woman who was killed many years ago because of being termed a witch is also a victim of a senseless tag about that spreads through people, causing great damage to her. In the end the ghost can kill everyone else but not Ragini despite torturing her, because she is innocent, un-

like Uday and can rightfully say "I have not done anything." The film is a combination of voyeurism in sex and in the supernatural. In a way you can say the film itself is a MMS, it's a MMS that tries to make the making of a MMS scary. (Quoted in Sen, "Spectral Pixels," 7)

71. Unlike the promiscuous young women in slasher films who are quickly dispatched by the monster, Ragini is the character who survives and the one we most identify with; she is the final girl, in a certain sense.

72. See, for example, the recent newspaper reportage involving alleged witchcraft and witch hunts in South Asia: Terrence McCoy, "Thousands of Women, Accused of Sorcery, Tortured and Executed in Indian Witch Hunts," *Washington Post*, July 21, 2014, accessed December 27, 2015, at www.washingtonpost.com/news/morning-mix/wp/2014/07/21/thousands-of-women-accused-of-sorcery-tortured; Sarita Santoshini, "Hunting Down Witches in Northeast India," *Al Jazeera*, September 3, 2015, accessed December 27, 2015, at www.aljazeera.com/indepth/features/2015/09/hunting-witches-northeast-india-150902092226394.html; and Jason Burke and Manoj Chaurasia, "Five Women Killed in India by Villagers Suspecting Witchcraft," *Guardian*, August 8, 2015, accessed December 27, 2015, at www.theguardian.com/world/2015/aug/08/five-women-killed-india-jharkhand-villagers-suspecting-witchcraft.

73. In *Click*, which is an unauthorized re-make of the Thai film *Shutter* (Banjong Pisanthanakun and Parkpoom Wongpoom, 2004), photographer Avi (Shreyas Talpade) and his girlfriend, Sonia (Sada), initially discover the presence of the ghost as a smudgy distortion in a series of digital photographs he has taken. Thereafter, whereas those who have wronged Aarti (Sneha Ullal) can see her everywhere, she appears to the rest of the world only as a wraithlike presence in photographs.

74. The planetary collaboration in an industrial sense is visible in the selection of this location. The government of Fiji provided many financial incentives for *3G* to be shot on its beautiful beaches and expensive resorts, hoping, no doubt, that this showcasing of the nation's natural wonders would boost tourism in the area.

75. In Takashi Shimizu's celebrated horror film (2002), which he remade in English as *The Grudge* in 2004, the rage of the dead protagonists continues to gather strength after their brutal murders.

76. Steven Shaviro, "What Is the Post-Cinematic?" August 11, 2011, accessed December 28, 2015, at www.shaviro.com/Blog/?p=992.

77. Despite the purchase of legal rights, however, Bhushan Patel, the director of *Alone*, insisted that the film was based on an "adapted screenplay" of the original Thai version, because "our sensibilities are very different." See "*Alone*: Interview with Director Bhushan Patel—Part 1," last modified January 5, 2015, accessed May 19, 2015, at www.youtube.com/watch?v=EBPz1sDoLjY.

1. *Talaash* is not a remake or adaptation of *Rouge*, and there has been no word from the producers of the latter that it was inspired by Kwan's film. However, the resonances are unmistakable, including the names of the ghostly protagonists, both of which, of course, invoke flowers.

2. Bliss Cua Lim describes the film's layering of time and space thusly: "In one of the film's most telling images, the revenant walks past a shop window, and we see reflected in it, as if on a screen, the shadowy performance of an old Cantonese opera at the theater that the storefront has replaced. In a visual palimpsest, this film sequence depicts one space, splintered yet whole: an antiseptic shopping mall in the late 1980s, in whose dark glass we glimpse the warm glamour of the demolished Tai Ping theater." Lim, *Translating Time* (Durham, NC: Duke University Press, 2009), 156.

3. It is interesting that the film is set in Bombay, yet large segments of it were actually shot in the coastal town of Pondicherry. Although there may have been production-related reasons for this masquerade of urban space, the swap does imbue the locations of *Talaash* with a strangely unreal character.

4. Combining jazz, electronic dance music (EDM), and other globally popular forms, the music of the film is an especially important component of this confident globality.

5. The phrase comes from the title of Melissa Gregg and Gregory Seigworth's introduction to *The Affect Theory Reader*, and they write, "[A]ffect is found in those intensities that pass body to body (human, nonhuman, part-body, and otherwise), in those resonances that circulate about, between, and sometimes stick to bodies and worlds, *and* in the very passages or variations between these intensities and resonances themselves. Affect, at its most anthropomorphic, is the name we give to those forces . . . that can serve to drive us toward movement, toward thought and extension. . . . Indeed, affect is persistent proof of a body's never less than ongoing immersion in and among the world's obstinacies and rhythms." Gregg and Seigworth, eds., "An Inventory of Shimmers," in *The Affect Theory Reader* (Durham, NC: Duke University Press, 2010), 1.

6. "It is necessary to speak *of the* ghost, indeed *to the* ghost and with it. . . . No justice . . . seems possible or thinkable without the principle of some responsibility, beyond all living present, within that which disjoins the living present, before the ghosts of those who are not yet born or who are already dead, be they victims of wars, political or other kinds of violence. . . . Without *this non-contemporaneity with itself of the living present*, without that which secretly unhinges it, without this responsibility and this respect for justice concerning those who *are not there*, of those who are no longer or who are not yet *present and living*, what sense would there be to ask the question 'where?' 'where tomorrow?' 'whither?'" Jacques Derrida, *Specters of Marx*, trans. Peggy Kamuf (London: Routledge, 2006), xviii.

7. For example, *Naagin* (2015) on Colors TV rehashes many of the myths of *ichchhadhari* snakes that were de rigueur in the snake films of the 1980s.

Bibliography

"A Nagin Without the Bite." *Statesman*, January 25, 1976.

Ahmad, Ashwin. "Bollywood Goes Global! Meet the Fans of Indian Cinema Across the World Who Know Their Shammi from Their Ranbir." *Daily Mail India*. Last modified April 26, 2014. Available at www.dailymail.co.uk/india home/indianews/article-2613971/Bollywood-goes-global-Meet-fans-Indian-cinema-world-know-Shammi-Ranbir.html.

———. "Memsaab: Bollywood's Phoren Fan Brigade." *Economic Times*. Last modified June 1, 2008. Available at http://articles.economictimes.indiatimes.com/2008-06-01/news/27698718_1_indian-cinema-hindi-film-bollywood.

Allocco, Amy. "Fear, Reverence and Ambivalence: Divine Snakes in Contemporary South India." In *Charming Beauties and Frightful Beasts: Non-Human Animals in South Asian Myth, Ritual and Folklore*, ed. Fabrizio M. Ferrari and Thomas Dähnhart, 217–235. Sheffield, UK: Equinox Publishing, 2013.

———. "Snakes in the Dark Age: Human Action, Karmic Retribution, and the Possibilities for Hindu Animal Ethics." In *Asian Perspectives on Animal Ethics: Rethinking the Nonhuman*, ed. Neil Dalal and Chloe Taylor, 179–201. London: Routledge, 2014.

"*Alone*: Interview with Director Bhushan Patel—Part 1." Last modified January 5, 2015. Accessed May 19, 2015. Available at https://www.youtube.com/watch?v=EBPz1sDoLjY.

Altman, Rick. *Film/Genre*. London: British Film Institute, 2006.

———. "Moving Lips: Cinema as Ventriloquism." *Yale French Studies* 60, Cinema/Sound (1980): 67–79.

"An Open Letter on the Subject of Filmi Snake Identification and Research." *Cinema Chaat: Masala, Movies, Moustaches, and More!* Last modified August 10, 2011. Available at http://cinemachaat.com/2011/08/10/an-open-letter-on-the-subject-of-filmi-snake-identification-and-research/.

Antarkar, Aruna. "Seven Cooks (De)Construct a Dish." Trans. Anjali Nerlekar. *Kesari*, July 14, 1981.

Appadurai, Arjun. *Modernity at Large: Cultural Dimensions of Globalization*. Minneapolis: University of Minnesota Press, 1996.

———. "Topographies of the Self: Praise and Emotion in Hindu India." In *Language and the Politics of Emotion*, ed. Catherine A. Lutz and Lila Abu-Lughod, 92–112. Cambridge, UK: Cambridge University Press, 1990.

Athique, Adrian. "Leisure Capital in the New Economy: The Rapid Rise of the Multiplex in India." *Contemporary South Asia* 17 (2) (2009): 123–140.

Auge, Marc. *Non-Places: Introduction to an Anthropology of Supermodernity*. Trans. John Howe. New York: Verso, 1995.

Baker, Aryn. "A Horror Movie on the Doorstep of the Taliban." Last modified June 12, 2007. Accessed February 7, 2015. Available at http://content.time.com/time/world/article/0,8599,1632168,00.html.

Baker, Brian. "Gothic Masculinities." In *Routledge Companion to the Gothic*, ed. Catherine Spooner and Emma McEvoy, 164–173. New York: Routledge, 2007.

"*Bandh Darwaza*: Howls, Cowls and Scowls." *Maharashtra Herald*, June 18, 1990.

Barker, Timothy Scott. *Time and the Digital: Connecting Technology, Aesthetics, and a Process Philosophy of Time*. Hanover, NH: Dartmouth College Press, 2012.

Basu, Anustup. "The Eternal Return and Overcoming 'Cape Fear': Science, Sensation, Superman and Hindu Nationalism in Recent Hindi Cinema." *South Asian History and Culture*, special issue, *South Asian Transnationalisms: Cultural Exchange in the Twentieth Century* 2 (4) (2011): 557–571.

———. "'The Face That Launched a Thousand Ships': Helen and Public Femininity in Hindi Film." In *Figurations in Indian Film*, ed. Meheli Sen and Anustup Basu, 139–157. Hampshire, UK: Palgrave Macmillan, 2013.

Basu, Mohar. "*Go Goa Gone*: 2nd Weekend Overseas Box Office Collections." *Koimoi*. Last modified May 21, 2013. Available at www.koimoi.com/box-office/go-goa-gone-2nd-weekend-overseas-box-office-collections/.

"*Bees Saal Baad*, a Murder Mystery: Good Time-Killer for the Masses." *Mother India*, July 1, 1962.

"'Bees Saal Baad' Grips, Despite Several Failings." *Filmfare*, June 1, 1962.

"Behind the Scenes." *Filmfare*, November 27, 1964.

Benshoff, Harry M. *Monsters in the Closet: Homosexuality and the Horror Film*. Manchester, UK: Manchester University Press, 1997.

Bhatt, Vikram. Interviewed by author. Digital recording. Mumbai, India, July 6, 2009.

Bhattacharya, Tithi. "Deadly Spaces: Ghosts, Histories and Colonial Anxieties in Nineteenth-Century Bengal." In *Postcolonial Ghosts*, ed. Mélanie Joseph-Vilain and Judith Misrahi-Barak, 143–156. Montpellier: Presses Universitaires de la Méditerranée, Collection Les Carnets du Cerpac, no. 8, 2009.

Bhaumik, Kaushik. "Querying the 'Traditional' Roots of Silent Cinema in Asia." *Journal of the Moving Image* 7 (2008). Accessed December 12, 2015. Available at www.jmionline.org/articles/2008/querying_the_traditional_roots_of_silent_cinema_in_asia.pdf.

Blake, Linnie. *The Wounds of Nations: Horror Cinema, Historical Trauma and National Identity*. Manchester, UK: Manchester University Press, 2012.

Bollywoodhungama. Available at www.bollywoodhungama.com/moviemicro/critic review/id/546910. 2015.

Boym, Svetlana. *The Future of Nostalgia*. New York: Basic Books, 2002.

———. "Nostalgia and Its Discontents." *Hedgehog Review* 9 (2) (2007): 7–18.

Brosius, Christine. *India's Middle Class: New Forms of Urban Leisure, Consumption and Prosperity*. New Delhi: Routledge India, 2014.

Burke, Jason, and Manoj Chaurasia. "Five Women Killed in India by Villagers Suspecting Witchcraft." *Guardian*, August 8, 2015. Accessed December 27, 2015. Available at www.theguardian.com/world/2015/aug/08/five-women-killed-india-jharkhand-villagers-suspecting-witchcraft.

Chakrabarty, Dipesh. *Provincializing Europe: Postcolonial Thought and Historical Difference*. Princeton: Princeton University Press, 2000.

Chakravarty, Sumita. *National Identity in Indian Popular Cinema, 1947–1987*. Austin: University of Texas Press, 1993.

Chatterjee, Shubhajit. "On Disreputable Genres: B Movies and Revisionary Histories of Bombay Cinema." *Marg* 64 (4) (2013): 32–41.

Cheah, Pheng. *Spectral Nationality: Passages of Freedom from Kant to Postcolonial Literatures of Liberation*. New York: Columbia University Press, 2003.

Chion, Michel. *Audio-Vision: Sound on Screen*. Trans. Claudia Gorbman. New York: Columbia University Press, 1994.

———. *The Voice in Cinema*. New York: Columbia University Press, 1999.

Chopra, Anupama. "Bollywood Is Prancing Far Abroad: Shah Rukh Khan and Bollywood's Global Fortunes Advance." *New York Times*. Last modified September 26, 2014. Available at www.nytimes.com/2014/09/28/movies/shah-rukh-khan-and-bollywoods-global-fortunes-advance.html?hpw&rref=movies&action=click&pgtype=Homepage&version=HpHedThumbWell&module=well-region&region=bottom-well&WT.nav=bottom-well&_r=1.)

Choudhury, Shubham Roy. "Sound of Horror: Sound and Dread in Hindi Cinema." *Journal of the Moving Image* (2007).

Christie, Deborah, and Sarah Juliet Lauro, eds. *Better Off Dead: The Evolution of the Zombie as Post-Human*. New York: Fordham University Press, 2011.

Clover, Carol J. *Men, Women, and Chainsaws: Gender in the Modern Horror Film*. Princeton: Princeton University Press, 1993.

Cohen, Jeffrey Jerome. "Undead (A Zombie Oriented Ontology)." *Journal of the Fantastic in the Arts* 23 (3) (2012): 397–412.

Collins, Jo, and John Jervis, eds. *Uncanny Modernity: Cultural Theories, Modern Anxieties*. New York: Palgrave Macmillan, 2008.

Creed, Barbara. *The Monstrous-Feminine: Film, Feminism, Psychoanalysis*. New York: Routledge, 1993.

Cubitt, Sean. "Phalke, Melies, and Special Effects Today." *Wide Angle* 21 (1) (1999): 115–130.

Davis, Colin. "*État Présent*: Hauntology, Specters and Phantoms." In *The Spectralities*

Reader, ed. María del Pilar Blanco and Esther Peeren, 53–60. New York: Bloomsbury, 2013.

Dayal, Geeta. "Studio 84: Digging into the History of Disco in India." *The Original Sound Track*. Last modified August 29, 2010. Accessed June 25, 2015. Available at www.theoriginalsoundtrack.com/2010/08/29/studio-84-the-history-of-disco-in-india/.

Dendle, Peter. "Zombie Movies and the 'Millennial Generation.'" In *Better Off Dead: The Evolution of the Zombie as Post-Human*, ed. Deborah Christie and Sarah Juliet Lauro, 175–186. New York: Fordham University Press, 2011.

Derrida, Jacques. *Specters of Marx*. Trans. Peggy Kamuf. London: Routledge, 2006.

Desai, Jigna. "The Scale of Diasporic Cinema: Negotiating National and Transnational Cultural Citizenship," *Routledge Handbook on Indian Cinema*, Routledge, 206–217, 2013.

Dharamsey, V. "The Advent of Sound in Indian Cinema: Theater, Orientalism, Action, Magic." *Journal of the Moving Image* 9 (2010). Accessed December 12, 2015. Available at www.jmionline.org/articles/2010/the_advent_of_sound_in_indian_cinema_theatre_orientalism_action_magic.pdf.

Dhusiya, Mithuraaj. "Bestiality, Compassion and Gender Emancipation: The Snake Woman in Hindi Horror Films." *Cineforum* 15 (2012): 105–134.

Dhusiya, Mithuraaj. "The Ramsay Chronicles: Non-Normative Sexualities in *Purana Mandir* and *Bandh Darwaza*." In *Bollywood and its Other(s): Towards New Configurations*, ed. V. Kishore, A. Sarwal, and P. Patra, 174–185. London: Palgrave Macmillan UK, 2014.

Doane, Mary Ann. "Paranoia and the Specular." In Doane, *The Desire to Desire: The Woman's Film of the 1940s*, 123–154. Bloomington: Indiana University Press, 1987.

Dube, Saurabh. *Enchantments of Modernity: Empire, Nation, Globalization*. Delhi: Routledge India, 2009.

Dudenhoeffer, Larrie. *Embodiment and Horror Cinema*. New York: Palgrave Macmillan, 2014.

Dudrah, Rajinder, and Priya Joshi. "Editorial: The 1970s and Its Legacies in India's Cinemas." *South Asian Popular Culture* 10 (1) (2012): 1–5.

Dwyer, Rachel. "The Biggest Star of All: The Elephant in Hindi Cinema." In *Charming Beauties and Frightful Beasts: Non-Human Animals in South Asian Myth, Ritual and Folklore*, ed. Fabrizio M. Ferrari and Thomas Dähnhardt, 181–198. Sheffield, UK: Equinox Publishing, 2013.

———. "Bombay Gothic: On the 60th Anniversary of Kamal Amrohi's *Mahal*." In *Beyond the Boundaries of Bollywood*, ed. Rachel Dwyer and Jerry Pinto, 130–155. New Delhi: Oxford University Press, 2011.

———. *Filming the Gods: Religion and Indian Cinema*. London: Routledge, 2006.

"Eleven Kinds of Zombies You'll Only Find in India." *Scoop Whoop*. Last modified March 28, 2014. Available at www.scoopwhoop.com/entertainment/11-kinds-of-zombies-youll-only-find-in-india/.

Fernandes, Leela. "The Politics of Forgetting: Class Politics, State Power and the Restructuring of Urban Space in India." *Urban Studies* 41 (12) (2004): 2415–2430.

Ferrari, Fabrizio M., and Thomas Dähnhardt. "Introduction." In *Charming Beauties and Frightful Beasts: Non-Human Animals in South Asian Myth, Ritual and Folklore*, ed. Ferrari and Dähnhardt. Sheffield, UK: Equinox Publishing, 2013.

"Filmi Snake Spotter's Field Guide." *Cinema Chaat: Masala, Movies, Moustaches, and More!* Last modified July 31, 2011. Available at http://cinemachaat.com/2011/07/31/filmi-snake-spotters-field-guide/.

Fisher, Mark. *Ghosts of My Life: Writings on Depression, Hauntology and Lost Futures*. Winchester, UK: Zero Books, 2014.

Gandhi, Maneka. "Tell It to the Birds." *Hindu*. Last modified February 24, 2013. Available at www.thehindu.com/todays-paper/tp-features/tp-sundaymagazine/tell-it-to-the-birds/article4448002.ece.

Ganti, Tejaswini. "No Longer a Frivolous Singing and Dancing Nation of Movie-Makers: The Hindi Film Industry and Its Quest for Global Distinction." *Visual Anthropology* 25 (4) (2012): 340–365.

———. *Producing Bollywood: Inside the Contemporary Hindi Film Industry*. Durham, NC: Duke University Press, 2012.

Ghosh, Bishnupriya. Lecture description for "The Security Aesthetic in Bollywood's High-Rise Horror." Available at http://web.international.ucla.edu/southasia/events/10334.

———. "On Grafting the Vernacular: The Consequences of Postcolonial Spectrology." *boundary 2, an international journal of literature and culture* 31 (2) (2004): 197–218.

———. "The Security Aesthetic in Bollywood's High-Rise Horror." *Representations*, special issue, *Financialization and the Culture Industry* 126 (1) (2014): 58–84.

Ghosh, Paramita. "King of Creeps." *Hindustan Times*. Last modified September 11, 2010. Available at http://www.hindustantimes.com/entertainment/king-of-creeps/story-SYtSoCGNc6OkoWpvFBMNWI.html.

Giles, Michelle. "Postcolonial Gothic and *The God of Small Things*: The Haunting of India's Past." *Postcolonial Text* 6 (1) (2011): 1–15.

Gopal, Sangita. *Conjugations: Marriage and Form in New Bollywood Cinema*. Chicago: University of Chicago Press, 2011.

———, and Sujata Moorti. "Introduction: Travels of Hindi Song and Dance." In *Global Bollywood: Travels of Hindi Song and Dance*, ed. Gopal and Moorti. Minneapolis: University of Minnesota Press, 2008.

Gopalan, K. "View from the Gallery: *Nagin*." *Filmfare*, March 5–18, 1976.

Gopalan, Lalitha. "Avenging Women in Indian Cinema." *Screen* 38 (1) (1997): 42–59.

———. *Cinema of Interruptions: Action Genres in Contemporary Indian Films*. London: British Film Institute, 2002.

Gordon, Avery F. *Ghostly Matters: Haunting the Sociological Imagination*. Minneapolis: University of Minnesota Press, 1997.

Govil, Nitin. *Orienting Hollywood: A Century of Film Culture Between Los Angeles and Bombay*. New York: New York University Press, 2015.

Grant, Barry Keith. "Digital Anxiety and the New Verité Horror and SF Film." *Science Fiction Film and Television* 6 (2) (2013): 153–175.

Gregg, Melissa, and Gregory J. Seigworth, eds. *The Affect Theory Reader.* Durham, NC: Duke University Press, 2010.

Gunew, Sneja. "Subaltern Empathy: Beyond European Categories in Affect Theory." *Concentric: Literary and Cultural Studies* 35 (1) (2009): 11–30.

Gunning, Tom. "An Aesthetic of Astonishment: Early Film and the (In)Credulous Spectator." *Art and Text* (Fall 1989).

———. "The Cinema of Attractions: Early Film, Its Spectator and the Avant-Garde." *Wide Angle* 8 (3 and 4) (1986).

———. "To Scan a Ghost: The Ontology of Mediated Vision." In *The Spectralities Reader*, ed. María del Pilar Blanco and Esther Peeren, 207–244. New York: Bloomsbury, 2013.

Gupta, Prachi. "Bollywood Embraces Zombie Culture." *Salon.* Last modified March 31, 2013. Accessed May 3, 2015. Available at www.salon.com/2013/03/31/bollywood_embraces_zombie_culture/.

Halberstam, Judith (Jack). *Skin Shows: Gothic Horror and the Technology of Monsters.* Durham, NC: Duke University Press, 1995.

Harper, Stephen. "*Night of the Living Dead*: Reappraising an Undead Classic." *Bright Lights Film Journal* (November 2005).

Harper, Sue. "Historical Pleasures: Gainsborough Costume Melodrama." In *Home Is Where the Heart Is: Studies in Melodrama and the Woman's Film*, ed. Christine Gledhill, 167–196. London: British Film Institute, 1987.

Holden, Philip. "The 'Postcolonial Gothic': Absent Histories, Present Contexts." *Textual Practice* 23 (3) (2009): 353–372.

Hsu, Wendy F. "Between Narrative and Expressive, Fantasy and Melodrama in Bombay (Bollywood) Film." *Virginia Review of Asian Studies* 5 (2003).

Hughes, William, and Andrew Smith. "Introduction: Defining the Relationships Between Gothic and the Postcolonial." *Gothic Studies* 5 (2) (2003): 1–6.

Iyer, Usha. "Nevla as Dracula: Figurations of the Tantric as Monster in the Hindi Horror Film." In *Figurations in Indian Film*, ed. Meheli Sen and Anustup Basu, 101–115. Hampshire, UK: Palgrave Macmillan, 2013.

James, Laura. "How *The Walking Dead* Destroyed Atlanta." *Atlanta Journal-Constitution.* Last modified February 6, 2015. Accessed May 28, 2015. Available at www.ajc.com/news/entertainment/television/how-walking-dead-destroyed-atlanta/nj585/.

Jameson, Fredric. "Postmodernism and Consumer Society." Lecture at the Whitney Museum of American Art. New York City, Fall 1982.

———. *Postmodernism, or, the Cultural Logic of Late Capitalism.* Durham, NC: Duke University Press, 1991.

Jamkhandikar, Shilpa. "Bollywood Launches Its First Zombie Films to Win Back Viewers." *Reuters.* Last Modified April 6, 2013. Accessed May 3, 2015. Available at http://in.reuters.com/article/2013/04/05/bollywood-film-zombies-idINDEE93405L20130405.

Jenkins, Henry. *Convergence Culture: Where Old and New Media Collide.* New York: New York University Press, 2006.

Jervis, John, "Uncanny Presences." In *Uncanny Modernity: Cultural Theories, Modern Anxieties*, ed. Jo Collins and John Jervis, 10–50. New York: Palgrave Macmillan, 2008.

Jha, Subhash K. "I Didn't Make *Hisss*: Jennifer Lynch." *Times of India*. Last modified October 25, 2010. Available at http://timesofindia.indiatimes.com/entertainment/hindi/bollywood/news/I-didnt-make-Hisss-Jennifer-Lynch/articleshow/6807314.cms.

Joshi, Priya. *Bollywood's India: A Public Fantasy*. New York: Columbia University Press, 2015.

Kabir, Nasreen Munni. "Palace of Delusion: Kamal Amrohi's *Mahal* Is Our First Reincarnation Thriller." *Outlook India*. Last modified June 4, 2012. Accessed May 11, 2013. Available at www.outlookindia.com/article.aspx?281005.

Kapur, Geeta. "Mythic Material in Indian Cinema." *Journal of Arts and Ideas* 14–15 (1987): 79–108.

Kavoori, Anandam P., and Christina Joseph. "*Nagina*: Conversations with a Snake." *Jump Cut* 43 (2000): 86–91.

Khan, Ali, and Ali Nobil Ahmad. "From Zinda Laash to Zibahkhana." *Third Text* 24 (1) (2010): 149–161.

Kirk, Gwendolyn S. "Working Class Zombies and Men in Burqas: Temporality, Trauma, and the Specter of Nostalgia in Zibahkhana." *BioScope* 5 (2) (2014): 141–151.

Klein, Amanda A. "Introduction: Love at First Sight." In Klein, *American Film Cycles*. Austin: University of Texas Press, 2011.

"Kohraa: The Beaten Track." *Filmfare*, May 1, 1964.

Kolowich, Steve. "A Brief History of Academics Writing Seriously About Zombies." *Chronicle of Higher Education*. Last modified October 41, 2014. Available at http://chronicle.com/article/A-Brief-History-of-Academics/149755.

Kristeva, Julia. *Powers of Horror: An Essay on Abjection*. New York: Columbia University Press, 1982 reprint.

Lalwani, Vickey. "Delhi's Deepika Is Ekta's Ragini." *Times of India*. Last modified May 6, 2011. Available at http://timesofindia.indiatimes.com/entertainment/hindi/bollywood/news/Delhis-Deepika-is-Ektas-Ragini/articleshow/8166499.cms.

Landy, Marcia. *Cinematic Uses of the Past*. Minneapolis: University of Minnesota Press, 1996.

Lauro, Sarah Juliet, and Karen Embry, "A Zombie Manifesto: The Nonhuman Condition in the Era of Advanced Capitalism," *boundary 2, an international journal of literature and culture* 35 (1) (2008): 85–108.

Lim, Bliss Cua. "Spectral Time, Heterogeneous Space: The Ghost Film as Historical Allegory." In Lim, *Translating Time: Cinema, the Fantastic, and Temporal Critique*, 149–189. Durham, NC: Duke University Press, 2009.

———. *Translating Time*. Durham, NC: Duke University Press, 2009.

Lowenstein, Adam. *Shocking Representation: Historical Trauma, National Cinema, and the Modern Horror Film*. New York: Columbia University Press, 2005.

Lutgendorf, Philip. "Jai Santoshi Ma." *Indian Cinema: Philip'sfil-ums.* Available at www.uiowa.edu/indiancinema/jai-santoshi-maa.

Majumdar, Neepa. "The Embodied Voice: Song Sequences and Stardom in Bombay Cinema." In Majumdar, *Wanted Cultured Ladies Only! Female Stardom and Cinema in India, 1930s–1950s*, 173–202. Chicago: University of Illinois Press, 2009.

Majumder, Rishi. "Ramsay International." *Motherland* 7 (2012). Last modified May 2012. Accessed December 2004. Available at www.motherlandmagazine.com/ghost-issue/ramsay-international.

Mankekar, Purnima. *Screening Culture, Viewing Politics: An Ethnography of Television, Womanhood, and Nation in Postcolonial India.* Durham, NC: Duke University Press, 1999.

Massumi, Brian. *Parables for the Virtual: Movement, Affect, Sensation.* Durham, NC: Duke University Press, 2002.

Masud, Iqbal. "*Nagina*—Passable as Fable." *Indian Express*, November 30, 1986.

Mathur, Suchitra. "From Capes to Snakes: The Indianization of the American Superhero." In *Comics as a Nexus of Cultures: Essays on the Interplay of Media, Disciplines and International Perspectives*, ed. Mark Berninger, Jochen Ecke, and Gideon Haberkorn, 175–186. Jefferson, NC: McFarland, 2010.

Mazumdar, Debu. "Snaky Sri Devi in *Nagina.*" *Indian Express*, November 24, 1986.

Mazzarella, William. *Shoveling Smoke: Advertising and Globalization in Contemporary India.* Durham, NC: Duke University Press, 2003.

McCoy, Terrence. "Thousands of Women, Accused of Sorcery, Tortured and Executed in Indian Witch Hunts." *Washington Post*, July 21, 2014. Accessed December 27, 2015. Available at www.washingtonpost.com/news/morning-mix/wp/2014/07/21/thousands-of-women-accused-of-sorcery-tortured-and-executed-in-indian-witch-hunts/.

McNally, David. *Monsters of the Market: Zombies, Vampires and Global Capitalism.* Leiden, The Netherlands: Brill, 2011.

Mishra, Vijay. *Bollywood Cinema: Temples of Desire.* New York: Routledge, 2001.

———. "Melodramatic Staging." In Mishra, *Bollywood Cinema: Temples of Desire*, 35–59. New York: Routledge, 2002.

Mitchell, Timothy, ed. *Questions of Modernity.* Minneapolis: University of Minnesota Press, 2000.

Morcom, Anna. *Hindi Film Songs and the Cinema.* Farnham, UK: Ashgate, 2007.

Moreland, Sean, and Summer Pervez. "Acts of Repossession: Bollywood's Re-Inventions of the Occult Possession Film." In *Fear and Learning: Essays on the Pedagogy of Horror*, ed. Aalya Ahmad and Sean Moreland, 75–94. Jefferson, NC: McFarland, 2013.

Mubarki, Meraj Ahmed. "Mapping the Hindi Horror Genre: Ghosts in the Service of Ideology." *History and Sociology of South Asia* 7 (1) (2013): 39–60.

"*Nagin*: Don't Mess with the Ladies." *Indiequill.* Last modified May 19, 2009. Available at http://indiequill.wordpress.com/2009/05/19/nagin-dont-mess-with-the-ladies/.

"*Nagin*—Our Review." *Nagpur Times*, March 28, 1976.

Naidu, Vinaya. "Fox Traveller India Engages with #IndianZombie Memes for the Walking Dead." *Business 2 Community*. Last modified March 31, 2014. Available at www.business2community.com/social-media/fox-traveller-india-engages-indianzombie-memes-walking-dead-0829360.

Nair, Kartik. "Fear on Film: The Ramsay Brothers and Bombay's Horror Cinema." *Sarai Reader* 8 (2008): 254–261.

———. "Taste, Taboo, Trash: The Story of the Ramsay Brothers." *Bioscope: South Asian Screen Studies* 3 (2) (2012): 123–145.

———. "Temple of Womb." *New Inquiry*. Last modified July 23, 2013. Accessed January 2015. Available at http://thenewinquiry.com/essays/temple-of-womb/.

Nandy, Ashis. "Slum's Eye View of Politics." Introduction to *The Secret Politics of Our Desires: Innocence, Culpability, and Indian Popular Cinema*, ed. Ashis Nandy. London: Zed Books, 1999.

Nardi, Carlo. "Reinventing Technology in Indian Popular Cinema." *Journal on the Art of Record Production* 5 (2011).

Nijhawan, Amita. "Excusing the Female Dancer: Tradition and Transgression in Bollywood Dancing." *South Asian Popular Culture* 7 (2) (2009): 99–112.

Phillips, Erica E. "Zombie Studies Gain Ground on College Campuses." *Wall Street Journal*. Last modified March 3, 2014. Available at www.wsj.com/articles/SB10001424052702304851104579361451951384512.

Pick, Anat. *Creaturely Poetics: Animality and Vulnerability in Literature and Film*. New York: Columbia University Press, 2011.

Pilar Blanco, María del. *Ghost-Watching American Modernity*. New York: Fordham Press, 2012.

———, and Esther Peeren. "Introduction: Conceptualizing Spectralities." In *The Spectralities Reader*, ed. María del Pilar Blanco and Esther Peeren. New York: Bloomsbury, 2013, 1–27.

———, and Esther Peeren, eds. *Popular Ghosts: The Haunted Spaces of Everyday Culture*. New York: Continuum, 2010.

Pinedo, Isabel. *Recreational Terror: Women and the Pleasures of Horror Film Viewing*. Albany: SUNY Press, 1997.

Posey, Sean. "A Country Walking Dead: The Zombie as Metaphor in American Culture and Film." *The Hampton Institute*. Last modified February 27, 2014. Available at www.hamptoninstitution.org/country-walking-dead.html#.VSxAuNzF_oU.

Prasad, M. Madhava. *Ideology of the Hindi Film: A Historical Construction*. New Delhi: Oxford University Press, 2001.

———. "Surviving Bollywood." In *Global Bollywood*, ed. Anandam P. Kavoori and Aswin Punathambekar, 41–51. New York: New York University Press, 2008.

———. "This Thing Called Bollywood." *Seminar* 525 (May 2003). Available at www.india-seminar.com/2003/525/525%20madhava%20prasad.htm.

Punathambekar, Aswin. *From Bombay to Bollywood: The Making of a Global Media Industry*. New York: New York University Press, 2013.

Punter, David, and Glennis Byron. *The Gothic*. Malden, MA: Blackwell, 2004.

Rabaté, Jean-Michel. *The Ghosts of Modernity*. Gainesville: University Press of Florida, 1996.

Rai, Amit. *Untimely Bollywood: Globalization and India's New Media Assemblage*. Durham, NC: Duke University Press, 2009.

Rajadhyaksha, Ashish. "The 'Bollywoodization' of the Indian Cinema: Cultural Nationalism in a Global Arena." *Inter-Asia Cultural Studies* 4 (1) (2003): 25–39.

Rajagopal, Arvind. *Politics After Television: Hindu Nationalism and the Reshaping of the Public in India*. Cambridge, UK: Cambridge University Press, 2001.

Ramadurai, Charukesi. "Bollywood's Foreign Appeal Finds Online Expression." *Sunday Guardian*. Last modified February 16, 2013. Available at www.sunday-guardian.com/masala-art/bollywoods-foreign-appeal-finds-online-expression.

Ramsay, Tulsi. Interviewed by author. Digital recording. Mumbai, India, July 8, 2009.

Rane, Ashok. "The Shortage of Newness in Ramsay Brothers' Story!" Trans. Anjali Nerlekar. *Mumbai Sakal*, May 13, 1988.

Rawal, Ravina. "Movie Review: *Rise of the Zombie* Bites Off More Than It Can Chew." *Firstpost*. Last modified April 6, 2013. Accessed March 5, 2015. Available at www.firstpost.com/bollywood/movie-review-rise-of-the-zombie-bites-off-more-than-it-can-chew-688801.html.

"Real 'Ragini' Speaks Up: BLASTS Ekta Kapoor—Bollywood Hungama Exclusive." Last modified May 12, 2011. Available at www.youtube.com/watch?v=BM-tRhEMVdc.

"Review: Mallika's 'Hisss' Fails to Charm the Box Office." *Zee News*. Last modified October 22, 2010. Available at http://zeenews.india.com/entertainment/movies/review-mallika-s-hisss-fails-to-charm-the-box-office_73701.html.

Review of *Nagin*. *Memsaabstory*. Last modified January 15, 2012. Available at http://memsaabstory.com/2012/01/15/nagin-1976.

Review of *Nagin*. *Screen*, February 6, 1976.

Risbood, Vaibhavi. "50 percent of 'Ragini MMS' Is True: Ekta Kapoor." *Daily Bhaskar*. Last modified March 1, 2011. Available at http://daily.bhaskar.com/news/ENT-50-of-ragini-mms-is-true-ekta-kapoor-1896512.html.

"*Rise of the Zombie* Movie Review." *Times of India*. Last modified April 4, 2013. Accessed March 5, 2015. Available at http://timesofindia.indiatimes.com/entertainment/hindi/movie-review/Rise-Of-The-Zombie/movie-review/18589066.cms.

Roscoe, Jane. "*The Blair Witch Project*: Mock-Documentary Goes Mainstream." *Jump Cut* 43 (2000): 3–8.

Rowan-Legg, Shelagh M. "Don't Miss a Bloody Thing: [REC] and the Spanish Adaptation of Found Footage Horror." *Studies in Spanish and Latin American Cinemas* 10 (2) (2013): 213–223.

"Russian Mafia and Not Government Controls Goa." *Times of India*, January 24, 2011. Accessed December 29, 2015. Available at http://timesofindia.indiatimes.com/city/goa/Russian-mafia-and-not-government-controls-Goa/articleshow/7349882.cms.

"Saamri: Horror's New Dimension." *Screen*, November 22, 1985.

Sahgal, Geety. "Mauritius Bound." *Indian Express*, September 5, 2014. Available at http://indianexpress.com/article/entertainment/screen/mauritius-bound/.

Santoshini, Sarita. "Hunting Down Witches in Northeast India." *Al Jazeera*, September 3, 2015. Accessed December 27, 2015. Available at www.aljazeera.com/indepth/features/2015/09/hunting-witches-northeast-india-150902092226394.html.

Sarkar, Bhaskar. "Metafiguring Bollywood: Brecht After *Om Shanti Om*." In *Figurations in Indian Film*, ed. Meheli Sen and Anustup Basu, 205–235. Hampshire, UK: Palgrave Macmillan, 2013.

Sayad, Cecelia. "Found Footage Horror and the Frame's Undoing," *Cinema Journal* 55 (2016): 43–66.

Schuessler, Jennifer. "Academic Zombies Attack! (Again)." *New York Times*. Last modified October 31, 2014. Available at http://artsbeat.blogs.nytimes.com/2014/10/31/academic-zombies-attack-again/?_r=0.

Sconce, Jeffrey. *Haunted Media: Electronic Presence from Telegraphy to Television*. Durham, NC: Duke University Press, 2000.

———. "'Trashing' the Academy: Taste, Excess, and an Emerging Politics of Cinematic Style." *Screen* 36 (4) (1995): 371–393.

———, ed. *Sleaze Artists: Cinema at the Margins of Taste, Style, and Politics*. Durham, NC: Duke University Press, 2007.

Sen, Aditi. "'I Wasn't Born with Enough Middle Fingers': How Low-Budget Horror Films Defy Sexual Morality and Heteronormativity in Bollywood." *Acta Orientalia Vilnensia* 12 (2) (2011): 75–90.

Sen, Meheli. "Haunted Havelis and Hapless Heroes: Gender, Genre and the Hindi Gothic Film." In *Figurations in Indian Film*, ed. Meheli Sen and Anustup Basu, 116–136. Hampshire, UK: Palgrave Macmillan, 2013.

———. "Terrifying Tots and Hapless Homes: Undoing Modernity in Recent Bollywood Cinema." *Literature Interpretation Theory* 22 (2011): 197–217.

———, and Anustup Basu, eds. *Figurations in Indian Film*. Hampshire, UK: Palgrave Macmillan, 2013.

Sen, Shaunak. "Spectral Pixels: Digital Ghosts in Contemporary Hindi Horror Cinema." *Wide Screen* 5 (1) (2015): 1–27.

Sharma, Neha. "Ekta Ruined My Life: Real Ragini." *Hindustan Times*. Last modified May 13, 2011. Available at http://www.hindustantimes.com/entertainment/ekta-ruined-my-life-real-ragini/story-OafS23hqgykSp5IAIPV4LN.html.

Sharma, Smrity. "Ekta Kapoor Challenges the Real Ragini." *Times of India*. Last modified May 13, 2011. Available at http://timesofindia.indiatimes.com/entertainment/hindi/bollywood/news/Ekta-Kapoor-challenges-the-real-Ragini/articleshow/8293159.cms.

Shaviro, Steven. *The Cinematic Body*. Minneapolis: University of Minnesota Press, 1993.

———. "Paranormal Activity: The Ghost Dimension," November 20, 2015. Accessed December 29, 2015. Available at www.shaviro.com/Blog/?p=1345.

———. *Post-Cinematic Affect*. Ropley, UK: Zero Books, 2010.

———. "What Is the Post-Cinematic?" August 11, 2011. Accessed December 28, 2015. Available at www.shaviro.com/Blog/?p=992.

"Shyam Ramsay: People Say the Ghosts in My Films Were Not Scary." *Rediff*. Last modified March 13, 2014. Accessed June 25, 2015. Available at www.rediff.com/movies/report/slide-show-1-shyam-ramsay-people-say-the-ghosts-in-my-films-were-not-scary/20140313.htm?print=true.

Sinha, Suvadip. "Ghostly Predicament: Narrative, Spectrality and Historicality in Rabindranath Tagore's 'The Hungry Stones.'" *Interventions: International Journal of Postcolonial Studies* 15 (7) (2015): 728–743.

Smith, Andrew. "Hauntings." In *Routledge Companion to the Gothic*, ed. Catherine Spooner and Emma McEvoy, 147–154. New York: Routledge, 2007.

Srivastava, Sanjay. "Voice, Gender and Space in Time of Five-Year Plans: The Idea of Lata Mangeshkar." *Economic and Political Weekly* 39 (4) (2004): 19–28.

Sundaram, Ravi. *Pirate Modernity: Delhi's Media Urbanism*. New York: Routledge, 2010.

Tarlo, Emma. *Unsettling Memories: Narratives of the Emergency in Delhi*. Berkeley: University of California Press, 2003.

Tewari, Mayank. "Indian Youth Is Not Just Ready for a Zombie Film, It Is Demanding One." *Tehelka*. Last modified September 12, 2011. Accessed May 12, 2015. Available at http://archive.tehelka.com/story_main50.asp?filename=Ws120911Cinema.asp.

Thomas, Rosie. *Bombay Before Bollywood: Film City Fantasies*. Albany: SUNY Press, 2013.

Tombs, Pete. "The Beast from Bollywood: A History of the Indian Horror Film." In *Fear Without Frontiers: Horror Cinema Across the Globe*, ed. Steven Jay Schneider, 243–253. Godalming, UK: FAB Press, 2003.

Uberoi, Patricia. "The Diaspora Comes Home: Disciplining Desire in DDLJ." *Contributions to Indian Sociology* 32 (1998): 305–336.

Varma, Ram Gopal. Interviewed by author. Digital recording. Mumbai, India, July 29, 2009.

Vasudevan, Ravi. "Disreputable and Illegal Publics: Cinematic Allegories in Times of Crisis." *Sarai Reader* 4 (2004): 70–79, 73.

———. "Shifting Codes, Dissolving Identities: The Hindi Social Film of the 1950s as Popular Culture." In *Making Meaning in Indian Cinema*, ed. Ravi Vasudevan, 99–121. New Delhi: Oxford University Press, 2000.

Vats, Rohit. "'Rise of the Zombie' Review: Monotony Kills the Novelty." *IBN Live*. Last modified April 5, 2013. Accessed March 5, 2015. Available at http://www.ibnlive.com/news/india/rise-of-the-zombie-review-monotony-kills-the-novelty-601103.html.

Vitali, Valentina. "The Evil I: Realism and Scopophilia in the Horror Films of the Ramsay Brothers." In *Beyond the Boundaries of Bollywood*, ed. Rachel Dwyer and Jerry Pinto, 77–101. New Delhi: Oxford University Press, 2011.

Watkins, Beth. "Adventures in a Subtitleless and Otherwise Wild and Woolly Land:

Sheshnaag." *Beth Loves Bollywood*. Last modified October 31, 2010. Available at http://bethlovesbollywood.blogspot.com/2010/10/adventures-in-subtitleless-and.html.

Weinstock, Jeffrey Andrew. "Introduction: The Spectral Turn." In *The Spectralities Reader*, ed. María del Pilar Blanco and Esther Peeren, 61–68. New York: Bloomsbury, 2013.

"Why All Gay Guys Love Sridevi." *Santa Banta: The Never Ending Show . . .* Last modified October 12, 2012. Accessed June 1, 2015. Available at www.santabanta.com/bollywood/59916/why-all-gay-guys-love-sridevi/.

Williams, Linda. "Film Bodies: Gender, Genre, and Excess." *Film Quarterly* 44 (4) (1991): 2–13.

"*Woh Kaun Thi?*: Sensitively Directed." *Filmfare*, March 6, 1964.

Wolfe, Cary. *What is Posthumanism?* Minneapolis: University of Minnesota Press, 2010.

Wolfreys, Julian. *Victorian Hauntings: Spectrality, Gothic, the Uncanny and Literature*. New York: Palgrave Macmillan, 2001.

Wood, Robin. "An Introduction to the American Horror Film." In *Planks of Reason: Essays on the Horror Film*, ed. Barry Keith Grant and Christopher Sharret, 146–192. Blue Ridge Summit, PA: Scarecrow Press, 2004.

Wright, Neelam Sidhar. "The Soul Gets Typecast: The Reincarnation Film in Hindi Popular Cinema." *New Cinemas: Journal of Contemporary Film* 12 (1 and 2): 113–132.

Zhang, Juwen. "Filmic Folklore and Chinese Cultural Identity." *Western Folklore* 64 (3–4) (2005): 263–280.

Index

Page numbers in *italics* refer to illustrations.